OCCASIO

G000153116

Financial Sector Crisis and Restructuring

Lessons from Asia

Carl-Johan Lindgren, Tomás J.T. Baliño, Charles Enoch, Anne-Marie Gulde, Marc Quintyn, and Leslie Teo

INTERNATIONAL MONETARY FUND
Washington DC
1999

© 1999 International Monetary Fund

Production: IMF Graphics Section
Typesetting: Joseph Ashok Kumar
Figures: In-Ok Yoon

Library of Congress Cataloging-in-Publication Data
Financial sector crisis and restructuring : lessons from Asia / Carl-Johan
   Lindgren... [et al.].
      p.   cm. — (Occasional paper ; 188)
    Includes bibliographical references.
    ISBN 1-55775-871-9
   1. Finance—Asia—Case studies.   2. Financial crises—Asia—Case studies. I. Lindgren, Carl-Johan   II. Occasional paper (International Monetary Fund) ; 188.

HC187.A2 F57 1999
332'.095—dc21   99-088474

Price: US$18.00
(US$15.00 to full-time faculty members and
students at universities and colleges)

Please send orders to:
International Monetary Fund, Publication Services
700 19th Street, N.W., Washington, D.C. 20431, U.S.A.
Tel.: (202) 623-7430   Telefax: (202) 623-7201
E-mail: publications@imf.org
Internet: http://www.imf.org

recycled paper

Contents

The following symbols have been used throughout this paper:

. . .   to indicate that data are not available;

—   to indicate that the figure is zero or less than half the final digit shown, or that the item does not exist;

–   between years or months (e.g., 1994–95 or January–June) to indicate the years or months covered, including the beginning and ending years or months;

/   between years (e.g., 1994/95) to indicate a fiscal (financial) year.

"Billion" means a thousand million.

Minor discrepancies between constituent figures and totals are due to rounding.

The term "country," as used in this paper, does not in all cases refer to a territorial entity that is a state as understood by international law and practice; the term also covers some territorial entities that are not states, but for which statistical data are maintained and provided internationally on a separate and independent basis.

Preface

This paper reviews the policy responses of Indonesia, Korea, and Thailand to the Asian crisis that erupted in 1997 and compares the actions of these three countries with those of Malaysia and the Philippines, which were buffeted by the crisis. Although work is still under way in all the affected countries, and thus any judgments are necessarily tentative, important lessons can be learned from the various experiences of the last two years.

The paper reflects these lessons and the emerging policies of the IMF's Monetary and Exchange Affairs Department (MAE). The material in this paper was originally prepared for discussion in the IMF's Executive Board in early September 1999. It was prepared under the direction of Stefan Ingves, Director of MAE, by a staff team led by Carl-Johan Lindgren and consisting of Tomás J.T. Baliño and Charles Enoch (who have been leading the department's work in Thailand, Korea, and Indonesia, respectively), Anne-Marie Gulde, Marc Quintyn, and Leslie Teo. Elena Budreckaite and Kiran Sastry provided research assistance, and Charmane Ahmed and Janet Stanford secretarial support. Jeff Hayden of the External Relations Department edited the report and coordinated its publication. The team benefited from contributions of numerous other MAE staff members involved in the department's work in the five countries, as is acknowledged in Appendices I–V. The paper thus reflects the hands-on experience of the MAE staff and experts involved.

The paper has also benefited from comments of the IMF's Executive Directors, colleagues in MAE, the Asia and Pacific Department (APD), and other departments in the IMF, as well as from colleagues in the World Bank. The views expressed in the paper are those of the IMF staff and do not necessarily reflect the views of the national authorities or IMF Executive Directors.

List of Abbreviations

ADB	Asian Development Bank
BAFIA	Banking and Financial Institutions Act (Malaysia)
BAP	Bankers Association of the Philippines
BAPINDO	Bank Pembangunan Indonesia
BBC	Bangkok Bank of Commerce
BCA	Bank Central Asia (Indonesia)
BDNI	Bank Dagang Nasional Indonesia
BIBF	Bangkok International Banking Facilities
BLR	Base lending rate (Malaysia)
BMB	Bangkok Metropolitan Bank (Thailand)
BNI	Bank Negara Indonesia
BRI	Bank Rakyat Indonesia
BTN	Bank Talringhan Nasional (Indonesia)
CAMEL	Capital, asset, management, equity, liquidity
CDRC	Corporate Debt Restructuring Committee (Malaysia)
CRA	Corporate Restructuring Agreement (Korea)
CRCC	Corporate Restructuring Coordinating Committee (Korea)
DBP	Development Bank of the Philippines
FIDF	Financial Institutions Development Fund (Thailand)
FRAC	Financial Restructuring Advisory Committee (Thailand)
FRA	Financial Sector Restructuring Agency (Thailand)
FSC	Financial Supervisory Commission (Korea)
FSS	Financial Supervisory Service (Korea)
IBRA	Indonesian Bank Restructuring Agency
KAMCO	Korean Asset Management Corporation
KDB	Korean Development Bank
KDIC	Korea Deposit Insurance Corporation
KEXIM	Korea Export-Import Bank
KTB	Krung Thai Bank (Thailand)
KTT	Krung Thai Thanakit (Thailand)
NIF	National Investment Fund (Korea)
PDIC	Philippine Deposit Insurance Corporation
SEC	Securities and Exchange Commission
SCR	Steering Committee on Restructuring (Malaysia)

I Overview

Financial and corporate sector weaknesses played a major role in the Asian crisis in 1997. These weaknesses increased the exposure of financial institutions to a variety of external threats, including declines in asset values, market contagion, speculative attacks, exchange rate devaluations, and a reversal of capital flows.[1] In turn, problems in financial institutions and corporations worsened capital flight and disrupted credit allocation, thereby deepening the crisis.

As a consequence, policy responses to the crisis emphasized structural reforms in the financial and corporate sectors in addition to the implementation of appropriate macroeconomic policies. These structural measures were also necessary for macroeconomic policies to achieve the intended stabilization. Structural measures included dealing with nonviable financial institutions, establishing frameworks for recapitalizing and strengthening viable institutions, restructuring the corporate sector, and improving prudential regulations and supervision and market discipline.[2]

This paper reviews the policy responses to the financial sector crisis in five Asian countries, focusing in particular on Indonesia, Korea, and Thailand. It complements Lane and others (1999) and draws lessons for the future, largely based on experience in these countries. Given that the restructuring is still ongoing, the study is necessarily selective in the issues it addresses and provisional in some of the answers it provides. Because of a combination of domestic and foreign factors, the crisis was particularly severe in Indonesia, Korea, and Thailand—in this paper referred to as the crisis countries—all of which obtained the IMF's financial support. Other countries in the region also experienced some of the effects of the financial turmoil. Although they did not suffer a full-blown crisis, some of those countries also adopted measures to deal with that turmoil and to strengthen their financial systems. Among these other countries, Malaysia and the Philippines are useful to compare with the three crisis countries, and therefore are also discussed in this paper when appropriate.

The structure of the paper is as follows. Section II briefly reviews vulnerabilities in the financial sector in the run-up to the financial crisis. Section III discusses measures taken during the initial stages of the crisis to stabilize the system. Section IV discusses issues involved in setting monetary and credit policies and the issue of a "credit crunch." Section V reviews issues related to the respective governments' strategies to restructure the financial sector. Section VI reviews institutional reforms undertaken to diminish the likelihood of future financial crises. Section VII discusses issues relating to IMF advice and IMF-supported programs. Conclusions and lessons are presented in Section VIII. Appendices I–V present case studies from Indonesia, Korea, Malaysia, the Philippines, and Thailand. The studies discuss in detail the financial sector problems and the steps taken to address them. They set the stage for the comparisons and lessons that are drawn in the main body of the paper.

The following paragraphs offer a brief analysis of the crisis and summarize the paper's main findings.

Origins of the Crisis

Financial and corporate sector weaknesses combined with macroeconomic vulnerabilities to spark the crisis (see Box 1 for a chronology of events). Formal and informal currency pegs, which discouraged lenders and borrowers from hedging, also contributed to the outbreak. Capital inflows had helped fuel rapid credit expansion, which lowered the quality of credit and led to asset price inflation. The inflated asset prices encouraged further capital inflows and lending, often by weakly supervised nonbank financial institutions. Highly leveraged corporate sectors, especially in Korea and Thailand,

---

[1]For simplicity, "bank" and "financial institution" are used interchangeably in this paper. When referring to a specific type of financial institution (e.g., commercial bank, merchant bank), that reference will be used in full.

[2]Nonviable financial institutions are those judged unable to maintain minimum thresholds of liquidity, solvency, and profitability.

Box 1. A Chronology of the Asian Crisis, March 1997–July 1999

1997

March 3	Thailand	First official announcement of problems in two unnamed finance companies, and a recapitalization program.
March–June	Thailand	Sixty-six finance companies secretly receive substantial liquidity support from the Bank of Thailand. Significant capital outflows.
April	Malaysia	Bank Negara Malaysia imposes limits on bank lending to the property sector and for the purchase of stocks.
June 29	Thailand	Operations of 16 finance companies suspended and a guarantee of depositors' and creditors' funds in remaining finance companies announced.
July 2	Thailand	Baht is floated and depreciates by 15–20 percent.
Early July	Indonesia	Pressure on the rupiah develops.
July 8–14	Malaysia	Bank Negara Malaysia intervenes aggressively to defend the ringgit: efforts to support the ringgit are abandoned; ringgit is allowed to float.
July 11	Indonesia	Widening of the rupiah's band.
July 11	Philippines	Peso is allowed more flexibility.
July 13	Korea	Several Korean banks are placed on negative credit outlook by rating agencies.
July 24	All	"Currency meltdown"—severe pressure on rupiah, baht, ringgit, and peso.
August 5	Thailand	Measures adopted to strengthen financial sector. Operations of 42 finance companies suspended.
August 14	Indonesia	Authorities abolish band for rupiah, which plunges immediately.
August 20	Thailand	Three-year Stand-By Arrangement with IMF approved.
August 25	Korea	Government guarantees banks' external liabilities; withdrawal of credit lines continues.
October 14	Thailand	Financial sector restructuring strategy announced; Financial Sector Restructuring Agency and asset management company established; blanket guarantee strengthened; new powers to intervene in banks.
October 24	Thailand	Emergency decrees to facilitate financial sector restructuring.
October 31	Indonesia	Bank resolution package announced; 16 commercial banks closed; limited deposit insurance for depositors in other banks; other bank closures to follow.
November 5	Indonesia	Three-year Stand-By Arrangement with IMF approved.
November 19	Korea	Exchange rate band widened. Won falls sharply.
Mid-November	Thailand	Change in government. Significant strengthening of economic reform program.
November	Korea	Korea Asset Management Corporation's (KAMCO) nonperforming asset fund is established.
December 4	Korea	IMF approves three-year Stand-By Arrangement but rollover of short-term debt continues to decline.
December 8	Thailand	Fifty-six suspended finance companies are permanently closed.
Mid-December	Indonesia	Deposit runs on banks, accounting for half of banking system assets.
December 18	Korea	New government is elected; commitment to program is strengthened.

December 24	Korea	Foreign private bank creditors agree to maintain exposure temporarily.
December 29	Korea	Legislation passed strengthening independence for Bank of Korea and creating Financial Supervision Commission.
December 31	Thailand	Bank of Thailand intervention in a commercial bank; shareholders' stakes eliminated.
December	Korea	Fourteen merchant banks are suspended and two large commercial banks taken over by the government.

1998

January 1	Malaysia	Measures announced to strengthen prudential regulations.
January 15	Indonesia	Second IMF-supported program announced. Indonesian Bank Restructuring Agency (IBRA) established and blanket guarantee announced.
January 20	Malaysia	Bank Negara Malaysia announces blanket guarantee for all depositors.
January 23	Thailand	Bank of Thailand intervenes in two commercial banks; shareholders eliminated.
January 26	Indonesia	Indonesian Bank Restructuring Agency (IBRA) established and blanket guarantee announced.
January 28	Korea	Agreement with external private creditors on rescheduling of short-term debt.
January	Korea	Ten of 14 suspended merchant banks closed; 20 remaining merchant banks are required to submit rehabilitation plans.
February 15	Korea	New president and government take office.
February	Indonesia	President Suharto reelected. Doubts about future of financial sector program grow stronger amid political uncertainty. Rupiah depreciates further and currency board is debated.
March 11	Thailand	One commercial bank purchased by foreign strategic investor.
March 25	Malaysia	Program to consolidate finance companies and to recapitalize commercial banks is announced.
March 31	Thailand	New loan classification and loss provisioning rules introduced.
March	Philippines	Three-year Stand-By Arrangement agreed with IMF.
April 4	Indonesia	IBRA closes seven banks and takes over seven others.
End of April	Korea	Four of 20 merchant banks' rehabilitation plans rejected; banks are closed.
May 18	Thailand	Bank of Thailand intervention in seven finance companies; shareholders eliminated.
Mid-May	Indonesia	Widespread riots. Rupiah depreciates, deposit runs intensify, and Bank Indonesia must provide liquidity.
May 21	Indonesia	President Suharto steps down.
May 29	Indonesia	A major private bank taken over by IBRA.
June 5	Indonesia	International lenders and Indonesian companies agree on corporate debt rescheduling.
June 29	Korea	For the first time, government closes commercial banks (five small ones). Two merchant banks are closed and two merged with commercial banks.
June 30	Korea	New loan classification and loss provisioning rules introduced.

Box 1 *(Concluded)*

June	Malaysia	Danaharta, an asset management company, is established.
Mid-July	Indonesia	Authorities allow market-determined interest rates on Bank Indonesia bills.
August 14	Thailand	Comprehensive financial sector restructuring plan announced, including facilities for public support of bank recapitalization. Intervention in two banks and five finance companies; shareholders' stakes eliminated.
August 30	Thailand	Majority ownership in one medium-sized commercial bank by foreign strategic investor.
August	Malaysia	Danamodal (bank restructuring and recapitalization agency) is established.
September 23	Indonesia	Indonesia's bilateral external debt to official creditors refinanced.
September 30	Indonesia	Bank Mandiri created through merger of four largest state-owned banks. Plans announced for joint government-private sector recapitalization of private banks.
September	Malaysia	Capital controls introduced, exchange rate pegged, disclosure requirements relaxed, and measures to stimulate bank lending adopted.
October 6	Indonesia	Amended Banking Law passed, which included strengthening of IBRA.
1999		
February 15	Malaysia	Capital controls replaced with declining exit levies.
March 13	Indonesia	Government closes 38 banks and IBRA takes over seven others. Eligibility of nine banks for joint recapitalization with government announced.
April 21	Indonesia	Closure of one joint-venture bank.
April	Indonesia	Government announces a plan to recapitalize the three other state banks (all insolvent).
June 30	Indonesia	Eight private banks recapitalized jointly through public and private funds.
July 5	Indonesia	Government announces plan for resolution of IBRA banks.
July 31	Indonesia	Legal merger of component banks of Bank Mandiri.
July	Thailand	One small private bank intervened and put up for sale; one major bank announces establishment of an asset management company.

and large unhedged short-term debt made the crisis countries vulnerable to changes in market sentiment in general and exchange and interest rate changes in particular. Malaysia and the Philippines were less vulnerable.

Weaknesses in bank and corporate governance and lack of market discipline allowed excessive risk taking, as prudential regulations were weak or poorly enforced. Close relationships between governments, financial institutions, and borrowers worsened the problems, particularly in Indonesia and Korea. More generally, weak accounting standards, especially for loan valuation, and disclosure practices helped hide the growing weaknesses from poli-

cymakers, supervisors, market participants, and international financial institutions—while those indicators of trouble that were available seem to have been largely ignored. In addition, inadequacies in assessing country risk on the part of the lenders contributed to the crisis.

The crisis was triggered by the floating of the Thai baht in July 1997. Changing expectations led to the depreciation of most other currencies in the region, bank runs and rapid withdrawals of foreign private capital, and dramatic economic downturns. When the crisis broke, Indonesia, Korea, and Thailand requested IMF assistance, both to obtain financial support and to restore confidence.

Coping with the Crisis

The initial priorities in dealing with the crisis were to stabilize the financial system and to restore confidence in economic management. Forceful measures were needed to stop bank runs, protect the payment system, limit central bank liquidity support, minimize disruptions to credit flows, maintain monetary control, and stem capital outflows. In the crisis countries, emergency measures, such as the introduction of blanket guarantees and bank closings, were accompanied by comprehensive bank restructuring programs and supported by macroeconomic stabilization policies.

Closings of the most insolvent or nonviable financial institutions were used initially to stem rapidly accumulating losses and central bank liquidity support. However, the experience of Indonesia showed that in a systemic crisis bank closings can lead to runs on other banks, if not accompanied by proper information, strong overall economic management, and a blanket guarantee.

Blanket guarantees for depositors and creditors were used in the crisis countries and in Malaysia to restore confidence and to protect banks' funding. Despite the enormous contingent costs and moral hazard problems involved, governments considered guarantees preferable to collapses of their banking systems. The guarantees were effective in stabilizing banks' domestic funding—although in some cases it took some time to gain credibility—but were less effective in stabilizing banks' foreign funding (Korea responded with voluntary debt rescheduling and Malaysia adopted capital controls). In Indonesia, a blanket guarantee was introduced only after an attempt to use a limited guarantee had backfired.

Liquidity support by central banks was reduced after the closure of the weakest financial institutions and the introduction of the blanket guarantees. Monetary control was maintained through sterilization measures—offsetting sales or purchases of securities by the central bank—in all countries, except initially in Indonesia. Monetary policy in all countries focused on the exchange rate, short-term interest rates, and the level of international reserves, rather than on traditional monetary aggregates, which had become unstable.

Credit growth slowed as demand contracted and supply plummeted, with bankers becoming more selective in their lending behavior. A heightened perception of credit risk, funding constraints, and a weakening capital position further constrained credit. In such circumstances, direct or indirect measures to stimulate new credit are unlikely to be sufficient to restore normal lending: that will take a return of profitability and solvency in the banking and corporate sectors.

Bank Restructuring

Comprehensive bank restructuring strategies in the crisis countries and in Malaysia sought to restore financial sector soundness as soon as possible, and at least cost to the government, while providing an appropriate incentive structure for the restructuring. (See Box 2 for a list of critical steps in resolving a systemic banking crisis.) The strategies included setting up appropriate institutional frameworks, removing nonviable institutions from the system, strengthening viable institutions, dealing with value-impaired assets, improving prudential regulations and banking supervision, and promoting transparency in financial market operations.

Key principles for bank restructuring strategies in the crisis countries have been the application of uniform criteria to identify viable and nonviable institutions, removal of existing owners from insolvent institutions, and encouragement of new private capital contributions, including from the foreign sector. Public support has sought to complement private sector contributions; liberalization of foreign ownership rules encouraged foreign participation.

Strategies must be adapted to fit countries' circumstances. Systemic bank restructuring is a complex medium-term process that requires careful tailoring. Accordingly, while the broad components of the restructuring strategies were similar, implementation details differed across countries according to the precise nature of the problems, legal and institutional constraints, and each government's preferences.

Valuation of bank assets is crucial for determining bank viability but is very difficult in a crisis environment, as markets are thin and values shift with changing circumstances. Tighter rules for loan classification, loss provisioning, and interest suspension were introduced to guide the valuation process. Different valuation procedures, including by banks themselves, external or international auditors, or supervisors, were used to provide the authorities with the best available data. Regardless of data quality, decisions had to be made as much as possible on the basis of uniform and fully transparent criteria.

Strengthening viable institutions involved asset valuation, loss recognition, and recapitalization. When banks breached minimum capital adequacy requirements, recapitalization and rehabilitation became mandatory, often under binding memoranda of understanding with the supervisory authorities. In the crisis countries loan-loss provisioning rules or capital adequacy requirements were implemented gradually—but transparently—to give banks time to restructure and mobilize new capital and to avoid aggravating credit supply problems. Public sector

---

Box 2. Ten Critical Points in Managing and Resolving a Systemic Bank Crisis

The sequence presented below describes the different phases one encounters when dealing with a major systemic financial sector crisis. This sequence is based on the assumption that a country's financial sector has public good aspects and, hence, that solving such a crisis warrants substantial public sector involvement. The different steps, from origin through recognition and resolution, and preventive measures are discussed in this paper. Although specific actions may differ among countries based on the depth of the crisis, the composition of the financial sector before the crisis, local circumstances and preferences, and the contents and sequence of the basic building blocks and strategies are similar across countries.

Steps 1–4. *The acute crisis phase: measures to stop the panic and stabilize the system.*

1. The crisis usually begins because, in one form or another, there is excessive leverage in the economy. In the early stages there may also be a degree of denial on the part of the banks and the government.

2. Bank runs by creditors and depositors start and intensify. The central bank responds by providing liquidity support to the affected banks.

3. When central bank liquidity is unable to stop the runs, the government announces a blanket guarantee for depositors and creditors. Such a measure is intended to reduce uncertainty and to allow time for the government to begin an orderly restructuring process.

4. All along, the central bank tries to sterilize its liquidity support to avoid a loss of monetary control.

Steps 5–8. *The stabilization phase: measures to restructure the system.*

5. The authorities design the tools needed for a comprehensive restructuring, including the required legal, financial, and institutional framework.

6. Losses in individual institutions are recognized. The authorities shift the focus from liquidity support to solvency support.

7. The authorities design a financial sector restructuring strategy, based on a vision for the postcrisis structure of the sector.

8. Viable banks are recapitalized, bad assets are dealt with, and prudential supervision and regulations are tightened.

Steps 9–10. *The recovery phase: measures to normalize the system.*

9. Nationalized banks are reprivatized, corporate debt is restructured, and bad assets are sold.

10. The blanket guarantee is revoked, which, if properly handled, is a nonevent because the banking system has been recapitalized and is healthy again.

---

equity support was also provided to viable banks, subject to stringent conditions.

The authorities intervened in institutions that failed to raise capital and faced insolvency through such techniques as government recapitalization/nationalization, mergers, sales, use of bridge banks and asset management companies, purchase and assumption operations, and liquidation. Shareholders typically absorbed losses until their capital was fully written off. In all the countries, the governments aim at reprivatizing the nationalized financial institutions as soon as possible; in this, Korea and Thailand have already made significant progress.

Management of impaired assets, including nonperforming loans, is one of the most complex parts of financial restructuring. Impaired assets can either be dealt with by the financial institutions themselves, by bank-specific or centralized asset management companies, or under liquidation procedures. Speed of disposal has to be considered. Assets have to be managed and disposed so as to preserve values and maximize recovery, while at the same time create the right incentives so as not to undermine borrower discipline throughout the system. The choice of asset management structure should depend on the nature of the asset and available management capabilities. Nonperforming loans with reasonable chances of recovery are generally better managed in banks.

A centralized asset management company typically involves government ownership, compared with decentralized asset management companies, which tend to be privately owned and bank specific. All asset management companies seek to provide better management structures for problem assets and to relieve banks' balance sheets. Asset sales by banks to asset management companies should not amount to back-door capitalization of banks (and bailout of shareholders) by receiving inflated prices, a matter complicated by the above-mentioned difficulty of valuing impaired assets. Because banks have to take a loss when they sell loans to an asset management company (public or private), capital scarcity may limit their capacity to do so. Indonesia, Korea, and Malaysia have opted for a centralized public asset management company, while Thailand established a public asset management company that only deals with residual assets of closed finance companies, and has encouraged the establishment of bank-specific asset management companies.

Cost of Restructuring

The gross costs of the bank restructurings are massive. Estimates put the public sector costs in the three crisis countries and Malaysia between 15 and 45 percent of GDP. The estimates may increase if further losses are uncovered, but they may also drop depending upon the proceeds from asset sales and privatization. The revenue generated by these sales will not be known for several years. There are, in addition, efficiency gains and wealth effects resulting from the restructuring. Initially, the costs were mainly carried by the central banks in the form of liquidity support to ailing banks. Only recently have governments started to refinance this liquidity by issuing domestic government bonds.

The fiscal implications of the crisis were estimated by imputing the carrying costs of the debt created to finance the restructuring. Full and transparent recording in the fiscal accounts of all costs incurred by the government, including capital costs, is important for fiscal analysis. The very large costs of the crisis may affect medium-term fiscal sustainability.

Other Issues

Government "ownership" of the reform programs and strong leadership are necessary to take charge of and implement the complex microeconomic processes that a systemic bank restructuring entail. In the crisis countries, political changes had a positive impact on the pace and resolve of the restructuring process. Only domestic constituencies can deal with the legal and institutional factors that are prerequisites for success, but that also can bring the process to a halt. Restructuring has to take into account human resource constraints and legal issues, given that it typically has major effects on private wealth.

Corporate sector problems represent the flip side of banks' nonperforming loans. Bank restructuring should be accompanied by corporate debt restructuring, which has been lagging and is now delaying the bank restructuring process. At the same time, financial sector restructuring should be given priority as the governance structure of banks and their prudential framework provide powerful levers to bring about the corporate restructuring reform.

Prudential regulation and supervision have been strengthened to foster better bank governance and stronger market discipline. In all the countries, domestic standards are being brought closer to international best practices, including areas such as foreign exchange exposure, liquidity management, connected lending, loan concentration, loan provisioning, data disclosure, and qualifications for owners and managers. Steps have been taken to strengthen the autonomy and authority of supervisors, upgrade their powers and skills, and improve on-site examination, off-site monitoring, and analysis techniques.

Role of the IMF

The IMF-supported programs in Indonesia, Korea, and Thailand centered on financial sector reform, not only because financial sector problems were a root cause of the crisis but also because reestablishing banking system soundness was crucial for restoring macroeconomic stability. Although the IMF was able to draw on both its past experience and its analytical work, the specific circumstances of each country added dimensions that required careful tailoring of the reform and resolution strategies for each country, often taking into account the authorities' sometimes strong preferences. The design of the reform strategies required access to bank-by-bank supervisory data, which was provided in the crisis countries.

Letters of Intent and Memoranda of Economic and Financial Policies laid out the strategies and sequencing. The IMF-supported programs required a delicate balance between the needs for short-term IMF conditionality and the medium-term nature of financial sector restructuring, which often involves steps and negotiations beyond the authorities' direct control.

Cooperation with the World Bank and other international organizations was close from, or soon after, the beginning, with somewhat different divisions of labor in each country. The IMF took the lead in assisting the authorities in designing the overall restructuring program of the three crisis countries, while the World Bank took charge of specific areas of program formulation and implementation. Most tasks have been done jointly to provide the authorities with the best possible advice and to use the resources of the two institutions as efficiently as possible.

Could the Crisis Have Been Prevented?

More transparency in macro- and microeconomic data and policies would have exposed vulnerabilities earlier and helped lessen the crisis. Better regulatory and supervisory frameworks would have helped, but supervisors would most likely not have been able to take necessary actions in the middle of the economic boom. No one foresaw the sudden massive erosion of loan values, once market sentiment changed and exchange rates collapsed.

Broad-based reforms are under way to strengthen the institutional, administrative, and legal frameworks in the crisis countries, based on evolving international best practices, codes, core principles, and standards. The crisis has shown the need to tailor prudential policies so that resilience is built up in times of economic booms to deal more easily with inevitable economic downturns.

International efforts have been undertaken to reduce the likelihood and intensity of future crises. Initiatives include work on the international financial architecture, the Financial Stability Forum, and financial sector stability assessments. The Basel Committee on Banking Supervision has formulated improvements to regulation and supervision of international lenders to address weaknesses that contributed to the Asian crisis.

II Vulnerabilities

The Asian financial crisis involved several mutually reinforcing events, starting with the devaluation of the Thai baht in July 1997, and followed by devaluations of other currencies, the attack on the Hong Kong dollar in October 1997, a rapid withdrawal of foreign private capital, bank runs, sovereign downgrades, and a dramatic decline in real economic activity.[3] A combination of financial system and corporate sector vulnerabilities and weaknesses contributed to the crises and magnified the negative impact of exchange rate devaluations and foreign capital withdrawals on financial institutions. This section highlights some of these vulnerabilities, which were present in all the crisis countries, albeit differing in specific aspects.

Macroeconomic and Financial Weaknesses

A key vulnerability arose from the large capital inflows—especially those deriving from foreign borrowing. These inflows were equivalent to 3.5 percent of GDP annually in Indonesia, 2.5 percent in Korea, and 10 percent in Thailand during 1990–96 (Figure 1). They were encouraged by high economic growth, low inflation, and relatively healthy fiscal performance (Tables 1 and 2, and Figure 2), financial sector and capital account liberalization, integration into global capital markets, formal or informal exchange rate pegs (Figure 3), and various incentives created by the government.[4] Capital flows also reflected conditions in the global financial system,

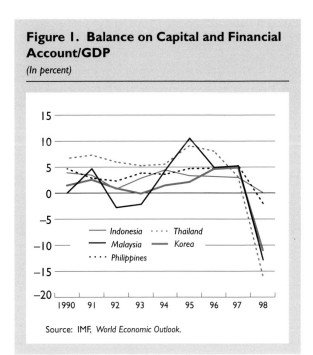

Figure 1. Balance on Capital and Financial Account/GDP

(In percent)

Source: IMF, *World Economic Outlook.*

including low interest rates and weaknesses in risk management by lenders in industrialized countries. The bulk of these inflows reflected direct borrowing by banks (Korea and Thailand) and corporations (Indonesia): this was especially evident in Thailand right before the crisis.[5] In contrast, in Malaysia, inflows of foreign direct investment were larger than direct borrowing and portfolio inflows, while capital inflows in the Philippines (particularly portfolio inflows) had only recently become significant.

Inflexible exchange rate regimes complicated macroeconomic management and increased vulnerability. The nominal exchange rate had depreciated in a predictable manner in Indonesia, and was

---

[3]This paper does not address the causes of the crisis. Detailed expositions on this subject can be found in Lane and others (1999), International Monetary Fund (1997), and International Monetary Fund (1998). Other studies, such as Furman and Stiglitz (1998), Goldstein (1998), and Radelet and Sachs (1998), have also addressed the subject.

[4]For example, in Thailand, bank lending and borrowing through Bangkok International Banking Facilities received favorable tax treatment, while in the Philippines, banks were subject to lower taxes on onshore income from foreign currency loans compared to that from domestic currency loans.

---

[5]In Thailand other inflows were 8 percent of GDP in 1996 compared to 3 percent of GDP for direct investment and portfolio inflows; in Indonesia and Korea, other inflows were on average 1 percent of GDP, and direct and portfolio investment 4 percent.

Table I. Selected Economic Indicators
(In percent or ratios)

	1990	1991	1992	1993	1994	1995	1996	1997	1998	1999[1]
Indonesia										
Real GDP growth	9.0	8.9	7.2	7.3	7.5	8.2	8.0	4.6	−13.6	−3.9
Inflation	7.8	9.4	7.5	9.7	8.5	9.4	7.9	6.6	60.7	25.4
Current account balance/GDP	−2.8	−3.4	−2.2	−1.5	−1.7	−3.3	−3.2	−3.0	−0.1	2.8
Central government balance/GDP	1.34	0.04	−1.15	−0.71	0.01	0.77	1.16	−0.67	−4.46	−6.48
Broad money growth	29.7	24.6	22.6	21.1	21.8	26.7	27.0	27.4	61.7	15.6
Private sector credit/GDP	46.1	45.8	45.5	48.9	51.9	53.5	55.4	61.0	51.6	...
Korea										
Real GDP growth	9.5	9.1	5.1	5.8	8.6	8.9	7.1	5.5	−5.5	2.0
Inflation	8.6	9.3	6.2	4.8	6.3	4.5	4.9	4.4	7.5	1.8
Current account balance/GDP	−0.8	−2.8	−1.3	0.3	−1.0	−1.9	−4.7	−1.8	13.1	7.1
Central government balance/GDP	−0.67	−1.62	−0.49	0.64	0.32	0.35	0.28	0.28	−3.78	−5.12
Broad money growth	17.2	21.9	14.9	16.6	18.7	15.6	15.8	14.1	25.2	...
Private sector credit/GDP	52.5	52.8	53.3	54.2	56.8	57.0	61.8	69.8	73.6	...
Malaysia										
Real GDP growth	9.6	8.6	7.8	8.3	9.3	9.4	8.6	7.7	−7.5	−1.6
Inflation	2.8	2.6	4.7	3.5	3.7	3.4	3.5	2.7	5.3	3.8
Current account balance/GDP	−2.1	−8.8	−3.8	−4.8	−7.8	−10.0	−4.9	−5.1	12.3	8.7
Central government balance/GDP	−3.08	−2.48	0.13	0.52	1.45	1.30	1.07	2.58	−1.91	−6.05
Broad money growth	18.2	24.4	18.1	23.8	15.8	18.2	23.7	9.6	1.3	6.1
Private sector credit/GDP	71.4	75.3	74.3	74.1	74.6	84.8	89.8	100.4	108.7	...
Philippines										
Real GDP growth	3.0	−0.6	0.3	2.1	4.4	4.7	5.8	5.2	−0.5	2.3
Inflation	14.1	18.7	9.0	7.6	9.1	8.1	8.4	6.0	9.7	8.5
Current account balance/GNP	−5.8	−1.9	−1.6	−5.5	−4.6	−4.3	−4.4	−5.1	1.8	2.1
Central government balance/GNP	−3.80	−2.40	−1.30	−1.60	−1.70	−1.30	−0.60	−0.70	−2.60	−2.70
Broad money growth	15.5	15.5	11.0	24.6	26.5	25.3	15.8	20.9	7.4	15.0
Private sector credit/GNP	20.5	18.9	21.5	27.2	30.0	38.2	50.0	57.6	50.5	46.9
Thailand										
Real GDP growth	11.6	8.1	8.2	8.5	8.6	8.8	5.5	−0.4	−8.0	1.0
Inflation	6.0	5.7	4.1	3.4	5.1	5.8	5.9	5.6	8.1	0.5
Current account balance/GDP	−8.3	−7.5	−5.5	−5.0	−5.4	−7.9	−7.9	−1.9	12.2	8.8
Central government balance/GDP	4.60	4.14	2.53	1.98	1.98	2.49	1.04	−1.62	−2.88	−3.84
Broad money growth	26.7	19.8	15.6	18.4	12.9	17.0	12.6	16.4	9.5	4.7
Private sector credit/GDP	64.5	67.7	72.2	79.8	90.9	97.5	100.0	116.3	109.5	...

Sources: IMF, *International Financial Statistics; World Economic Outlook*; and national authorities.
[1] 1999 IMF estimates.

closely linked to the U.S. dollar (or a basket of currencies) in Korea, Malaysia, the Philippines, and Thailand. The broadly stable exchange rate created incentives for borrowing in foreign exchange as borrowers underestimated the risks associated with foreign currency exposure.[6] Lenders, meanwhile, ignored the fact that lending in foreign exchange involved substantial credit risk. Maturity mismatches in banks' portfolios, and currency mismatches on corporations' balance sheets aggravated the problem. A long history of stable exchange rates also undermined incentives to introduce adequate prudential rules on, and monitoring of, foreign currency exposures. The three crisis countries were especially vulnerable to capital outflows and exchange rate devaluations because of the significant amount of short-term foreign currency debt, which was mostly unhedged. Furthermore, the growth of this debt outpaced growth in usable foreign exchange reserves during most of the 1990s, making these countries increasingly susceptible to a deterioration in market sentiment and large capital

---

[6] In addition, domestic nominal interest rates were above foreign rates, especially with regard to yen rates.

Table 2. Selected Indicators of Vulnerability
(Period ended December 1996)

	Indonesia	Korea	Malaysia	Philippines	Thailand
Macro indicators					
Inflation >5%	•			•	•
Fiscal deficit >2% of GDP					
Public debt >50% of GDP				•	
Current account deficit >5% of GDP					•
Short-term flows >50% current account deficit[1]	•	•	•	•	•
Capital inflows >5% of GDP		•	•	•	•
Ratio of short-term debt to international reserves >1 [2]	•	•			•
Financial sector indicators					
Recent financial sector liberalization	•	•		•	•
Recent capital account liberalization		•			
Credit to the private sector >100% of GDP		•	•		•
Credit to the private sector, real growth >20%			•	•	
Emphasis on collateral when making loans	•	•	•	•	•
Estimated share of bank lending to the real estate sector >20%[3]	•	•	•		•
Stock of nonperforming loans >10% of total loans					
Stock market capitalization (as percent of GDP)	40	30	310	98	56

Source: IMF, *International Financial Statistics; World Economic Outlook;* World Bank and IFC.

Note: The cutoff points are based on the relevant literature that attempts to predict currency and banking crises (Kaminsky, Lizondo, and Reinhart, 1997, for currency crisis; and Hardy and Pazarbaşıoğlu, 1998, for banking crisis).

[1]Defined as the sum of net portfolio and other investments in the financial accounts.

[2]As of June 1997.

[3]At the end of 1997. Includes indirect exposure through collateral.

outflows.[7] In addition, material adverse change clauses in debt contracts shortened the effective maturity of long-term debt, increasing vulnerability to negative events.[8] Malaysia was less vulnerable because foreign currency borrowing was lower due to a requirement of official approval above a certain limit.

The capital inflows helped fuel rapid credit expansion that led to strains—asset price inflation and excessive risk taking—which increased the vulnerability of the financial systems. In Korea, Malaysia, and Thailand private sector credit in nominal terms expanded rapidly during the 1990s, at an average rate of 15 to 20 percent compared to inflation rates of 3 to 10 percent (Figure 4). Total commercial bank and near-bank assets grew from between 50 and 100 percent of GDP in 1992 to between 150 and 200 percent of GDP at the end of 1996 (Box 3). As a comparison, deposit money banks held assets equal to 30 percent of GDP in Mexico, 48 percent in Brazil, 80 percent in the United States, 136 percent in the European Union, and 300 percent in Japan.[9] The Asian economies were in a self-reinforcing cycle—growth in credit reinforced the investment booms, which in turn encouraged further capital inflows and lending. This growth also led to asset price inflation (especially in Malaysia and Thailand), which encouraged lending to the real estate sector and inflated collateral values. Meanwhile, banks were increasingly exposed to credit and foreign exchange risks and to maturity mismatches, to the extent that foreign borrowing was short term and domestic lending long term, thus increasing the countries' vulnerability to

---

[7]By mid-1997, total outstanding claims held by foreign banks on domestic residents in the three crisis countries amounted to $232 billion, of which $151 billion was short term. Short-term debt amounted to 20 percent of total foreign debt in Indonesia, 44 percent in Korea, 50 percent in Malaysia, 60 percent in the Philippines, and 30 percent in Thailand. In Indonesia, Korea, and Thailand, the ratio of short-term liabilities to international reserves was above 1; in Malaysia it was 0.6, and in the Philippines it was 0.8 (see also Lane and others, 1999).

[8]In some cases, such clauses would permit the lender to require immediate repayment if a country's bond or sovereign rating were downgraded.

[9]Data for the end of 1998 for the European Union and the end of 1996 for the other countries. Data for nonbank financial institutions in these countries are not readily available.

Figure 2. Real GDP Growth
(In percent)

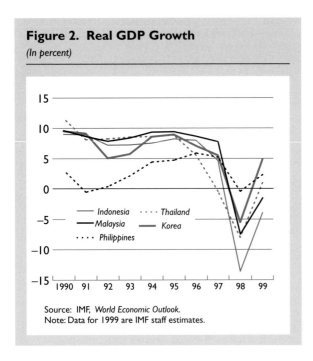

Source: IMF, *World Economic Outlook.*
Note: Data for 1999 are IMF staff estimates.

Figure 3. Real Effective Exchange Rate
(June 1997 = 100)

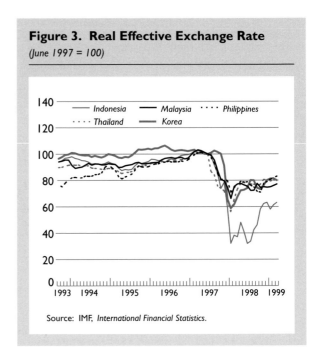

Source: IMF, *International Financial Statistics.*

outflows.[10] Rapid growth also strained banks' capacity to assess risk adequately.

In most countries, the growing nonbank financial institutions held riskier assets and more volatile financing than commercial banks, which made them increasingly vulnerable to a decline in asset quality and to a change in investor and depositor sentiment.[11] Nonbank financial institutions had grown very rapidly in recent years; they were favored by the easier licensing requirements (Thailand) and less stringent regulations, including lower capital requirements (Korea and the Philippines) than those applied to commercial banks.[12] Merchant banks in Korea and finance companies in Thailand were the first institutions to face liquidity shortfalls, and many became insolvent and had to be closed.[13]

---

[10]Banks had lent substantial amounts in foreign currency to borrowers without secure foreign exchange revenue streams. The corporate sector's repayment capacity became severely impaired once the currencies started to depreciate, leading to corporate insolvencies and major problems for the banks.

[11]Nonbank financial institutions had become increasingly important compared to commercial banks in Korea and Thailand. This trend has been particularly striking in Korea, where commercial banks' share of total deposits has fallen from 71 percent in 1980 to 30 percent at the end of 1996 to the benefit of investment trust companies, insurance companies, and other nonbank financial institutions.

[12]There is an argument for less stringent prudential requirements for nonbank financial institutions, insofar as they perform a narrower range of activities. However, these institutions in the Asian crisis countries operated broadly like commercial banks.

[13]Finance companies in Malaysia also faced liquidity shortfalls. There, the government's policy has been to strengthen the sector through mergers (see Section V).

The corporate sector in Korea and Thailand was highly leveraged, a factor that, in combination with the pervasive nature of the corporate crisis, significantly deepened the banking crisis. Average debt to equity ratios of listed companies were around 400 percent in both countries at the end of 1996. By contrast, ratios in Indonesia, Malaysia, and the Philip-

Figure 4. Nominal Credit Growth to the Private Sector
(In percent)

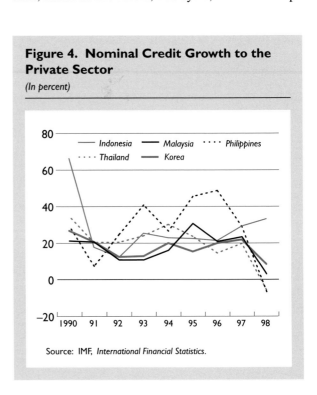

Source: IMF, *International Financial Statistics.*

Box 3. Structure of the Financial System at the End of 1996

Commercial banks dominated the financial system in *Indonesia*. Out of a total of 238 commercial banks, there were 7 state-owned banks, 27 regional government banks, 160 private banks, 34 joint-venture banks, and 10 foreign banks. In addition, there were approximately 9,200 rural banks. Nonbank financial institutions included 252 finance companies, 163 insurance companies, about 300 pension and provident funds, and 39 mutual fund companies. Total assets of the system were equivalent to about 90 percent of GDP. Commercial banks held 84 percent of total assets while rural banks held about 2 percent. The remaining assets were held by finance companies (7 percent of total assets), insurance companies (5 percent), and other nonbank financial institutions (2 percent).

Korea's financial system was the most differentiated among these countries, with 26 commercial banks, 52 branches of foreign commercial banks, 7 specialized and development banks, 30 merchant banks, 30 investment trust companies, 33 life insurance companies, 17 nonlife insurance companies, 56 securities companies, 19 investment advisory companies, 230 mutual savings companies, 2 credit guarantee funds, and approximately 6,000 credit unions, mutual credit facilities, and community credit cooperatives. Total assets of the system were close to 300 percent of GDP. Commercial banks alone accounted for 52 percent of total assets, while specialized and development banks accounted for 17 percent.[1] Merchant banks held a further 5 percent; insurance companies 7 percent; while the remaining 19 percent were held by other types of institutions.

In *Malaysia*, the financial system included 35 commercial banks, 39 finance companies, 12 merchant banks, 7 discount houses, 4 pension and provident funds, 62 insurance companies, 6 unit trusts, 7 development institutions, and a savings bank. Total assets of the system were equivalent to 300 percent of GDP. Commercial banks accounted for 70 percent of total assets of the banking system (comprising the commercial banks, finance companies, and merchant banks), and merchant banks and finance companies for 30 percent of total assets.

Although the financial sector in the *Philippines* included different types of banks and nonbanks, the sector was dominated by commercial banks. At the end of 1996, there were 49 commercial banks, 3 specialized government banks, 109 thrift banks, approximately 800 rural banks, 129 insurance companies, 12 nonbank financial institutions with quasi-banking functions, and a large number of small nonbank institutions without quasi-banking functions. The number of foreign banks that operate wholly owned branches in the Philippines is currently capped at 14. Total assets of the system were equivalent to 115 percent of GDP. Commercial banks held 82 percent of total assets, thrift banks accounted for 9 percent, rural banks 1 percent, and nonbanks the remaining 8 percent.

In *Thailand*, the financial system included 29 commercial banks, 91 finance and securities companies, 7 specialized state-owned banks, approximately 4,000 savings and agricultural cooperatives, 15 insurance companies, 880 private provident funds, and 8 mutual fund management companies. Out of the 29 commercial banks, 14 were branches of foreign banks. In addition, 19 foreign banks were established under the offshore Bangkok International Banking Facilities, which lent to residents in foreign currency. Total assets of the system amounted to the equivalent of 190 percent of GDP. Commercial banks alone accounted for 64 percent of total assets, while finance companies accounted for 20 percent of total assets. State-owned specialized banks accounted for a further 10 percent.

In all countries, except Indonesia, banks were mostly private, with many of the larger private banks publicly listed. The degree of ownership concentration differed across countries: in Korea, a single ownership limit of 4 percent meant that banks were owned by diverse groups of individuals, while in Thailand, despite a similar rule, several of the large banks were owned or controlled by family groups. Similarly, in Indonesia, Malaysia, and the Philippines, banks were owned or controlled by corporate conglomerates.

At the same time, a significant part of the banking sector was owned by the public sector, especially in Indonesia where public sector banks accounted for over 40 percent of total assets of the financial system. In Korea and Thailand, state-owned institutions represented about 15 percent of total assets. In Malaysia one large commercial bank was government-owned.

There were also foreign banks (branches or subsidiaries) with substantial stakes (5–20 percent of total banking system assets) in the domestic financial system in all five countries, although the degree of financial openness in each country differed, with Korea, Malaysia, and Thailand being the most restrictive and the Philippines the least. In Indonesia, foreign banks were allowed to own up to 85 percent of a joint venture.

---

[1]Assets include trust accounts, which are a significant share of commercial bank assets (about 40 percent). Trust accounts have grown rapidly and are subject to weaker regulation and fewer restrictions than regular bank accounts.

Box 4. Weaknesses in Disclosure Practices in the Asian Crisis Countries

The following shortcomings in accounting and disclosure practices undercut market discipline and fueled the crisis.

- High corporate leverage was hidden by related-party transactions and off-balance sheet financing.
- High-level foreign exchange risk exposure by corporations and banks resulting from large, short-term borrowing in foreign currency was not evident.
- Disclosure of loan classification, loan-loss provisioning, and accrual of interest was weak. Although most banks disclosed the accounting policy for loan-loss provisioning, they did not disclose in the balance sheet the aggregate amount of loans and advances for which they had stopped accruing interest.

- In Korea, the practice of cross-guarantees made it hard to assess the solvency of the largest borrowers.
- Consolidation of accounts was generally absent.
- Detailed information on sectoral concentration was largely absent, even though all countries had large exposure limits in place.
- Disclosure regarding derivative financial instruments was weak.
- Contingent liabilities of the parent of a conglomerate, or of financial institutions, for guaranteeing loans (particularly foreign currency loans) were generally not reported.

---

pines were about 150 to 200 percent.[14] With the exception of Indonesia, corporate leverage had increased significantly over the 1990s.[15] The high corporate leverage in Korea was largely the outcome of government policies that emphasized aggressive export-oriented growth and included measures such as directed credit, subsidized loans, and explicit or implicit credit guarantees that biased funding in favor of borrowing rather than equity placements. In Thailand, corporate borrowing reflected optimistic growth projections and a push to gain market share. At the same time, equity markets in the three crisis countries were undeveloped, since large family-controlled corporations were hesitant to raise funds through equity financing lest their control be diluted. In Malaysia, the stock market was particularly highly developed (with a capitalization of over 300 percent of GDP at the end of 1996; see Table 2), reducing the need for bank financing.

Structural Vulnerabilities

Bank lending practices in the five countries have traditionally relied on collateral rather than credit assessment and cash flow analysis, making banks especially vulnerable to excessive risk taking and declines in asset values. For example, during the years of high economic growth, credits were increasingly

used to fund investments that turned out to be economically unsound. When the exchange rate devaluation and contraction in demand rapidly eroded companies' repayment capacity (see footnote 10), banks and supervisors were suddenly faced with sharply increasing nonperforming loans, loan-loss provisioning needs, declines in collateral values, and eroding capital bases. Other inadequate lending practices including connected lending, high exposure to individual clients, and excessive sectoral concentration of loans, aggravated the problem.

In addition, ineffective market discipline allowed excessive risk taking. Inadequate accounting and disclosure practices (see Box 4) and implicit government guarantees weakened market discipline. A tradition of forbearance and "lifeboat" schemes for nonviable institutions instead of firmer corrective action or government intervention encouraged excessive risk taking, increased moral hazard, and prevented market agents from exerting discipline. As a result, risk premiums, credit ratings, and analyst reports, including reports of international financial institutions, indicate that market participants did not identify the weaknesses and did not predict crisis.

In the crisis countries, prudential regulation and supervision had serious deficiencies. These deficiencies included lax prudential rules, or application of rules, particularly on connected lending, loan concentration, cross guarantees, and foreign currency mismatches. A significant problem was the lack of strict loan classification criteria and weak rules on loan provisioning and interest suspension. In addition, financial sector regulators and supervisors lacked autonomy, making them susceptible to political and industry pressure. Supervisors frequently waived prescribed limits, a significant problem in

---

[14]In comparison, such ratios were about 110 in the United States, 140 in Germany, and 200 in Japan; see the World Bank (1998).

[15]For example, between 1991 and 1996, leverage had doubled in Malaysia and Thailand; see the World Bank (1998).

Korea and Thailand.[16] The prudential framework also failed to keep up with the developments in the system. For example, in some countries prudential rules on foreign currency exposures failed to limit excessive foreign open positions or maturity mismatches. More broadly, building up supervisory capacity was not a priority during the boom years.

---

[16]In addition, in Korea, commercial, development, and merchant banks were regulated and supervised by different agencies, allowing for regulatory arbitrage and making consolidated supervision difficult.

Weaknesses in supervision were compounded by the close links between governments and financial institutions. The government's interference in credit allocation in Indonesia and Korea (through directed credits) circumvented the need for thorough risk assessment by the banks, made the governments co–responsible for the quality of banks' assets, and provided an implicit government guarantee on banks' liabilities. Furthermore, given the governments' historic role of promoting investment through policy loans and guarantees to corporations, supervisors were constrained in their ability to penalize banks for making bad loans.

III Addressing the Emergency

In all the countries discussed in this paper, urgent measures had to be taken to contain the crisis (Indonesia, Korea, and Thailand) or prevent growing pressures from developing into a full-blown crisis (Malaysia and the Philippines).

In systemic banking crises, major government intervention is required even in countries strongly committed to market-oriented policies. Such intervention is justified by negative externalities associated with widespread bank failures, such as a breakdown in the payment system, disruptions to credit flows, and depositor losses. Moreover, financial sector soundness facilitates macroeconomic stabilization and creates the conditions for the resumption of growth. In all the crisis countries and Malaysia, the authorities weighed the effects of these externalities against the potential fiscal costs of intervention and the moral hazard problems and decided to implement proactive restructuring strategies.

Strategies for dealing with the financial sector crisis have sought to incorporate good practices from international experience and have the following components: stabilization of the financial system; changes in the institutional framework to deal effectively with the crisis; resolution of nonviable financial institutions; strengthening of viable financial institutions; management of nonperforming assets; and restructuring of the corporate sector (see Box 5 for an overview of bank resolution procedures). While the broad strategies were similar across the crisis countries, each country adapted them to take into account national circumstances and preferences (see Appendices I–V for a detailed description of country-specific circumstances). These components are discussed in detail in Section V.

The initial priorities of such a strategy were to stabilize the financial sector and lay out a restructuring strategy. They were complemented by a macroeconomic stabilization plan. Stabilization of the financial sector was accomplished by providing central bank liquidity support and a blanket guarantee on depositors and most creditors.[17] To stabilize foreign funding, countries used voluntary debt restructuring where feasible (notably Korea), and capital controls on outflows (Malaysia). To cut the flow of central bank liquidity support, prevent further losses, and demonstrate their commitment to implement necessary reforms, authorities closed institutions judged to be insolvent or nonviable. These measures were the first elements of broader restructuring plans.

Macroeconomic Policies

A credible macroeconomic stabilization program was essential to restore depositor and creditor confidence.[18] After the initial shocks—that is, withdrawals of foreign funds and exchange rate depreciation leading to further withdrawals of capital—all countries sought to implement macroeconomic stabilization policies. Monetary policy was used to dampen overshooting of nominal exchange rates and avert depreciation–inflation spirals. Following the initial depreciations, however, uncertainty over the success of stabilization efforts and continued efforts of foreign creditors to cut their exposure in Asia led to continued capital flight, further exchange rate depreciation, and higher interest rates, all of which aggravated problems in the corporate and financial sectors. In Indonesia, confidence was further undermined by policy reversals.

A well-designed, comprehensive, and credible financial sector restructuring strategy was necessary for a sustainable macroeconomic stabilization and resumption of high growth. Progress in structural reforms was also critical for improving domestic and foreign confidence in these economies. Questions arose over which to put first: should the economic programs have focused exclusively on macroeconomic policies, leaving the structural re-

---

[17]In Korea, the government initially announced a guarantee on foreign debt, but this failed to stem capital outflows, probably because of uncertainty about the legal status of the measure and about the government's ability to honor it. In Indonesia, the government initially announced a limited deposit guarantee that soon had to be replaced by a blanket guarantee.

[18]See Lane and others (1999) for a more detailed discussion of macroeconomic policies in the crisis countries.

Box 5. Bank Resolution Procedures: Terminology and Definitions

A variety of resolution procedures have been employed in the Asian crisis countries. This box defines the terminology used in this paper.

A bank *closure* is the act whereby a bank is physically closed to the public and, thus, prevented from doing business. A closure can be final or temporary (it may also be partial, involving continued management of existing assets and liabilities). In a legal final closure of an institution, there are several resolution options: the institution can exit the system either through liquidation or through a complete or partial transfer of its assets and liabilities to other institutions, as discussed below. In a temporary closure, the terms *suspension* and *freeze* may also be used. The purpose of a temporary closure is to allow time for a more careful evaluation of the institution's situation, or to allow owners time to present recapitalization and restructuring plans.

Intervention by the authorities in insolvent or nonviable institutions refers to the authorities' assuming control of a bank, taking over the powers of management and shareholders. An intervened bank usually stays open under the control of the authorities, while its financial condition is better defined and decisions are made on an appropriate resolution strategy. Resolution strategies include liquidation, nationalization, mergers/sales, purchase and assumption operations, and the use of bridge banks.

Liquidation is the legal process whereby the assets of an institution are sold, its liabilities are settled to the extent possible, and its license is withdrawn. A bank liquidation can be voluntary or forced, within or outside general bankruptcy procedures, and with or without court involvement. In a liquidation assets are sold to pay off the creditors in the order prescribed by the law. In a systemic crisis with several institutions to be liquidated simultaneously and quickly, special procedures or special institutions may be needed for the liquida-tion, as existing structures (e.g., the regular court system) cannot carry out the job in a timely manner.

Nationalization means that the authorities take over an insolvent bank and recapitalize it. It differs from the traditional use of the term "nationalization," which describes a government takeover of a solvent private bank. Governments in the crisis countries distinguish such temporarily nationalized banks from other state-owned banks and often seek to divest/privatize the nationalized institutions at an early date.

In a *merger* (or sale) of an institution, all the assets and liabilities of the firm are transferred to another institution. Mergers can be voluntary or government assisted. A key issue is to avoid situations in which a merger of weak banks results in a much larger weak bank, or in which an initially strong bank is substantially weakened.

In a *purchase and assumption (P&A) operation*, a solvent bank purchases a portion of the assets of a failing bank, including its customer base and goodwill, and assumes all or part of its liabilities. In a publicly supported P&A operation, the government typically will pay the purchasing bank the difference between the value of the assets and liabilities. Variations of P&A operations could be a purchase of assets, entitling the acquiring bank to return certain assets within a specified time period, or a contractual profit/loss-sharing agreement related to some or all the assets. P&A operations in the context of bank resolution can involve the liquidation or transfer of bad assets to an asset management company.

A variation of a P&A operation involves the use of a temporary financial institution—a *bridge bank*—to receive and manage the good assets of one or several failed institutions. The bridge bank may be allowed to undertake some banking business, such as providing new credit and rolling over existing credits. Bad assets would be liquidated or transferred to an asset management company.

---

forms for a later time, or should structural reforms have been made at a slower pace? Several considerations regarding the financial sector argued against delay. First, a banking system saddled with large amounts of nonperforming loans would have maintained an excessively cautious lending policy, which would have caused an even greater credit slowdown and further delayed the restoration of normal credit flows. Second, where banks (and companies) were insolvent, allowing them to continue operating without restructuring would have allowed market distortions and moral hazards to build. Third, bank and corporate restructuring was necessary to facilitate the rollover of maturing foreign loans and new private investment that was crucial to ensuring the necessary financing of the economies; it would have been difficult for such flows to resume if domestic banks and corporations were perceived to remain financially shaky and inadequately supervised. Fourth, keeping insolvent banks (and companies) in operation could have entailed higher fiscal costs and further complicated monetary management.

The crises themselves created a demand for structural reforms. There was a widespread perception domestically and abroad that serious structural flaws in banking and corporate practices had been key determinants of the crisis. Thus, economic programs that failed to address those flaws and practices would likely have been viewed to be incomplete or have only a temporary success. Moreover, there was a momentum and a social pressure for reform. For instance in Korea, labor unions demanded that the chaebols—the large diversified industrial groupings—be reformed not only on economic grounds but also on equity considerations. In particular, the union view that the unavoidable social cost of the crisis be borne also by the owners of the chaebols helped to mobilize government support for the reforms. In Thailand, there was also widespread acceptance of a need for changes to the financial and corporate infrastructure to ensure that excessive risks and vulnerabilities of the kind that had led to the crisis would not be repeated. The sharp reduction in demand put pressure on corporations in all the countries to restructure their business. For some time, the authorities had identified and prepared many of the structural reforms that became part of IMF-supported programs; the crisis brought the pressure for many such reforms to be implemented. For instance, in Korea, a program of financial reform had been prepared but was only implemented when the crisis broke.

It is doubtful that the crisis economies could have been stabilized and confidence returned—even temporarily—without implementing major structural reforms. Malaysia, which did not have an open liquidity crisis, also found it essential to implement far-reaching reforms of its bank and corporate sectors. Without structural reforms, forbearance regarding loss recognition would have allowed inefficient and unsound enterprises and banks to continue operations, leading to growing distortions, discouraging new private investment, and constituting a major burden on economic growth. As a result, the fiscal costs of the restructuring—which already raise medium-term sustainability concerns—would have been even higher. Also, not addressing the key sources of the crisis would have cast a cloud over the success of any program. All these elements suggest that, had the structural reforms been delayed or very weak—for example, the continued financing of non-viable institutions—this would have cast strong doubts on the sustainability of any macroeconomic adjustment.

Liquidity Support

The central banks in all five countries provided liquidity to financial institutions to offset the withdrawal of deposits and credits at some institutions. Many banks were subject to withdrawals both from domestic depositors and creditors, as well as external creditors. Central banks provided liquidity under various emergency lending and lender-of-last-resort facilities. The amounts were especially large in Indonesia and Thailand (Table 3). Most liquidity support was in domestic currency except for Korea, where the Bank of Korea also provided support in foreign currency ($23.3 billion) to commercial

banks. In Korea, Malaysia, and Thailand, support was also provided to nonbank financial institutions, such as merchant banks and finance companies.

To preserve monetary control these massive amounts of liquidity support had to be sterilized. Sterilization enabled central banks to recycle liquidity from banks gaining deposits to those losing deposits and credit lines. Sterilization had to take place amid underdeveloped money and interbank markets.[19] Sterilization was largely effective in Korea and Thailand but not in Indonesia where, for several months, protracted political and macroeconomic uncertainties resulted in continued deposit withdrawals and capital outflows from the system as a whole, making it impossible for the central bank to recycle liquidity. The resultant highly expansionary monetary policy led to a continued flight from the currency and to the collapse of the rupiah. Since July 1998, when overall conditions stabilized, monetary policy exercised through market-based auctions became more effective. In Malaysia, sterilization was partial, because of concerns about the effect of high interest rates on economic activity.

Blanket Guarantees

To stabilize banks' funding and prevent bank runs, Indonesia, Korea, Malaysia, and Thailand announced full protection for depositors and creditors. In all four countries this blanket guarantee was introduced as soon as the severity of the crisis became apparent. Such a guarantee entails a firm commitment by the government to depositors and most creditors of financial institutions that their claims will be honored.[20] A blanket guarantee generally aims at providing confidence in the banking system; stabilizing the institutions' liability side; buying time while the restructuring work is being organized and carried out; and preserving the integrity of the payment system. Thailand had announced the major elements of the guarantee in July 1997, which was reconfirmed under the IMF-supported program in August 1997. Korea established a full guarantee in November of that year, before negotiations with the IMF had started. In Indonesia, the blanket guarantee

---

[19]Low levels of public debt meant that there was a lack of government paper—usually a core element of well-developed money markets. In Indonesia, the development of a market for central bank bills had been stunted by the authorities' failure to allow full market determination of interest rates.

[20]The guarantees were, as a rule, not applied to shareholders and holders of subordinated debt. In Indonesia, insider deposits were not covered by the guarantee. In Thailand, directors' and related persons' deposits and/or claims were not covered by the guarantee unless they could prove that these transactions were at "arms length."

Table 3. Liquidity Support Provided to Financial Institutions, June 1997 to June 1999

	Stock of Support (at peak)	Form	Repaid as of End of April 1999	Notes
Indonesia	170 trillion rupiah in June 1998 (17 percent of GDP).	Overdrafts.	10 trillion rupiah.[1]	Stock of liquidity support increased from 60 to 170 trillion rupiah between November 1997 and June 1998.
Korea	10.2 trillion in won in December 1997 (2 percent of GDP).	Deposits and loans.	9.2 trillion won.	Most of the liquidity support provided in November and December 1997.
	23.3 billion in U.S. dollars (5 percent of GDP).		20 billion U.S. dollars.	
Malaysia	35 billion ringgit in early 1998 (13 percent of GDP).	Deposits.	n.a.	Most liquidity support in early through mid-1998.
Philippines	18.6 billion pesos (0.8 percent of GDP) in May 1998.	Emergency loans and overdrafts.	5.6 billion pesos.	Provided in late 1997 to mid-1998.
Thailand	1,037 billion baht in early 1999 (22 percent of GDP).	Loans from the Financial Instititions Development Fund (FIDF) and capital injections.	54 billion baht.[2]	Most liquidity support provided in mid-1997 through mid-1998.

Source: IMF staff estimates.
[1]Excluding commitments from former shareholders of banks that received liquidity support to make repayments over four years.
[2]The total would be 561 billion baht, if debt-equity conversions were included.

was established as part of an IMF-supported program (January 1998), after a limited guarantee had failed to stabilize the situation. Although never faced with a full-blown crisis, the government in Malaysia introduced a blanket guarantee in January 1998. The Philippine authorities, in contrast, have not seen a need for a blanket guarantee. The country had a well-established limited deposit insurance scheme that had been tested in the precrisis period. In none of the countries was any sort of government guarantee extended to entities or shareholders in the nonfinancial sector.

The modalities of the guarantees differed slightly from country to country. In Thailand, the guarantee was preceded by the announcement that the operations of 58 finance companies would be suspended pending acceptable recapitalization proposals and that depositors and some creditors in those companies would be compensated in full or in part, in line with the government's earlier announcement.[21] All depositors and creditors of remaining finance compa-

nies and commercial banks were fully guaranteed. In Indonesia, delays in recognizing the systemic nature of the crisis slowed the introduction of the blanket guarantee. Thus, the Indonesian government initially attempted to control the crisis by extending liquidity support to problem banks and instituting a limited deposit insurance scheme.[22] However, such limited depositor protection was ineffective, and when a large number of banks experienced runs, making apparent the systemic nature of the problem, the government announced a blanket guarantee for all depositors and creditors. The Korean government announced a full guarantee on all depositors and most creditors of financial institutions. Malaysia offered the blanket guarantee on deposits to all commercial banks, finance companies, and merchant banks, including the overseas branches of domestic banking institutions. In all countries, the guarantees were announced to be temporary and meant to maintain public confidence during the period of restructuring.[23] All the countries'

---

[21]A cabinet decision in July 1997 had already guaranteed the deposits in finance companies. There were two phases in the suspension of these companies. In the first phase, 16 companies were suspended and only depositors were covered by the guarantee. In the second phase, 42 companies were suspended, and both depositors and creditors were covered by the guarantee.

[22]This partial scheme had been planned by the authorities for some time.

[23]No explicit expiration date was announced in Thailand and Malaysia. The Indonesian government extended the guarantee for at least two years, with a six-month notification period before it would be lifted. In Korea, the guarantee would expire by the end of the year 2000.

Box 6. Emergency Capital Control Measures

Indonesia imposed limits on forward sales of foreign exchange contracts by domestic banks to nonresidents (excluding trade and investment related transactions) in August 1997.

Malaysia attempted to minimize the impact of short-term capital flows on the domestic economy by first restricting (August 1997) and later (September 1998) eliminating the offshore ringgit market. As such, the measures eliminated practically all legal channels for transfer of ringgit abroad; required the repatriation of ringgit held offshore to Malaysia; blocked the repatriation of portfolio capital held by nonresidents in Malaysia for a 12-month period; and imposed tight limits on transfers of capital abroad by residents. In February 1999, the 12-month holding period rule was replaced with a graduated system of exit levy on repatriation of portfolio investments, with the rate of the levy decreasing with the duration of investment.

In July 1997, the *Philippines* began to require prior approval for the sale of nondeliverable forwards to nonresidents and lowered the limit on residents' foreign currency purchases from banks for nontrade purposes. The latter limit was further reduced in April 1998.

As soon as the pressure on the exchange rate started to build up (May–June 1997), *Thailand* took a series of measures to limit baht lending to nonresidents through transactions that could facilitate a buildup of baht positions in the offshore market. Genuine underlying business related to current international transactions, FDI flows, and various portfolio investments were exempt. These measures in reality led to the creation of a two-tier exchange market with separate exchange rates for investors who buy baht in domestic and overseas markets (the spreads between both rates were narrow).

---

central banks announced that they would provide the necessary liquidity to make it possible to honor the guarantee.

A blanket guarantee must be credible to stop the need for liquidity support and the run on banks. Credibility can be enhanced by stating the terms of the guarantee explicitly, and by confirming the government's commitment by law and making the guarantee part of a comprehensive restructuring strategy and part of the macroeconomic program. Most countries faced credibility issues initially. In Thailand, where the full guarantee was announced as part of the IMF-supported program, markets did not trust the government's commitment until the legal status of the guarantee had been strengthened, and the guarantee had been tested following the intervention of some banks at the beginning of 1998. In Korea, the comprehensive IMF-supported program bolstered the credibility of the authorities' rehabilitation plan, including the blanket guarantee. In Indonesia, a blanket guarantee was introduced as part of a new bank restructuring and macroeconomic program in January 1998. As a result of these measures, the exchange rate stabilized and deposit runs subsided slowly and stopped after the guarantee was tested during the closure of seven banks in April 1998.[24]

While a blanket guarantee may be a necessary condition to stop bank runs by depositors, it is not a

sufficient one. A blanket guarantee—backed by a willingness to provide the necessary liquidity—can restore market confidence in a bank's ability to pay back deposits and other protected liabilities in local currency. However, if people are fleeing the currency (e.g., because of political uncertainties or economic turmoil), bank runs will continue because a blanket guarantee cannot restore confidence in the currency or prevent capital flight. Also, external credit lines may not be rolled over despite the guarantee, even at higher interest rates.

If the authorities wish to impose losses on depositors and creditors of failing financial institutions, they must do so before the blanket guarantee is extended. In systemic crises, however, drawing clear distinctions between categories of institutions in the initial stages may not be possible due to a lack of information or equity considerations. In Thailand, the authorities inflicted losses on some creditors of the suspended and subsequently closed finance companies.[25] The other countries did not take such a measure and covered depositors and creditors of all financial institutions still operating at the time of the announcement. Indonesia even applied the blanket guarantee retroactively to the 16 banks closed in October 1997.

Countries have introduced a variety of measures to limit moral hazard problems. These measures include intensifying the supervision of banks; capping deposit rates at a maximum premium above the av-

---

[24]Subsequently, the guarantee protected the banking system in the weeks following President Suharto's resignation in May 1998 even though there were further runs on the largest private bank, the owners of which were closely associated with the President, and the rupiah depreciated to its lowest level ever.

[25]Creditors of 16 finance companies suspended in June 1997 were treated more harshly than those of 42 companies suspended in August.

Box 7. Considerations Regarding the Immediate Closure of Banks in a Systemic Crisis

During a systemic crisis, deciding when to close banks, and which banks, is not easy. The benefits and drawbacks of immediate closure are outlined below.

Advantages

• Reduces bank losses and minimizes cost to depositors, creditors, or provider of guarantee.

• Ceases central bank liquidity support.

• Allows distribution of losses to shareholders, holders of subordinated debt, and other creditors.

• Eliminates moral hazard and adverse selection problems associated with insolvent institutions remaining in operation.

• Removes excess capacity from the financial sector.

• Helps to restore confidence in other banks and in government strategy, if done quickly and effectively.

Disadvantages

• Restricts access to deposits and disrupts payment system.

• Severs relationship between lender and borrower, causing a credit contraction.

• Fuels contagion and runs on other banks, if not executed properly (for example, without blanket guarantee).

• Leads to further loss of value of bank assets.

• May entail a base money expansion when deposits are paid out.

For closures to be successful

• Must be accompanied by a credible blanket guarantee.

• Owners and subordinated debt-holders must absorb losses.

• The right set of institutions must be included; markets should be reassured that all nonviable institutions are dealt with.

• Must include measures to protect payment system and minimize disruptions to the credit market.

• Must be accompanied by clear and consistent public announcements.

• Must be part of a broader strategy to make future banking system more efficient.

---

erage levels being offered by the "best" banks to prevent weak banks from bidding too aggressively for deposits (in Indonesia and Thailand); covering the principal of the deposit only, above a specific threshold amount (and not the interest); explicitly announcing that the blanket guarantee was a temporary measure (Indonesia, Korea, and Thailand); requiring institutions to contribute a guarantee fee (Indonesia, Korea, and Thailand);[26] and, in case of insolvent banks, completely writing down current owners' shares and removing existing management.

Blanket guarantees entail a very large contingent liability for the government. Initially, the guarantee is mainly a confidence booster, but by giving a blanket guarantee, the government acquires a sizable contingent liability against assets of uncertain value—which most often will be insufficient to pay for the contingent liability that the government will be called to honor. Even though the blanket guarantees entail large costs, these may well be lower than the potential economic and social cost of a collapse of the banking system. But since the blanket guarantee protects not just small depositors, it may entail a regressive wealth distribution effect because taxpay-

ers' funds are also used to protect large depositors and creditors, including external creditors. All these factors suggest that in each situation the costs and benefits of the blanket guarantee have to be weighed carefully. In case of a systemic crisis, however, a blanket guarantee will be necessary, provided that the government can make such a system credible and that the financial sector is deemed to be sufficiently large and of major importance to the economy.

Capital Controls and Debt Rescheduling

To stabilize foreign funding, specific measures had to be taken. The five countries followed different paths to stabilize and reverse the capital outflows. Korea continued to keep its capital account open and renegotiated the country's short-term foreign debt. In response to declining rollover rates of short-term foreign debt, Korea reached an agreement with foreign banks in January 1998 to reschedule some $22 billion in interbank deposits and short-term loans due in 1998. This marked the beginning of the stabilization of capital flows and of the rapid reduction in central bank liquidity support. Indonesia, the Philippines, and Thailand imposed temporary capital controls measures to fight currency speculation (Box 6). These controls were lifted in Indonesia and Thailand

---

[26]In Korea, there is no special contribution to the blanket guarantee as such, but financial institutions must contribute to the insurance fund administered by the Korean Deposit Insurance Company.

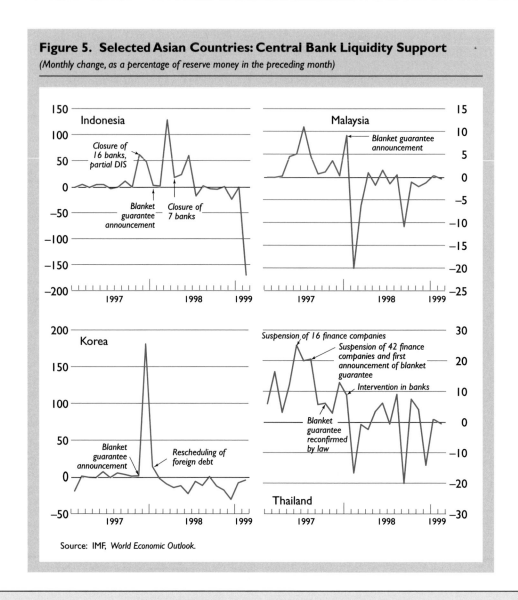

Figure 5. Selected Asian Countries: Central Bank Liquidity Support
(Monthly change, as a percentage of reserve money in the preceding month)

Source: IMF, *World Economic Outlook.*

Box 8. Indonesia: Closure of 16 Banks

At the outset of the crisis (October 1997), 16 banks (3 percent of assets of banking system) were closed. These banks had been deeply insolvent for several months and had been subject to fraud. Depositor protection was limited to the equivalent of $2,000 (this covered over 90 percent of depositors, but only 20 percent of the deposit base).

Problems

The closure of these 16 banks, unlike in Korea and Thailand, did not assist in stemming the general loss of confidence in the government and the banking sector. The main reasons for this failure appear to be:

• Some politically well-connected banks known to be insolvent were kept open (despite the recommendations of IMF staff).

• The announcement of the bank closures suggested that more banks would be closed later. This news, in conjunction with the lack of a full guarantee on depositors, led to a flight to safety because depositors expected to incur further losses.

• One politically well-connected closed bank was allowed to reopen under a new name within weeks, showing ineffectiveness in pursuing the resolution process.

• Failure on part of the government to implement key reform measures in its IMF-supported program.

• After an initial fall-off of bank runs, depositors started to withdraw funds in sizable amounts from many banks, with a tendency to redeposit in state banks.

once an IMF-supported program was in place. Malaysia introduced more comprehensive controls over capital flows. Indonesia, Korea, and Thailand all liberalized foreign ownership rules during the crisis to attract additional foreign capital to the financial and corporate sectors.

Immediate Closing of Financial Institutions

Closing of insolvent or nearly insolvent financial institutions in the three crisis countries was needed to stem accumulating losses and rapidly growing liquidity support and to give markets a signal that there was a break from the past practice of extensive forbearance (Box 7, see page 21). In Thailand, 58 finance institutions had their operations suspended—56 of which were later closed (for liquidation) after failing to present acceptable recapitalization plans. The Korean government initially suspended 14 merchant banks, 10 of which were later liquidated. Subsequently, seven more merchant banks would be closed. In Indonesia, the closure of 16 small, deeply insolvent private banks was soon followed by intensified bank runs. The partial nature of guarantees provided to depositors, the perception that other weak institutions remained in the system, a loss of confidence in the government's overall economic management, and a flight from the currency fueled the runs. Indonesia's experience, contrasted with that of Korea and Thailand, underscores the fact that bank closures are only successful if all clearly nonviable institutions are closed; the action is part of a comprehensive and credible restructuring strategy; appropriate macroeconomic policies are in place; and the process is clearly and credibly explained to the public (Box 8).

The selection of nonviable institutions to be closed relied largely on liquidity indicators, such as borrowing from the central bank. This was necessary given the typical lack of meaningful information on bank solvency and the realization that insolvent banks can operate as long as they remain liquid. The liquidity triggers typically included the size of central bank credit as a multiple of bank capital.[27] Only later, as more information became available either through special audits or the supervisory process, could solvency indicators be used as criteria for choosing nonviable institutions (see Section V). In Korea, solvency data were available from the beginning and insolvency was the criterion for the suspension of merchant banks and for corrective action vis-à-vis the two most distressed commercial banks.

The combined emergency measures reduced the need for central bank liquidity support (see Figure 5). In Korea, these measures, in conjunction with the macrostabilization plan, and the announcement of a restructuring strategy, had an immediate effect on the demand for central bank liquidity support. A similar effect can be observed from the announcement of the blanket guarantee in Malaysia as part of a restructuring plan. In Thailand, the demand for central bank credit from finance companies abated in the aftermath of the suspensions, although several small- and medium-sized banks required support until they were intervened in early 1998. As explained earlier, the impact in Indonesia was different; even after the introduction of the blanket guarantee, banks' demand for central bank liquidity did not subside until after the closing of another seven banks in April 1998.

---

[27]For example, four times bank capital was used in Indonesia and three times in Thailand for the suspension of the 58 finance companies.

IV Monetary and Credit Policies

The crisis had profound effects on the overall monetary environment and on policymakers' ability to use financial policies to steer the economy. This section examines the difficulties encountered and discusses the possible interaction between measures to reestablish monetary control and the observed decline in credit to the economy in the crisis countries.

Monetary Management

Monetary management is particularly challenging during a banking crisis because the relationships between money and intermediate and final targets of monetary policy tend to become unstable.[28] Banking crises can affect the short-run stability of money demand, the money multiplier, velocity, the transmission mechanism, and various signa l variables for monetary policy. In the first instance, this occurs because of changes in the composition of money and credit aggregates.[29] Table 4 shows how the variability of a set of monetary aggregates increased during the period. In addition, the segmentation of the interbank market in some countries complicated the choice of interest rate for the central bank to target. (Figure 6 illustrates how interbank rates diverged significantly across groups of banks in Indonesia in early 1998.) In this context, monetary policy focused on the exchange rate, short-term interest rates and the level of international reserves (see Section VII for a discussion of the implications of the shift in relationships for IMF programs).

Credit Crunch

Whether there was a credit crunch in the Asian crisis countries has been a matter of debate.[30] A credit crunch has been traditionally defined as an excess demand for credit under prevailing interest rates, or a situation where credit is rationed through non-price mechanisms. Frequently, however, the term has been used more loosely to describe a fall in real credit to the private sector. In all countries, the growth rate of real credit has indeed declined sharply since late 1997, which has been interpreted as a credit crunch (Figure 7). However, care is needed when measuring and interpreting credit developments in a crisis situation. Measurement of credit developments is generally blurred by such factors as the treatment of loans that are written off or transferred to an asset management company, the rollover of credits, and the effects of bank closures and valuation changes on the data.[31]

When an economy is hit by a negative shock, it is often difficult to determine whether a decline in the growth of credit is the result of a shift in demand or in the supply of credit. In Asia, both demand and supply were affected. On the one hand, demand for credit declined as consumption and investment were sharply reduced because of uncertainty, overcapacity, weakening economic conditions, and the negative wealth effect arising from a fall in asset prices.

---

[28]Garcia-Herrero (1997) discusses the monetary impact of a banking crisis.

[29]For example, in Korea, credit aggregates would have shown a decline in credit over 1998 unless adjustments were made to take into account the large amounts of nonperforming loans being sold to the public asset management company. Monetary aggregates should also be adjusted for the large exchange rate valuation changes.

[30]For a discussion, see Lane and others (1999), in particular Box 6.5, which, based on several empirical studies, concludes that the findings are mixed. Empirical work is presented in Ghosh and Ghosh (1999), who found evidence for a credit crunch in Indonesia (in late 1997), and in Korea and Thailand (from late 1997 to early 1998), although in the latter two countries, credit demand fell so sharply that supply was not a binding constraint. Dollar and Hallward-Driemeier (1998) found that in Thailand, from late 1997 to early 1998, the lack of access to credit was regarded as the least important factor by manufacturing firms as reasons for slowing down output; Ding, Domaç, and Ferri (1998) found evidence for a widespread credit crunch in Thailand, particularly in the first few months of the crisis.

[31]For a discussion of these and related issues, as well as enhancements to the monetary survey to address these weaknesses, see Frécaut and Sidgwick (1998).

Table 4. Standard Deviation of Selected Monetary Indicators

	June 1996 to June 1997	June 1997 to June 1998
Indonesia		
Demand deposits/M2	0.53	0.95
Time, savings, foreign currency deposits/M2	0.55	0.96
Money multiplier	0.14	0.27
Korea		
Demand deposits/M3	0.19	0.45
Time, savings, foreign currency deposits/M3	0.44	0.72
Money multiplier	0.27	0.55
Malaysia		
Demand deposits/M2	0.89	1.77
Time, savings, foreign currency deposits/M2	0.91	3.06
Money multiplier	0.09	0.36
Philippines		
Demand deposits/M3	0.50	0.64
Time, savings, foreign currency deposits/M3	0.02	0.02
Money multiplier	0.16	0.21
Thailand		
Demand deposits/M2	0.30	0.28
Time, savings, foreign currency deposits/M2	0.39	0.51
Money multiplier	0.34	0.58

Sources: IMF, *International Financial Statistics*; and national authorities.

Figure 6. Indonesia: Daily Interbank Money Market Rates by Type of Bank

(In percent per year)

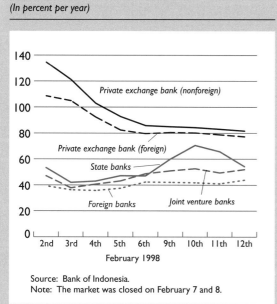

Source: Bank of Indonesia.
Note: The market was closed on February 7 and 8.

On the other hand, borrowers lost creditworthiness, which made banks reluctant to lend, even at higher interest rates. A self-reinforcing dynamic may develop where negative economic shocks may lead to a decline in the demand for credit. Such a situation will also affect the financial system—leading to a decline in the supply of credit, which, in turn, will aggravate the distress in the real sector, further weakening the demand for credit. The following paragraphs discuss the supply-side factors in more detail. A full analysis of the demand-side factors is beyond the scope of this paper.

Even though, in aggregate, deposits did not fall, many institutions had liquidity problems because of a shift of deposits to higher-quality institutions. In addition, the drying up of foreign credit lines forced banks to preserve liquidity by recovering assets as quickly as possible and slowing new lending, thus reducing growth in the supply of credit. For example, foreign claims on banks in Indonesia declined by about 43 percent between the end of December 1997 and the end of June 1998; the decline was much slower (21 percent) during the second half of 1998. Corresponding declines for Korea are 27 percent and 15 percent for the same periods, and 31 percent and 27 percent for Thailand.

Figure 7. Growth Rate of Real Credit to the Private Sector
(In percent)

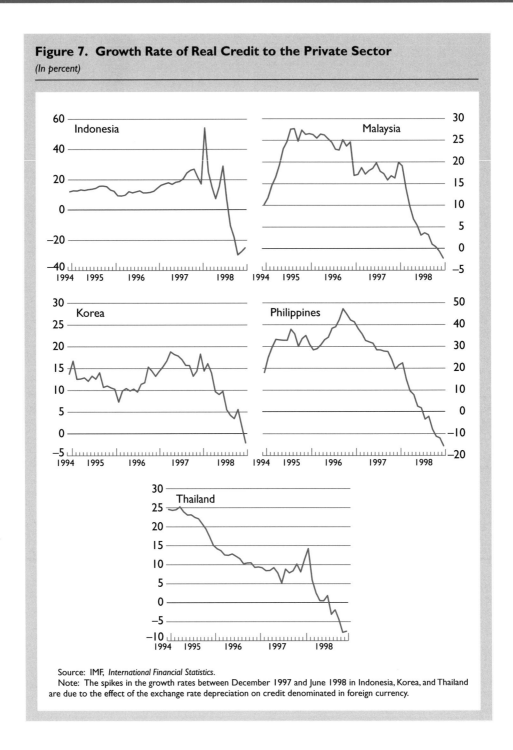

Source: IMF, *International Financial Statistics.*
Note: The spikes in the growth rates between December 1997 and June 1998 in Indonesia, Korea, and Thailand are due to the effect of the exchange rate depreciation on credit denominated in foreign currency.

The need to increase loan-loss provisions and maintain capital adequacy affected banks' ability to lend. Stricter capital adequacy requirements and/or provisioning rules are likely to have further reduced banks' willingness to lend. Instead of lending banks would increase their holdings of more liquid and safer assets, which carry lower weights in the computation of capital adequacy requirements, thus reducing the supply of credit.[32] To mitigate these ef-

---

[32]Growth in security holdings other than those acquired as part of recapitalization exceeded the growth in loans for Korea, Malaysia, and Thailand during 1998.

Table 5. Measures to Alleviate the Credit Slowdown

	Measures
Indonesia	Credit facility to small- and medium-sized enterprises; allow negative interest rate spreads; Indonesian Bank Restructuring Agency (IBRA) takeover of certain insolvent banks; export credit guarantee scheme; recapitalization assistance.
Korea	Discount facility at central bank for loans to small- and medium-sized enterprises; credit guarantee scheme; moral suasion to lend to small- and medium-sized enterprises; bridge banks and purchase and assumption operations for bank closures; recapitalization assistance; purchases of nonperforming loans.
Malaysia	Moral suasion on banks to lend; lower interest rates (or interest margins); lower reserve and liquid asset requirements; mandated targets on lending to private sector; purchases of nonperforming loans.
Philippines	Suspended the general provisioning requirement for loans in excess of outstanding stock at the end of March 1999; lower reserve requirements.
Thailand	Special credit facility for small- and medium-sized enterprises and exporters; moral suasion on lending rates; recapitalization support.

Source: IMF.

fects, in each country banks were given time to phase in tighter prudential standards (see Section V). Banks also became extremely risk averse in a situation where the creditworthiness of potential borrowers rapidly deteriorated.

The closure of financial institutions may also have affected the availability of credit. Customers of closed institutions had difficulty building up a credit relationship with other financial intermediaries in the middle of the crisis. For instance, in Korea and Thailand, groups of borrowers served by merchant banks and finance companies lost access to credit as a result of closures. In addition, liquidation processes can have varying effects on credit availability, in that they can accelerate repayment (as in Korea), or require customers to repay loans on maturity that would otherwise have been rolled over, or, on the contrary, remove pressure from repayment or servicing the debt for some or all customers. To reduce the negative effects on credit, regulators at first closed only those institutions that were most deeply insolvent, applying other resolution procedures that would allow customers to continue their credit relationship (such as nationalization, intervention, mergers, purchase and assumption operations, or bridge banks; see Box 5) to remaining institutions.

All countries used a variety of measures in an effort to alleviate the credit slowdown in their economies. These include direct measures, such as special credit facilities for small- and medium-sized enterprises, credit guarantees, and mandated credit targets, as well as indirect ones, such as "moral suasion" on banks to lend or keep interest rates or inter-

est margins low and gradualism in the application of prudential rules and public resources to help banks meet their capital adequacy requirements (Table 5).[33]

Among the measures taken to overcome the banks' unwillingness to lend was the attempt by some governments to lower the risk of lending to certain categories of borrowers by taking over part of the credit risk. Such measures, including guarantees on export or import credits or on lending to small- and medium-sized companies, may be useful but have to be designed so that guarantees do not fully eliminate the banks' credit risk, or relieve them from performing a proper credit assessment, even if this means that guarantee schemes are not fully used. Thus, in Indonesia and Thailand, the partial nature of the export guarantee schemes led banks to more carefully evaluate credit risks, but it has resulted in undersubscription to these schemes because banks are unwilling to increase exposures to corporations that they judge to be insolvent. To address the same concern, the Korean authorities intend to phase in reductions in the coverage of the credit guarantees offered by public guarantee funds, which in most cases had been 100 percent of the loan.

Measures to alleviate the credit crunch that coerce banks to lend, or that result in the compression or elimination of positive interest margins, can only further damage already weak banks. Such measures

---

[33]Some measures that existed before the crisis, such as credit or guarantee facilities for exporters, were augmented.

create perverse incentives in that they make banks more unwilling to lend. Negative spreads in Indonesia made it profitable for clients to borrow and redeposit their proceeds (such "round-tripping" forces banks to ration credit). Low margins will discourage new lending and compromise bank profits and their capital base and, therefore, undermine the entire restructuring process. The soundest way to alleviate a slowdown in credit is through a combination of measures to stabilize the economy and enhance profitability and solvency of banks and their corporate customers.

V   Bank Restructuring

The three crisis countries and Malaysia implemented comprehensive bank restructuring strategies. This section discusses selected issues related to the design and implementation of these strategies. It reviews broad principles and policies underlying such strategies and discusses operational issues related to the restructuring, such as institutional arrangements, issues in valuing financial institutions, the speed of recapitalization, methods to deal with troubled institutions, management of value-impaired assets, the cost of the restructuring, institutional constraints, and linkages with corporate restructuring.

Broad Principles and Policies

A broad-based restructuring strategy should achieve the following economic objectives: (1) restore the viability of the financial system as soon as possible so that it can efficiently mobilize and allocate funds (a core banking system must be in place to preserve the integrity of payment systems, capture financial savings, and ensure essential credit flows to the economy); (2) throughout the process, provide an appropriate incentive structure to ensure effectiveness and, as far as possible, avoid moral hazard for all market participants, including bank owners and managers, borrowers, depositors and creditors, asset managers, and government agents involved in bank restructuring and supervision; and (3) minimize the cost to the government by managing the process efficiently and ensuring an appropriate burden sharing (by distributing losses to existing shareholders). To achieve these objectives, governments had to ensure effective governance of intervened banks, application of appropriate resolution procedures, maximization of the value of nonperforming assets, and optimal involvement of private investors. While all the crisis countries followed these broad objectives, strategies varied according to local circumstances, government preferences, and the depth of the crisis.

Systemic bank restructuring requires strong government leadership because the restructuring seeks to preserve an essential economic infrastructure and entails major macroeconomic and wealth distribution effects, even if in essence it is a microeconomic process. Key steps include decisions on institutional arrangements to deal with the crisis; criteria for evaluating institutions; a strategy to deal with nonviable institutions and to restructure the viable ones consistent with macroeconomic goals; the extent and modalities of public sector support for restructuring; the arrangements for loan recovery and workouts and asset management; arrangements to ensure operational restructuring; and the pace of restructuring and compliance with prudential norms (see Box 9). Experience also indicates that clear information to the public on the steps to be undertaken is a crucial part of the strategy; a nontransparent restructuring process may fail to restore the public's confidence in the government and the financial system.

The strategies adopted by the crisis countries have been broadly similar, in that they all have aimed at removing nonviable institutions and requiring strict compliance with international best practices for capital adequacy, loan classification, and loan-loss provisioning by the end of the restructuring period (Table 6). All countries aimed at maximizing (domestic and foreign) private sector involvement in the recapitalization process. In the event, the extent of private sector involvement has depended on country-specific circumstances, such as the depth of the crisis, the availability of domestic private funds amidst a deteriorating macroeconomic situation, and the legal framework for attracting foreign investors.

Malaysia and the Philippines never experienced a full-blown crisis and applied different restructuring strategies from those in the three crisis countries. In Malaysia, the emergency measures assisted in containing pressures on the system and were followed by a package of proposals that focused on recapitalizing banks that were expected to become undercapitalized in the course of 1998; strengthening the finance company sector through consolidation (mergers); establishing a strong institutional framework to manage the restructuring; and strengthening of regulatory and supervisory frameworks. Faced with the threat of a crisis, the Philippines adopted a

---

Box 9. Principal Issues in Devising a Bank Restructuring Strategy

The following issues need due attention in developing a strategy for restructuring banks.

- Institutional and legal frameworks for the restructuring, including the allocation of qualified human resources;

- Criteria for discriminating between those institutions that are sound and need no public support, those that are viable but require public support, and those that should exit the system;

- Modalities to assess the financial condition of institutions (deciding on who will do the valuation, and on the valuation rules to be applied, including loan classification, loan-loss provisioning, and collateral valuation);

- Methods for dealing with troubled institutions (liquidation, mergers, nationalization, use of bridge banks, or purchase and assumption operations);

- Treatment of existing and new shareholders;

- Role of government and private (domestic and foreign) sectors in contributing equity and subordinated debt;

- Financing arrangements, including target level of recapitalization, types of instruments, terms and conditions for the government's support of restructuring (guided by the principle of minimizing the government's contribution);

- Arrangements for loan recovery and workouts and management of problem assets;

- Appropriate linkages with corporate restructuring;

- Operational restructuring of banks;

- Timeframe for the different steps in bank restructuring;

- Information campaign and transparency on the restructuring strategy to ensure credibility and public confidence;

- Exit strategy from government ownership of banks; and

- Exit strategy from blanket guarantee.

---

financial sector reform program in early 1998 to strengthen the ability of the system to withstand shocks. The main ingredients were a streamlining of the resolution procedures of troubled banks, encouragement of mergers, the privatization of the remaining government equity stake in the Philippine National Bank (the second largest bank in the country), now planned for mid-2000, and an enhancement of the prudential and supervisory frameworks.[34]

The cost of restructuring the financial sector is typically high and largely falls on the public sector. This reflects a severe lack of equity capital in the banking system and the corporate sector at the outset of a crisis. In the crisis countries, seeking efficient ways to restructure objectives at the least fiscal cost was a key concern of the authorities. A poor fiscal situation could severely constrain the public sector's capacity to absorb the cost of the restructure. This was not the case in Indonesia, Korea, and Thailand, which all had relatively sound fiscal positions at the onset of the crisis.[35] However, the immense scale of public support needed will most likely require special efforts to preserve medium-term fiscal sustainability.

---

[34]These policies were components of the Stand-By Arrangement with the IMF, approved in March 1998, and of the Banking Sector Reform Loan with the World Bank, approved in December 1998.

[35]However, the perceived sound fiscal positions concealed the costs of directed credits, liquidity support to banks, and other rapidly increasing government contingency liabilities.

Institutional Arrangements

The allocation of responsibilities for handling the restructuring was a crucial first step in the strategy. Taking into account not only technical considerations but also political circumstances and institutional and legal frameworks already in place, governments put in place a variety of institutional structures:

- In Indonesia, no institution was in charge of restructuring until the Indonesian Bank Restructuring Agency (IBRA) was established in January 1998 under the auspices of the ministry of finance. Initial problems in providing adequate legal and regulatory powers to the IBRA delayed the effective start of bank restructuring and asset management. Bank Indonesia remained the principal supervisory authority, though its powers vis-à-vis state-owned banks and IBRA had not been clearly defined.

- In Korea, responsibility for restructuring was given to the newly established Financial Supervisory Commission. The Financial Supervisory Commission also coordinated the work of the other agencies involved in addressing the crisis, including the Korean Asset Management Corporation (KAMCO), a bridge bank (Hanaerum Merchant Bank), and the Korean Deposit Insurance Company (KDIC).

- In Malaysia, a well-designed institutional framework supported by strong legislation was already in place. The restructuring has been coor-

Table 6. Summary of Measures to Address the Financial Sector Turmoil

Measure	Indonesia	Korea	Malaysia	Philippines	Thailand
Emergency measures					
Liquidity support	Yes	Yes	Yes	Yes	Yes
Introduction of a blanket guarantee	Yes	Yes	Yes	No	Yes
Institutional measures					
Establishment of an overarching restructuring authority	Yes	Yes	Yes[1]	No	No
Establishment of a separate bank restructuring authority	Yes	No	Yes	No	No
Establishment of a centralized asset management corporation	Yes	Yes[2]	Yes	No	No[3]
Adoption of a special corporate debt restructuring framework	Yes	Yes	Yes	No	Yes
Operational autonomy of restructuring agencies	Limited	Yes	Yes	n.a.	n.a.
Restructuring measures					
Intervention in financial institutions that were weak or insolvent. This would include:	Yes	Yes	Yes	Yes	Yes
Mergers of weak institutions	Yes[4]	Yes	Yes	Yes	Yes[4]
Closure of insolvent institutions	Yes	Yes	No	Yes	Yes
Use of public funds to purchase nonperforming assets	Yes	Yes	Yes	No	No
Use of public funds to recapitalize institutions, including:	Yes	Yes	Yes	No	Yes
State intervention in banks	Yes	Yes	Yes	No	Yes
Elimination or dilution of current shareholder stakes of insolvent banks	Yes	Yes	Yes	Yes	Yes
New direct foreign investment	Yes	Yes	Limited[5]	Yes	Yes
Other measures					
Measures to encourage corporate restructuring	Yes	Yes	Yes	Yes	Yes
Steps to improve prudential supervision and regulation	Yes	Yes	Yes	Yes	Yes

Source: IMF.
[1]Steering committee chaired by the central bank.
[2]The powers and resources of a preexisting asset management company were substantially increased.
[3]The Financial Sector Restructuring Agency (FRA) was established to liquidate 56 closed finance companies, and the asset management company to deal with residual FRA assets.
[4]Between government-owned intervened institutions.
[5]Foreign banks are allowed to purchase up to a 30 percent stake.

dinated by an overarching steering committee chaired by Bank Negara Malaysia, which is also the supervisory authority, and includes managers of the three other agencies involved, that is, Danaharta (the asset management company), Danamodal (the bank recapitalization company), and the Corporate Debt Restructuring Committee (the corporate restructuring agency).

- In Thailand, no new agency was set up with specific responsibilities for bank restructuring. The Financial Institutions Development Fund, a legal entity within the Bank of Thailand, which is also the supervisory authority, has been in charge of managing liquidity and solvency support to intervened banks. However, most decision making has been left with the Ministry of Finance. The Financial Institutions Development Fund has been hampered by a lack of clear legal powers. The Financial Sector Restructuring Agency (FRA) was set up to assess the viability of the 58 suspended finance companies and to liquidate the assets of the 56 companies that were closed. A public asset management company was established to purchase residual assets from FRA. Moreover, the Corporate Debt Restructuring Advisory Committee was set up to facilitate corporate debt restructuring.

- In the Philippines, no new institutional arrangements were introduced. The central bank's role in bank restructuring has been based on its role as regulator and supervisor. The Philippines Deposit Insurance Corporation (established in 1963) has continued to be involved with the resolution of insolvent banks; problems of weak but solvent banks have been addressed by encouraging mergers.

Issues in Valuing Bank Assets

Realistic valuation of banks' assets is an important factor in establishing the viability of individual banks, but it is difficult during a crisis. In fact, in these circumstances there is no precise method for valuing nonperforming loans.[36] There are no market prices for nonperforming loans. Valuation based on appropriately discounted present values becomes less reliable as estimates of cash flows, interest rates, and underlying business conditions become volatile. The valuation can be particularly difficult when the viability and repayment capacity of borrowers is in doubt. Also, it is hard to value collateral, not only because of uncertain prices and a limited market, but because of uncertainty as to whether, and when, the bank can seize the collateral.

Differing approaches to valuation were used to improve self-assessments by banks in the three crisis countries. While banks continued to be responsible for valuing their assets and making provisions for losses, they were also subject to intensified on-site examinations by supervisors and assessments by external auditors. These on-site examinations and external audits generally revealed situations that were worse than those reported by the banks. In Indonesia and Korea, these assessments were further supplemented with audits by internationally recognized accounting firms. In Thailand, the authorities questioned the value of additional assessments by international auditors of banks meeting all prudential and regulatory requirements. Each approach has advantages and drawbacks. Self-assessments are often biased due to conflicts of interests; external audits by local firms and supervisory evaluations may not carry sufficient credibility in the market; and foreign assessors may have a limited understanding of a borrower's repayment capacity and other local circumstances. In addition, international auditors might be too cautious in their valuations, perhaps to limit their potential liability in case they overvalued assets. Resorting to international audits, however, seems essential for credibility purposes in cases of pervasive government interference or insider lending.

The information collected through either of these valuation methods serves as a basic input for the restructuring authority's decisions on the viability of financial institutions. Thus, regardless of the valuation methods used, the end result must allow the restructuring agency to compare banks, based on uniform and transparent criteria.[37] This implies that the restructuring agency or the bank supervisor has to choose the valuation procedures, including the possible use of external valuation boards. It also implies

that the agency be able to issue regulations on how banks should assess the value of their assets, but be prepared (and have the power) to overrule valuations by others where deemed appropriate. This power to overrule needs to be used judiciously, particularly in cases where the assessment has been done by independent outsiders. Moreover, valuations should be subject to revisions as economic conditions change. In any event, most prospective private investors will undertake their own due diligence valuations prior to any investment in or acquisition of assets or financial institutions.[38]

Speed of Recapitalization

In all countries, the bank restructuring strategy relied on a tightening of rules for loan-loss provisioning and the observance of minimum capital requirements.[39] This gave banks a basis for recognizing their losses based on international best practices, identifying their capital shortfalls, and putting forward recapitalization plans. The tightening of regulations was gradual, however.[40] On the one hand, markets were demanding more information about banks' financial conditions and strengthened regulation and supervision. Meeting those demands was viewed as necessary for investors to restore the flow of funds to the affected countries and resume lending and provide capital to domestic financial institutions. On the other hand, insufficient resources (e.g., capital funds to meet minimum capital adequacy requirements or long-term foreign financing to eliminate maturity mismatches) made it impossible for banks to meet strict prudential standards in the short run. Requiring banks to meet international standards for capital adequacy requirements and loan-loss provisions in a very short timeframe would have forced them to shrink their balance sheets drastically. This would have further reduced credit to the private sector and aggravated the recession. Thus, a gradual approach was used. Moreover, it would have been impossible for banks to effect a reduction in their outstanding loans sufficient to meet the capital adequacy requirement.

Gradualism for achieving compliance with international standards can apply to loan-loss provisioning or capital adequacy. The former overstates capital adequacy while the latter shows a capital

---

[36]Nonperforming or value-impaired loans or assets are those whose estimated value is below their original book or contractual value.

[37]Valuations should, of course, be based on consistent assumptions regarding key economic variables and on best practice accounting and valuation standards.

[38]Such due diligence valuations typically take three to six months and are preconditions for investors to buy assets or take strategic ownership interests.

[39]These new regulations are discussed in Section VI.

[40]Gradualism, as discussed here, differs from prudential forbearance in that the latter refers to the authorities' providing ad hoc exemptions and waivers from prudential norms for individual financial institutions in a nontransparent way.

adequacy requirement below the regulatory minimum. Countries have used both approaches. IMF staff has emphasized that full transparency of the policy considerations behind the decisions should be assured to enable investors to make educated decisions.[41] In Indonesia and Korea, banks have been given time to meet their normal capital adequacy requirements. The minimum capital adequacy requirement is currently at 4 percent in Indonesia, but is to increase to 8 percent by the end of 2001. In Korea, commercial banks were required to meet a capital adequacy requirement of 6 percent by March 1999 and 8 percent by March 2000 (a different schedule was applied to merchant banks). In Thailand, an 8.5 percent capital adequacy requirement for commercial banks (8 percent for nonbank financial institutions) applies in full while the loan-loss provisioning requirements are increased each semester until the end of year 2000.[42] In Malaysia, valuation and provisioning rules were strengthened, but some gradualism was allowed with respect to public disclosure of nonperforming loans. In the Philippines, higher minimum capital requirements were phased in gradually, aiming at full compliance by the end of 2000.

Dealing with Troubled Institutions

Once nonviable banks were separated from viable ones, governments in all crisis countries and Malaysia devised strategies to rehabilitate those institutions deemed viable. To minimize the fiscal cost for the government and to preserve private ownership of banks, each government encouraged banks to rehabilitate themselves. In cases where market-based solutions were not forthcoming, governments sought to assist in forging such solutions. In case of insolvency, governments intervened. The degree of government involvement largely related to the degree of insolvency of the banks.

The main vehicle for seeking private-sector-based resolutions was for the respective governments to request recapitalization and rehabilitation plans from existing shareholders. In all countries, owners of undercapitalized banks were requested to provide timetables to raise the banks' capital adequacy requirements to prescribed levels and to show their viability.[43] In Korea, the government requested from banks with capital adequacy requirements below 8 percent self-improvement plans to reach that threshold, including contributions of new capital from existing or new shareholders. Approval of those plans was a requirement for banks to keep their license and for them to receive public sector support through the sale of nonperforming loans to KAMCO or in the form of equity. The precise content of individual plans varied depending on the circumstances and the size and significance of the institution. Memoranda of understanding between the banks and supervisory agencies were used to document the approval of the plans and the conditions attached to them. The conditions typically included operational improvement benchmarks on matters such as cost reduction, labor shedding, and rate of return on assets. Likewise, the Bank of Thailand requested half-yearly capitalization plans from all undercapitalized institutions, spelling out how they would bring in equity (domestic and foreign) to meet their capital adequacy requirements. These plans were agreed upon under binding memoranda of understanding with the Bank of Thailand.

The initial lack of private capital in the three crisis countries forced the governments to promote plans whereby new private capital contributions would be matched in varying proportions by the government. Under Indonesia's joint recapitalization program, for banks with a capital adequacy requirement between +4 percent and –25 percent, owners have to submit a business plan demonstrating medium-term viability, in addition to passing a fit-and-proper test. Schedules to eliminate excess connected lending also had to be agreed upon. Owners had to provide 20 percent of the capital shortfall and the government the remaining 80 percent.[44] Korea followed a case-by-case approach, under which the government was prepared to arrange for KAMCO purchases of nonperforming loans, purchase subordinated debt, or subscribe new capital, to assist private banks' recapitalization efforts. In Thailand, the government will match any amount of capital injected by private investors, provided (1) the bank has brought forward and fully implemented the end of year 2000 loan classification and provisioning rules; (2) the new capital (public and private) is injected with preferred status; (3) the government and the new investor have the right to change management; and (4) an acceptable operational restructuring plan has been presented to the authorities, including procedures for dealing with nonperforming loans and for improving internal

---

[41]In principle, showing the actual capital adequacy requirement is more transparent and is in line with international accounting standards.

[42]However, full up-front application of final provisioning rules is required in cases where banks seek public funds to match new private equity contributions.

[43]In Korea and Thailand, this was also done for institutions that had been suspended, to give them a last chance to prove their viability.

---

[44]In these banks, owners will keep day-to-day control of their banks and have first right of refusal to buy back the government's stake at the end of three years.

control and risk management systems.[45] This scheme has contributed to restoring confidence in the Thai banking system, and hence, inducing private banks to find private investors with or without the public matching funds.

To facilitate foreign participation in the restructuring process, governments have liberalized regulations on foreign ownership of financial institutions. In addition to bringing in foreign capital, these measures have also aimed at introducing international banking expertise into the domestic financial system to enhance competition. All countries have allowed foreign investment in existing financial institutions. In Indonesia, two sizeable private banks have recently been bought by foreign banks and further purchases are expected. In Korea, the banking law has been changed to allow foreigners to acquire a controlling interest in domestic banks, including full ownership, and the government is seeking to sell a controlling interest to foreign investors in two of the largest commercial banks. In addition, foreign investors have contributed capital to other major commercial banks and have started negotiations to invest in other segments of the financial sector, such as in insurance companies. In Malaysia, foreign shareholders are allowed to take a stake in domestic banking institutions to up to 30 percent. In Thailand, foreign ownership in excess of 49 percent in existing banks has been allowed to help restructure the system. Strategic foreign investors have taken a majority stake in two small private banks, and foreign ownership in some large banks is approaching 50 percent. Malaysia has indicated that foreign banks with operations in the country will be allowed to buy finance companies. The Philippines has not yet been fully opened to new foreign ownership of existing banks, but further liberalization is planned. Recently drafted legislation has been submitted to allow 100 percent ownership of distressed banks, but this is to be reduced to 70 percent over 10 years.

When self-rehabilitation was beyond reach, governments resorted to a variety of bank resolution methods to deal with troubled institutions. Such methods included interventions, nationalizations, mergers, purchase and assumption operations, and the use of bridge banks.

A general principle in resolving troubled institutions is that existing shareholders should bear losses until their capital has been fully written off. This principle was generally applied in the crisis countries, although in some countries shareholders were left with nominal stakes to take into account legal restrictions on a full write-down or to avoid costly legal challenges by the old shareholders. In Indonesia, for example, the shareholders in the largest bank taken over in April 1998 were diluted to 1 percent of total equity. In Korea, until amended in mid-1998, legislation prevented shareholder stakes from being written down below the minimum capital required for a bank to operate. In Thailand, the shares of owners in intervened banks have been written down to token values.[46] Furthermore, in Indonesia, the authorities are pursuing former shareholders of failed banks for personal indemnification for past central bank liquidity support in those cases where banks have been in violation of prudential regulations, especially for connected lending.

The contribution of new shareholders is of key importance to help strengthen bank finances and governance. All countries have revised the rules and regulations governing new shareholders. Existing shareholders are required to meet fit-and-proper tests to remain eligible, and rules regarding conflicts of interest for shareholders have been strengthened. A key issue is the maximum size of the equity share of each individual shareholder: concentration of equity may facilitate governance and capital injections, but concentration may also lead to excessive connected lending and large exposure risks. New or amended banking laws in Indonesia and Korea address this trade-off. In Korea, for instance, the law limits the maximum shareholding stake of domestic residents in commercial banks unless that stake is matched by a foreigner's stake.

In the three crisis countries, deep insolvency of private banks led to the nationalization of a significant part of the private bank sector. In Indonesia, IBRA has acquired control of 12 banks, representing 20 percent of the banking sector. The authorities continue to distinguish between the "banks taken over," however, and the seven state banks existing before the crisis, because the aim is to resolve the former through privatization, mergers, or closures within a relatively short period. In Korea, public equity support was very extensive because the limits on single ownership of commercial banks meant that there were no significant strategic shareholders that could be called upon to inject funds into the banks. Thus, five of the six major corporate lending banks have ended up with government shareholdings in excess of 90 percent. In Thailand, public equity support has mainly been provided to the institutions that

---

[45]The new investor has the option to buy back the government shares within three years at the government's initial cost plus carrying costs. If after full provisioning, the Tier 1 capital adequacy requirement falls below 2.5 percent, the government will recapitalize the bank up to this level before matching private funds.

[46]A legal restriction has prevented the writing down of subordinated debt except in cases of legal closure and liquidation.

were state-owned at the outset of the crisis, to the six commercial banks and 12 finance companies that have been intervened, and to match private equity contributions in a few private banks.[47] All the governments have expressed their commitment to privatize their state-owned banks as soon as feasible. Korea and Thailand have already made some progress in this direction.

Closures, mergers, purchase and assumption operations, and bridge banks were useful techniques to consolidate the financial sectors in most countries, and governments adopted them flexibly under the circumstances. As mentioned before, closures were an important measure in all three crisis countries, as indicated by the proportion of the closed entities in the sector. Government-assisted mergers were used in all countries to consolidate the banking system. In Korea and Malaysia, mergers involved private sector banks, but in Indonesia and Thailand such operations were limited mostly to the state-owned sector. In Indonesia, four of the seven state banks are in the process of being merged into a single bank. In Thailand, the authorities are merging the intervened banks and finance companies into three new banks. The 56 closed finance companies are being liquidated by FRA through public auctions; the liquidation continued through the end of 1999. Mergers, purchase and assumption operations, and bridge banks have been used in Korea.[48] The strategy in Malaysia was different for commercial banks and finance companies. For the commercial banks, a recapitalization strategy was set up for 14 banks that were identified as undercapitalized, or projected to become undercapitalized in the course of 1998; in addition, four banks would be merged into two. One such operation, involving two banks, has been completed. For the finance companies, the government initially aimed at consolidating the 39 companies to less than half that number through mergers. As of August 15, 1999, 15 had been absorbed or merged.[49] In the Philippines, private-sector-led mergers were encouraged through easing of accounting and prudential regulations.

In the event, governments used a wide variety of resolution strategies. In a deep systemic crisis, no standard solution can be prescribed within the broad overall restructuring strategy. Governments had to deal with troubled institutions on a case-by-case basis. The final solution for each institution had to take into account the interest of the parties involved (existing shareholders, potential domestic or foreign investors, the government, and creditors) as well as the legal and regulatory framework, and, often, the political situation. As a result, the outcome for the sector as a whole necessarily varied from country to country (Table 7).

Dealing with Impaired Assets

Proper management and disposition of nonperforming assets is one of the most critical and complex aspects of successful and speedy bank restructuring. The government's overarching objective should be to maximize the value of the impaired assets in the system, minimize fiscal costs, and prevent credit discipline of borrowers from deteriorating. Various approaches can be adopted to achieve those objectives. Impaired assets may either be held and dealt with by the financial institutions themselves or sold to special companies or agencies created to handle bad assets. The likelihood that the borrower will be able to honor his loan contract should determine whether the asset should be handled as a loan subject to collection or as a case for liquidation, including collateral. The more likely that the borrower will honor the loan contract, possibly after renegotiation, the more reason there is to keep it in a bank. If the borrower is bankrupt, or otherwise unlikely to repay, and the bank has to seek recovery of collateral—which often takes the form of real estate or other physical assets—a separate institution with special knowledge in asset resolution techniques most likely should undertake the recovery.

The optimal strategy for managing and disposing of impaired assets has many variations, depending on factors such as the nature of the problem assets, their overall size and distribution, the structure of the banking system, the legal framework, and available management capacity in the banks and in the public sector. There is no single optimal solution but rather a combination of solutions for each country that may vary over time and for each bank. The strategy will need to consider the speed of disposition of the assets and whether to use a centralized or decentralized process and institutional framework (Table 8).

Speed of disposition is determined by the quantity, quality, and type of assets; market demand for such assets; and whether the assets belong to a bank that has been closed or to one in operation. While economic recovery requires some asset sales or liquidations to help markets find new price levels, the mar-

---

[47]The intervened institutions were insolvent and not in a position to raise capital. Financial Institutions Development Fund took control, recapitalized them, and is preparing them for reprivatization.

[48]In Korea, the bridge bank, a subsidiary of the KDIC, was given a life span of three years and was used only for the good assets of closed merchant banks.

[49]According to the most recently announced merger exercise (July 29, 1999), the domestic commercial banks, finance companies, and merchant banks will be consolidated into six large financial groups.

Table 7. Mergers, Closures, and State Interventions of Financial Institutions
(June 1997 to June 1999)

	Mergers	Closures	State Interventions
Indonesia	Four of the seven state commercial banks to be merged into a single commercial bank (54 percent).	64 commercial banks (18 percent).	12 commercial banks (20 percent).
Korea	Nine commercial banks and two merchant banks to create four new commercial banks (15 percent).	Five commercial banks, 17 merchant banks, more than 100 other nonbank financial institutions (15 percent).	Four commercial banks (14 percent).[1]
Malaysia	15 mergers (6 percent)(finance companies and commercial bank).	None.	One merchant bank and three finance companies under central bank control (3 percent).
Philippines	Four commercial bank mergers (2 percent).	One commercial bank (1 percent).[2]	None.
Thailand[3]	Three mergers involving five commercial banks and 12 finance companies (16 percent).	56 finance companies (11 percent) and one commercial bank (2 percent).	Six commercial banks and 12 finance companies (12 percent).

Source: IMF.

Note: Figures in parentheses refer to percentage of total banking system assets held by the corresponding group of institutions.

[1]Banks with over 90 percent government ownership. The government owns varying amounts of shares in seven other commercial banks.

[2]Closures of a number of rural banks and small thrifts are not included. Such closures are routine operations in the Philippines.

[3]In Thailand, most of the intervened institutions were later merged. Thus, columns one and three include the same institutions.

kets may be extremely thin and care needs to be taken not to destroy values for the entire banking system through "fire-sale" liquidations. This is of particular concern in a systemic crisis when the amount of problem assets typically is very large. The value of impaired assets may be better preserved through careful management and gradual sales by specialized institutions (in this paper all such units located outside banks are referred to as asset management companies). At the same time, it is important not to "park" severely impaired assets for years in asset management companies while waiting for an economic upturn. Such an approach may result in accrual of carrying costs and ultimately bigger losses. Moreover, poor management of the assets may deteriorate their value. In the case of failed banks, it is important to move the better quality loans to other operating institutions as fast as possible to preserve value. In Korea this was done through bridge banks, while in Thailand most of the assets of the 56 closed finance companies have been sold to the private sector through public auctions carried out by the FRA.[50]

Each country considered the advantages and disadvantages of dealing with impaired assets in a centralized or decentralized asset management company structure and related ownership issues in its own circumstances (Table 9). Centralized asset management companies, which typically need to be state-owned, have been used in Korea and Malaysia, and more recently in Indonesia. Advantages and disadvantages of state-owned, centralized asset management companies are shown in Box 10. A key objective of a state-owned centralized asset management company is to buy nonperforming loans from banks and thus help banks clean up their balance sheets as fast as possible. It is also useful in cases of mergers or bank sales when the merging or purchasing party may not wish to get a large amount of nonperforming loans as part of the deal. Thailand has chosen a decentralized process, encouraging each commercial bank to establish its own separate asset management company. However, a public asset management company was established to purchase residual assets from FRA. In Indonesia private asset management companies to deal with failed banks were ruled out due to governance concerns.[51] The sale of banks' assets

[50]So far, more than half of the assets of the 56 finance companies have been sold to the private sector and most of the remainder will be sold to the public asset management company that was set up as the residual buyer of all FRA managed assets that could not be sold in the auctions.

[51]This was done to prevent associates of some of the failed banks from setting up private asset management companies, which could have circumvented rules for pricing and prudent governance.

Table 8. Framework for Managing Impaired Assets

Speed of Disposition	Decentralized	Centralized
Rapid (sale or liquidation)	Direct asset sales by banks; Liquidation of a bank.	Rapid resolution vehicles (Thai Financial Sector Restructuring Agency, or FRA).
Long-term (asset management)	Individual asset management companies (Thailand); bank workout units (all countries).	Long-term disposition (asset management).

to an asset management company forces immediate recognition of the value of the loan. This may deter such sales in cases where banks have been carrying these loans at inflated values.

Pricing is the most difficult issue for a public asset management company purchasing assets from private banks. The issue is less severe for a public asset management company buying assets from a state-owned bank or a private asset management company buying assets from a private bank.[52] This is due to the valuation difficulties for impaired assets discussed earlier. Purchases of a bank's assets at inflated values by an asset management company amount to a back-door recapitalization of the bank and a bailout of the bank's shareholders.[53] The impossibility of determining an unambiguously fair market price for nonperforming loans has so far deterred the Thai authorities from setting up a public, centralized asset management company and they have instead opted for a decentralized approach. Proper transfer pricing is also of key importance for the incentive structures for both the asset management company and the banks—there is a need to set up a system that provides the right balance. Excessive prices for nonperforming loans may also induce banks to reduce their recovery efforts, which could lead to a general deterioration of credit discipline and loan values throughout the banking system.

A decentralized approach that encourages each bank to set up its own asset management company allows arrangements to suit each bank's conditions (see Table 10). Thailand followed such a route, encouraging banks to set up their own asset management companies to which they can transfer assets at

market value. Five private banks are in the process of setting up asset management companies and other banks (including state-owned ones) are expected to follow. Until recently, however, this process has been held up due to capital scarcity.

The final results of the various strategies will only be known when the process of recovering impaired assets has been completed. This process will take time. As noted earlier, it would be unwise to undertake massive sales of assets in the midst of the crisis. Also, practical problems—such as the need to acquire proper legal title to collateral and to prepare an inventory of the assets—require time to be solved. Nonetheless, sales of impaired assets have begun in Korea, Malaysia, and Thailand.

Cost of Restructuring

Estimating the cost of financial restructuring is one of the more challenging issues. There are costs both in the private and public sectors to cover losses and contribute new capital. The private sector outlays will not be considered here. The government's *gross costs* for the restructuring arise from paying out guaranteed bank liabilities; providing liquidity support; assisting in meeting capital adequacy requirements; and purchasing nonperforming loans. The *net costs* will only be known after proceeds from (re)privatization of banks and recoveries of loans accruing to the government have been taken into account.[54] A more complete picture of the cost would also include the indirect effects of the crisis and subsequent reforms. The magnitude of these costs and the need for political support for the process require transparent accounting rules and disclosure of information.

---

[52]Consolidated accounting needs to ensure that transfers to private asset management companies are not used as an artificial way of cleaning up the banks.

[53]In Korea, the asset management company had to change its criteria for determining the purchasing price, since the purchase prices determined initially appeared to be too high; even after the adjustment the asset management company had no difficulty in getting banks willing to sell assets.

---

[54]In Indonesia, a significant offset to the cost of restructuring is also likely to come from the disposal of assets pledged by shareholders of failed banks in violation of legal lending limits. IBRA also hopes to secure significant recoveries based on forensic examinations of illegal transactions of some of the failed banks.

Table 9. Public Asset Management Companies in the Asian Crisis Countries

	Centralized/Public Asset Management Companies	Amount Purchased by the End of April 1999 (face value as a percent of GDP)	Eligible Loans	Pricing Policy
Indonesia	Became fully operational in April 1998 within Indonesian Bank Restructuring Agency (IBRA).	20	Loss loans from state banks, and private banks eligible under the government's joint recapitalization scheme.	Zero value.
Korea	Korean Asset Management Corporation (KAMCO) was reconstituted as an asset management company in late 1997.[1]	10	All financial institutions.	45 percent of face value for secured loans; 3 percent for unsecured loans.
Malaysia	Danaharta was established in mid-1998.	17[2]	All financial institutions, including Labuan Subsidiaries of Malaysian banks and development financial institutions.	Average discount has been 37 percent (excluding one large loan, it has been 60 percent).
Philippines	No asset management company.	…	…	…
Thailand	Financial Sector Restructuring Agency (FRA) established on October 24, 1997, to deal with suspended finance companies.	17.5	Assets of the closed financed companies.	Auctions. In a first round only private bidders and, if not sold, to the asset management companies.
	An asset management company was set up to act as bidder of "last resort" for assets of closed finance companies.	4[3]	Finance companies or intervened banks (so far only finance companies).	In the second round, the asset management companies purchased at 20 percent of book value on average.

Source: IMF.
[1]KAMCO existed before the crisis.
[2]End of June 1999.
[3]This 4 percent is included in the 17.5 percent.

Gross costs in the three crisis countries and Malaysia are likely to range from 15 percent to 45 percent of GDP (Table 11). Estimating the cost of restructuring is an evolving exercise because loss recognition is still taking place as part of the corporate restructuring process.[55] The cost of restructuring will depend on several factors, including domestic and external macroeconomic conditions, the effectiveness of corporate restructuring, and the efficiency of bank restructuring efforts. As a result, estimates for the cost of restructuring vary widely, with government numbers generally lower than market estimates.[56] While

IMF staff has continuously made estimates based on different scenarios to discuss policy options with the authorities, it has refrained from including any estimates in official documents because of their sensitive and crude nature.

The need for immediate liquidity support at the onset of the crisis meant that the central banks in the crisis countries were the main providers of funds. In Indonesia and Thailand, formal arrangements to allocate costs between the central bank and the government were weak or did not exist. Meanwhile, in Indonesia, the government has issued 150 trillion rupiah (13 percent of GDP) of indexed bonds to the central bank to compensate it for past liquidity support. In Thailand, the government was authorized to issue bonds for 500 billion baht (10 percent of GDP) to cover losses in the Financial Institutions Development Fund, and the government has announced its intention to cover additional losses in a similar way.

---

[55]Banks' accounts may continue to show additional losses for some time even if economic conditions improve because the positive effect of recovery on the loan portfolio may be offset by losses from existing loans.

[56]For example, Merrill Lynch estimated recapitalization requirements for commercial banks—just one component of gross costs—at 42 percent for Indonesia, 10 percent for Korea, 11 percent for Malaysia, and 26 percent for Thailand (Merrill Lynch, 1999).

Box 10. Advantages and Disadvantages of a Centralized Public Asset Management Company

The crisis countries considered the following when deciding whether to adopt a centralized, public asset management company.

Advantages

• Serves as a vehicle for getting nonperforming loans out of troubled banks, based on uniform valuation criteria.

• Allows government to attach conditions to purchases of nonperforming loans in terms of bank restructuring.

• Centralizes scarce human resources (domestic and foreign).

• Centralizes ownership of collateral, thus providing more leverage over debtors and more effective management.

• Serves as a third party for insider loans (Indonesia).

• Can better force operational restructuring of troubled banks.

• Can be given special legal powers to expedite loan recovery and bank restructuring.

Disadvantages

• Management is often weaker than in private structures, reducing the efficiency and effectiveness of its operations.

• Such agencies are often subject to political pressure.

• Values of acquired assets erode faster when they are outside a banking structure.

• Nonperforming loans and collaterals are often "parked" long-term in an asset management company, not liquidated.

• If not actively managed, the existence of a public asset management company could lead to a general deterioration of credit discipline in financial system.

• Cost involved in operating an asset management company may be higher than a private arrangement.

• If dealing with private banks, determining transfer prices is difficult.

Bonds issued or guaranteed by the governments of Indonesia, Korea, and Thailand are the main instruments for financing the government's contribution to the restructuring costs (Table 12). Market interest rates and regular coupon payments are needed, because, as opposed to zero coupon bonds, they help banks' cash flows. Tradable bonds help banks manage their liquidity, as they can sell the bonds if liquidity is needed.[57] Given the large amount of bonds to be issued, making them tradable also assists the development of a government bond market and reduces the cost for the government; thus, the development of an efficient microstructure for government securities markets becomes critically important.[58] Only Korea and Malaysia used a combination of cash and bonds to provide capital, although cash injections in both cases were so minimal that they did not interfere with monetary policy. The government of Indonesia has recently approved the issuance of another 100 trillion rupiah of bonds (9 percent of GDP) to the banks to finance the first wave of bank recapitalization. The interest cost of all the bonds is borne by the budget. In Korea, parliament approved the issuance of 64 trillion won of bonds to finance KAMCO and KDIC (15 percent of GDP).

A full and transparent recording of the cost of bank restructuring is important. While the initial support by the central banks was not very transparent, bringing the outlays into the budget would imply more transparency. All of the crisis countries have incorporated into their budgets the interest payments on the governments' recapitalization bonds. However, the cost of earlier liquidity support and the capital cost of government bonds have not yet been accounted for in the budgets. Incorporating the total restructuring costs into the budget is crucial, not only to have a clear overview of the total cost, but also to be in a position to better assess the countries' medium-term fiscal sustainability. This can be achieved through the use of an augmented fiscal balance that would explicitly incorporate all major quantifiable fiscal costs of bank assistance operations (Box 11). For financial programming purposes, however, the carrying costs of financial sector restructuring is a more appropriate concept.

Institutional Constraints

Restructuring a banking system following a systemic crisis of the magnitude experienced in Asian countries is a complex process that goes far beyond purely technical operations. Restructuring strategies have to take into account local business practices, the availability of human resources, the deficiencies

---

[57]Under special circumstances, governments could decide to issue non-negotiable bonds, for instance to prevent insolvent banks from selling those bonds and investing the proceeds in risky assets (as in Indonesia).

[58]For a discussion of the development of a microstructure for government securities, see Dattels (1997). The importance of smooth functioning money markets for the development of central bank open market operations is discussed in Quintyn (1997).

Table 10. Pros and Cons of Decentralized Asset Management

	Advantages	Disadvantages
Within banks	Knowledge of the borrower may facilitate debt restructuring. Access to borrower through branch network.	Lack of skills for restructuring of troubled debt, operations of companies, debt-equity swaps, etc. Hampers "normal" banking functions (lending activities), particularly if the nonperforming loan portfolio is large. Less loss recognition up front. Does not clean up the bank's books.
In private asset management companies	Specialized skill mix. Focus on restructuring function. Creation of an asset management industry and secondary market for distressed assets. Loss recognition up-front. Cleans up the bank's books.	Lack of knowledge of the borrower. Bank may not have sufficient capital to recognize losses up front.

in the legal and judiciary framework, and depend largely on the degree of political support. In the three crisis countries, the changeover in the political regime had a clear positive impact on the pace of restructuring. Full recognition by the new governments of the magnitude of the crisis not only increased their resolve to implement the restructuring strategy, but also made it easier to gather broad-based support for the restructuring.[59]

Bank restructuring requires a large number of people with a wide variety of skills. Countries seldom have such resources readily available because crises are only sporadic occurrences. Governments often had to rely on outside expertise to help develop their strategy and carry out specialized tasks. In addition, the number of people needed was considerable. For instance, approximately 5,000 people (foreign and local experts, officials from different agencies, and security forces) were involved in the final closing of the 56 finance companies in Thailand. Similar numbers were involved in such operations in Indonesia.

Deficiencies in national legal and judicial frameworks have been major obstacles to the restructuring process in the crisis countries. Key issues include the initial lack of proper and tested exit policies for banks (especially insufficient authority to take early action against weak banks and to eliminate shareholders); the lack of legal protection of officials (the absence of immunity from prosecution and civil

suits of officials in the exercise of their duties is still a major problem in the Philippines and Thailand); the inadequacy of foreclosure procedures and bankruptcy laws and an appropriate judicial infrastructure to deal with the massive corporate debt restructuring problem; a legal framework that often favored debtors over creditors; and the slowness and inexperience of the courts. Once deficiencies were recognized, it took a considerable amount of time before laws could be changed, and parliaments sometimes introduced counterproductive amendments, further delaying the process.

Table 11. Authorities' Estimates for the Gross Cost of Financial Sector Restructuring

	In Percent of GDP
Indonesia	45
Korea	15
Malaysia	12
Philippines	n.a.
Thailand	n.a.

Source: National authorities.

Note: Gross costs do not include recoveries. The cost will depend on a number of factors, including macroeconomic conditions, effectiveness of corporate restructuring, and the efficiency of the bank restructuring effort. Estimates of these costs are based on different assumptions and methodologies and may therefore not be comparable across countries.

[59]Public recognition of the size of the crisis was delayed because these economies had for long been viewed as highly successful, and therefore unlikely to face a major crisis.

Table 12. Instruments Used to Recapitalize and Purchase Nonperforming Loans

	Instrument	Received	Description
Indonesia	Bonds.	Equity.	Variable and fixed coupon bonds. Owners under the private bank scheme may purchase back shares after three years; tradable.
	Bonds.	Nonperforming loans.	Variable coupon bonds; tradable.
	Debt to equity conversions.	Equity.	Index-linked bonds; tradable.
Korea	Bonds or cash.	Equity or preferred shares.	Variable coupon bonds issued by KAMCO and KDIC and guaranteed by the government; tradable.
	Shares.	Equity or preferred shares.	Governments share in public enterprises.
	Bonds.	Nonperforming loans.	Fixed (initially) and variable coupon bonds; traded.
Malaysia	Bonds or cash.	Convertible preferred shares or subordinated debt.	Zero coupon bonds; not easily traded.
	Bonds.	Nonperforming loans.	Zero coupon bonds; not easily traded.
Philippines	Not applicable.		
Thailand	Debt to equity conversions.	Equity.	FIDF loans converted to equity.
	Bonds.	Equity.	Fixed-coupon bonds; tradable.
	Bonds.	Subordinated debt.	Fixed-coupon bonds; nontradable.

Source: IMF.

Linkages to Corporate Sector Restructuring

The severity of the corporate sector crisis in the three crisis countries has affected bank restructuring more than in most other bank crises. In most crisis countries, corporate sector restructuring began slowly and is lagging behind bank restructuring. This stems from the fact that the loss recognition process took longer, legal frameworks for addressing the issues were not or only partially in place, additional skills were needed that were not readily available, and the sector itself is more complex and diversified than the banking sector. Most important, unlike the banking sector, the private, corporate sector is not under the control of one single regulatory and supervisory agency. Moreover, corporate debt restructuring (the part that has a direct bearing on bank restructuring) largely depends on a broader business restructuring, which is usually a slow process. To the extent that corporate restructuring continues to lag behind, bank restructuring might be delayed. Generally, the two processes should proceed as simultaneously as possible, although bank restructuring should take the lead. This is so, not only because it is more feasible because banks are fewer and are already subject to an established supervisory regime, but also because it is necessary to have functioning financial institutions as counterparties to facilitate the corporate restructuring. Several initiatives have been taken to expedite corporate sector restructuring (Box 12).

Box 11. The Augmented Fiscal Balance

The concept of augmented fiscal balance would explicitly incorporate the major quantifiable fiscal costs of bank assistance operations that are not included in the current definitions of the overall balance.[1] The augmented balance is not intended to replace the overall balance, but to present an additional measure of the fiscal stance for countries where bank assistance operations are important. Use of the augmented balance would allow a transparent, comprehensive, and reasonably comparable presentation of government financial assistance for bank restructuring across countries. If not using an augmented balance framework, complete details of the capital cost of bank restructuring operations should be recorded separately, regardless of whether they are budgetary or quasi-fiscal costs.

[1]See Daniel, Davis, and Wolfe (1997).

Box 12. Linkage to Corporate Restructuring

Corporate restructuring is lagging behind bank restructuring, and has been hampered by a lack of leverage of most banks vis-à-vis their borrowers. The countries generally lacked frameworks for restructuring failing borrowers, such as coordinating credit committees under the guidance of a lead bank. Moreover, in many countries, the courts have tended to be lenient and provided little support for creditors, at least in the initial stages. Companies have been able to continue to operate under the court's protection, allowing interest to be deferred. This has undermined credit discipline. In some countries, measures have been taken to address this problem: first, through strengthened bankruptcy and foreclosure procedures to lessen the balance in favor of the borrowers, and second, by providing incentives and mechanisms for banks and corporate clients to restructure before reaching the courts. Initiatives also have been taken to improve court procedures.

The speed at which corporate restructuring takes place depends on a variety of factors, including the legal and regulatory framework at the onset of the crisis, the vigor of its enforcement, the structure of the corporate sector, and the nationality of the creditors. Corporate restructuring in Indonesia has so far been slow because new bankruptcy and foreclosure laws have not been enforced, in particular by the state-owned institutions. Korea is more advanced than the others because it adopted new laws fairly rapidly, has a corporate sector concentrated around the chaebols, and has clearly specified its restructuring objectives and provided strong leadership. The legal framework is strongest in Malaysia. Thailand suffered from delays in adopting a new legal framework for bankruptcy and disclosure.

Countries have given a variety of incentives to banks to address and expedite corporate debt restructuring. The "London Approach," which provides a framework whereby creditors would jointly approach the debtor and work out a mutually beneficial (out-of-court) arrangement, has so far been used most aggressively for government-led restructuring in Korea, where a number of medium-sized corporate groups have been dealt with in this way (debt rescheduling with some interest rate reduction, or issuance of convertible bonds and debt/equity swaps). In Thailand, the Corporate Debt Restructuring Advisory Committee (CDRAC) was formed by the Bank of Thailand and representatives from debtor and creditor groups, which agreed upon a framework for corporate debt restructuring based on the London Approach (the "Bangkok Approach"). The CDRAC initially targeted large debt restructuring cases but has recently expanded its coverage to small- and medium-size cases. A scheme that would combine government support for recapitalization with corporate debt settlement (Tier 2 options) has also been in place to encourage corporate debt restructuring. In Indonesia, the government has adopted a four-way classification of delinquent borrowers, based on their degree of cooperation with the workout process and business prospects. The state institutions and Indonesian Bank Restructuring Agency (IBRA) are adopting a coordinated approach vis-à-vis each major delinquent borrower, beginning with the largest, broadly along the lines of the London Approach (the "Jakarta Initiative"). In Malaysia, the asset management company (Danaharta) has been given very extensive powers in dealing with the borrowers of any loans it buys. These powers seem to have had a significant effect on borrowers, because banks threatened to sell to Danaharta if the borrower failed to resume servicing the debt.

The banking system provides a key lever for corporate restructuring, in particular as regards corporate debt. Tightening and stronger enforcement of prudential regulations can make a major contribution. For instance, in Korea, tighter regulations on maximum exposure limits, connected lending, liquidity mismatches, and cross guarantees have required corporations to seek other sources of finance or shrink their balance sheets. Also, Korean banks—following strong government leadership—have been instrumental in approving and monitoring corporate restructuring plans. International financial institutions, particularly the World Bank, have strongly supported this process, including the banks' heavy involvement as key counterparts.

VI   Institutional Reform

Early in the crisis, all countries took initiatives to strengthen prudential regulation and supervision, bank governance, and market discipline. The nature and direction of these initiatives was similar in all countries: to bring domestic standards closer to internationally accepted practices. Preparations have also started for the eventual removal of the blanket guarantees. Initiatives have also been taken to improve prudential regulation and supervision of international creditors in their home countries.

Prudential Supervision

In the crisis countries, the autonomy of the supervisory authority has been strengthened. In Indonesia, a new central bank law, passed in May 1999, established independence for Bank Indonesia. Under the law, responsibility for supervision moves from Bank Indonesia to a new agency in 2002. In Korea, before the crisis, a proposal for a new autonomous supervisory authority met with considerable resistance, but after the crisis broke the legislature swiftly passed new legislation establishing such an autonomous body. More recently, additional powers for licensing and supervision have been transferred to the new authority. In Thailand, supervision has been strengthened and become more autonomous. The new Bank of Thailand and Financial Institutions Acts are being drafted to give the Bank of Thailand greater supervisory authority. These laws are expected by early 2000.

All countries have made efforts to upgrade their supervisory capacity and strengthen the powers of supervisors. Supervisory reporting by banks has been much improved, and countries are relying more on on-site examinations. Moreover, supervisors can now demand additional loan-loss provisioning from banks, corrective actions when problems are detected, and more support from banks' external auditors. The use of memoranda of understanding to enhance the supervisory authorities' ability to monitor and enforce compliance with prudential ratios and performance benchmarks of financial institutions has become common. Supervisors now have more power over entry of banks, supported by new fit-and-proper rules (in all countries, the policy generally is not to allow new entrants until the restructuring is over). Most of the countries have introduced procedures that will remove some earlier supervisory discretion that allowed them to waive compliance with regulations on a case-by-case basis, for example regarding loan concentration. To strengthen supervisors' hands in dealing with problem institutions, mandatory "prompt corrective action" procedures have been or are being introduced for situations where capital adequacy falls below certain trigger points.

Prudential Regulation

Regulations concerning loan classification, provisioning, and income recognition have been brought closer to compliance with international best practices (see Tables 13 and 14). Loan classification rules were strengthened in all countries. The period overdue for interest suspension was shortened to three months in Indonesia and Thailand (this rule had already been tightened in the Philippines). All the countries tightened their specific loan-loss provisioning requirements and introduced or tightened their general provisioning requirements. All the countries, with the exception of the Philippines, have made required loan-loss provisions tax deductible. The definitions of capital have been improved and, in some countries, the absolute minimum levels of capital have been increased. As discussed earlier, banks were given time to comply with these new regulations, according to specific timetables.

Several other key prudential regulations are being improved. These include foreign exchange exposure limits in all countries; liquidity management rules in Indonesia, Korea, and Malaysia; connected lending regulations in Indonesia and Korea; single borrower and group exposure limits in Korea and Malaysia; and cross guarantees within chaebols in Korea. Fit-and-proper rules for owners and managers were introduced or strengthened in all countries. In addi-

Table 13. Time Period for Overdue Criteria for Interest Suspension and Loan Classification

Country	Period Overdue for Interest Suspension	Substandard	Doubtful	Loss
Indonesia				
Old[1]	1–12 months	1–12 months[2]		21 months[3]
New	3 months	3 months	6 months	9 months
Korea				
Existing	Immediately when past due	Normally not classified until 3 months past due unless declared bankrupt		
Proposed	No changes currently proposed	3 months	3–12 months	12 months
Malaysia				
Old	6 months	6 months	9 months	12 months
New[4]	6 months	3 months	6 months	9 months
Philippines[5]	3 months	3 months (unsecured)	...[6]	6 months (unsecured)
Thailand				
Old	6 months[7]	6 months (unsecured)	Over 6 months (unsecured)	Over 6 months
		12 months (secured)	Over 12 months (secured)	Over 12 months
New	3 months	3–6 months	6–12 months	Over 12 months

Source: IMF; national authorities.

[1]Varies by type of credit and installment period.

[2]Credit exceeds overdue criteria for substandard but is considered collectible and the value of collateral is not less than 75 percent or credit cannot be collected, but value of collateral not less than 100 percent.

[3]Refers to 21 months after a credit has been classified as doubtful and there is no repayment.

[4]Effective March 1999.

[5]New rules issued October 1997, which tightened overdue criteria for classifying loans depending on number and amount of arrearages, refer only to installment loans.

[6]A loan previously classified as substandard in the last examination is reclassified as doubtful if principal has not been reduced by atleast 20 percent during the preceeding 12 months.

[7]Effective January 1998 irrespective of collateral; previous limit (since July 1995) was 12 months for secured loan.

tion, other imprudent banking practices, such as government directed lending, where applicable, are being phased out. The speed with which new regulations could be phased in had to take into account not only bank and supervisory agency constraints in introducing any new regulation, but also crisis-specific elements, such as the ability of their clients to comply with such rules.

Most countries have taken measures to improve transparency and disclosure, as well as the quality of data disclosed. Quality of data has been improved by new loan classification, provisioning, and income recognition rules and by extensive involvement of onsite examiners and international auditors and analysts to support banks' recapitalization efforts. This is expected to enhance governance and market discipline over time. In Malaysia, following an initial tightening, authorities in 1998 relaxed disclosure requirements, allowing disclosure to be less frequent (semi-annual); however, the regulatory reporting was not changed.[60] New bank laws (under preparation in Thailand) or regulations (in Korea and Indonesia) also require banks to report to the public their financial statements more frequently (mostly quarterly) or make their requirements more explicit. Consolidated financial reporting and disclosure by groups will also enhance transparency; in Korea this is promoted by the consolidation and concentration of supervisory functions. In the Philippines, banks listed on the stock exchange are now required to disclose to the public on a quarterly basis key indicators on their soundness.

The countries with blanket guarantees intend to remove them as soon as feasible. All countries in-

[60]Banking institutions were given an option of reporting nonperforming loans using either the standard of three months or six months past due. Of the 78 financial institutions, 21 (representing 46 percent of the system's loans) have retained the three-month nonperforming loan classification criteria.

Table 14. Loan Provisioning Requirements: Comparative Information
(In percent)

Country	Unclassified Standard	Special Mentioned	Substandard	Doubtful	Loss
Indonesia					
Old[1]	.5	n.a.	10[2]	50[2]	100[3]
New	1	5	15	50	100
Korea					
Existing	.5	2[3]	20	75[4]	100[4]
Proposed No changes currently proposed					
Malaysia					
Old[5]	0	0	20[6]	50[6]	100[6]
New[5]	0	0	20[6]	50[6]	100[6]
Philippines					
Old	0	0	0[7]	50	100
New[8]	0	5	25[9]	50	100[9]
Thailand					
Old	0	0	15[10,11]	100[10]	100[10]
New[12]	1	2	20[10]	50[10]	100[10]

Source: IMF.

[1] Based on uncollateralized portion.

[2] Effective at the end of 1996 for Substandard and 1993 for Doubtful and Loss.

[3] Classified as precautionary loans.

[4] That portion of a loan classified doubtful or loss that is fully secured will normally be classified substandard to the extent of the market value of the collateral.

[5] Effective 1998 general provision increased from 1 percent to 1.5 percent of total outstanding loans (including interest), net of interest in suspect and specific provisions.

[6] Provision computed against uncollateralized portion.

[7] For collateralized; 25 for uncollateralized.

[8] Effective October 1997 a general provision of 2 percent on gross loan portfolio to be phased in through October 1999. adopted.

[9] For both collateralized and uncollateralized.

[10] Provision computed against uncollateralized portion.

[11] Since June 1997.

[12] Stricter criteria for secured loans.

tend to move from a blanket guarantee to a limited coverage of all depositors.[61] There are major dangers, such as deposit runs, in removing the guarantee before the financial system is sound, however. For a limited scheme to work, a number of preconditions have to be met, including the banking system's return to solvency and profitability, the adoption of mechanisms to deal with the exit of individual banks, and the restoration of public confidence. The public should be provided ample notice of the removal of the guarantee and detailed information on the limited guarantee scheme that replaces it. The lifting of the blanket guarantee, when it occurs, should be a nonevent.

Regulations Governing Creditors

Efforts are being undertaken to address weaknesses in the operation and supervision of international lenders, as they have been identified during the Asian crisis. Initiatives include work on a new international financial architecture, the Financial Stability Forum, enhanced financial sector surveillance by international financial institutions, and work by the Basel Committee on Banking Supervision, whose *Supervisory Lessons to be Drawn from the Asian Crisis* proposes a review of various elements of the existing capital rules and of the Basel Committee's guidance on country risk. (See Basel Committee on Banking Supervision, 1999.)

[61] Korea's limited deposit insurance scheme, which existed before the crisis, is scheduled to replace the current blanket guarantee as of the end of the year 2000. Thailand did not have a deposit insurance scheme and is now working on the design of such a scheme to be introduced by special legislation.

VII   Financial Sector Reforms in IMF-Supported Programs

Financial sector reforms have been at the core of the IMF-supported programs for the Asian crisis countries. The focus was on the financial sector because (1) distress and weaknesses in the sector were widely perceived as a major cause of the crisis; (2) reestablishing banking system soundness was crucial to restoring macroeconomic stability; (3) restoring confidence in banks was essential for the return of funding into the financial system; and (4) the crisis generated demands for the authorities to address the causes of the crisis by carrying out major reforms, thus providing impetus for implementing reform that in some cases had been planned for years. In the Philippines, the structural component in the program was smaller, because major shortcomings of the financial system had been addressed earlier. Malaysia's strategy, although different in some respects from the IMF-supported programs in the crisis countries, also had a major focus on financial sector reforms.

While the magnitude of the financial sector crises was larger than anything experienced before, IMF staff was able to draw on its experience in recent years both from actual crisis involvement and analytical work.[62] Although many of the events in the unfolding crisis were familiar, differences in key elements added new dimensions to the crisis requiring particular care in choosing the restructuring approach. Such elements were the structure of the banking and corporate sectors, business practices, limitations in the legal systems, and the authorities' strong preferences for certain institutional arrangements. The magnitude of the crisis and the speed at which it developed required immediate responses. Thus, the development of strategies and policies involved extensive discussions among the authorities and IMF staff, and new approaches and procedures needed to be developed, taking into account the characteristics and constraints of each country at that particular point in time, while maintaining a certain amount of uniformity of policies among the countries.

The reform strategy for each country was incorporated in letters of intent and memoranda of economic and financial policies, both of which spell out the details of the IMF-supported programs. These strategies included measures to ensure the exit of nonviable institutions, the strengthening of those that remained in operation, the restructuring of the corporate sector, and the adoption of institutional reforms to help prevent future crises. Box 13 summarizes the measures included in letters of intent and memoranda of economic and financial policies of the countries that received IMF financial support. From the onset, these documents included both immediate actions and broad outlines of the medium-term strategy for restructuring and its sequencing. Given that the precise nature and timing of future actions could not be determined at the outset, the programs left sufficient flexibility in implementation. Subsequently, they were refined in the course of reviews as new information became available and as required by the evolving circumstances in each country. The market sensitivity of certain actions required in the initial stages of the program ruled out the inclusion of such actions in the letters of intent.

Several issues arose in adapting complex medium-term bank restructuring strategies to the format and conditionality of IMF-supported programs. IMF conditionality has usually been quantitative and strictly time-bound, involving actions under the control of the authorities. In the case of bank restructuring, however, conditionality has to be set cautiously, as the process involves steps that are seldom amenable to measurement, often take longer than planned, are not directly under the control of the authorities, require legal steps to be adhered to, and involve negotiations between different parties in the public and private sector. Moreover, since restructuring actions have a significant impact on private property and wealth, they must be undertaken in a manner consistent with each countries' legal and judicial framework.

The timing and pace of reforms requires a delicate balance between short-term IMF conditionality and the medium-term nature of financial sector restructuring. To maintain momentum and credibility,

---

[62]See, for example, Sundararajan and Baliño (1991), Lindgren, Garcia, and Saal (1996), Alexander and others (1997), Enoch and Green (1997), and Folkerts-Landau and Lindgren (1998).

Box 13. Financial Sector Restructuring Measures in IMF-Supported Programs

Financial sector measures included in IMF-supported programs in Indonesia, Korea, Thailand, and the Philippines included:

Measures to stabilize the system

- Provide liquidity support at penal rates and subject to conditionality (Indonesia, Korea, and Thailand).

- Introduce a blanket guarantee (Indonesia and Thailand).

- Cap deposit rates to reduce the ability of weak banks to capture deposits and further weaken the system (Indonesia and Thailand).

- Identify and close fundamentally unsound financial institutions. These included commercial banks (Indonesia), commercial and merchant banks (Korea), and finance companies (Thailand).

- Require owners of closed institutions to lose their stakes in these institutions (Indonesia, Korea, and Thailand).

- Share losses of closed finance companies with creditors; restructure some depositor claims to longer maturities (Thailand).

Measures to restructure the financial sector

- Establish a restructuring agency (Indonesian Bank Restructuring Agency, IBRA, in Indonesia).

- Complete diagnostic reviews of financial institutions (Indonesia and Korea).

- Tighten loan classification and loan-loss provisioning rules (Indonesia, Korea, Thailand, and the Philippines).

- Allow for full tax deductibility on income for loan-loss provisioning (Indonesia, Korea, and Thailand).

- Establish a transparent timetable for banks to meet capital adequacy requirements (Indonesia and Korea) or provisioning requirements (Thailand).

- Intervene in insolvent banks (all countries).

- Agree on memoranda of understanding between undercapitalized banks and the authorities to specify a timetable for raising capital to meet capital adequacy requirements and attain performance benchmarks (Indonesia, Korea, the Philippines, and Thailand).

- Issue guidelines on the modalities for the use of public funds to recapitalize banks (Thailand) and to purchase nonperforming loans from private institutions (Indonesia and Korea).

- Issue guidelines for stricter bank licensing (Thailand).

- Take steps to privatize nationalized banks (Indonesia, Korea, and Thailand).

Measures to reform the institutional framework

- Enact legislation to enhance the operational independence of the supervisory authority (Korea) and central bank (Indonesia).

- Take steps to strengthen bank supervision (Indonesia and the Philippines).

- Improve accounting, disclosure, and auditing standards (Korea, the Philippines, and Thailand).

- Issue strengthened regulations regarding connected lending, liquidity management, foreign currency exposure, and large exposures (Indonesia and Korea); cross guarantees were also to be eliminated for the top 30 chaebols in Korea.

- Introduce a new bankruptcy law (Indonesia and Thailand).

---

reforms must proceed rapidly, but the complexity of the process and country-specific constraints have to be taken into account. For instance, rapid recapitalization of financial institutions was a desirable goal in principle, but in reality, too rapid a pace would have meant that necessary concomitant measures, such as operational restructuring and banks' search for private capital, would not have been feasible and that banks would have had to cut credits even more drastically, thus aggravating the crises. Thus, the recapitalization was phased and strictly monitored under the IMF-supported programs. Similarly, in Korea, policies to address the excessive maturity mismatches between foreign exchange assets and liabilities had to be phased in, taking into account the difficulty in converting short-term to longer-term foreign financing at the time. To introduce meaningful benchmarks for

measures like privatization, which involves complex negotiations with private parties, is even more challenging.

Detailed information on the financial condition of individual banks was necessary in order to assess the situation of the system, design a restructuring strategy, and monitor compliance with the program. Generally, it is impossible to deal with a systemic banking crisis efficiently without access to bank-by-bank data. IMF staff had access to detailed supervisory data for individual banks in the three crisis countries. Such access was necessary to evaluate the quality of the restructuring policies and to monitor their implementation. In Malaysia and the Philippines, access to such data was more restricted. Handling of bank information had to be done according to agreed-upon procedures and in accordance with bank secrecy laws in each country.

While the Asian crisis showed that the IMF would need to play a central role in assisting the authorities in the management of the initial crisis and in the design of the overall restructuring strategy, it also demonstrated the need for close cooperation with other multilateral agencies, particularly the World Bank. Cooperation with the World Bank was close from the beginning in all countries, although the division of labor differed. In particular, the urgent nature of many of the tasks and the heavy demand on IMF staff resources required very close collaboration between the staffs of both institutions and flexibility in their approach to the division of labor.

The IMF assumed the lead role in the three crisis countries and the World Bank made important contributions in specific aspects of program formulation and implementation. The IMF relied on its capacity to develop programs quickly and develop the linkages between macroeconomic stability and financial sector soundness. The World Bank provided expertise, and financing, to assist the authorities in program implementation and institution building, increasing its role in the crisis countries over time. In all crisis countries, the staffs of the IMF and World Bank have cooperated closely from the early stages, taking into account each other's views in the program discussions with the authorities—which often included staff of both institutions attending meetings with the authorities on financial restructuring issues. Also, World Bank staff took the lead in the area of corporate restructuring and nonbank financial institutions. Work on strengthening legal and regulatory frameworks has been done jointly.

An important source of difficulties was related to the design and implementation of the immediate steps required to stabilize and restructure the financial system. In all three crisis countries, letters of intent were negotiated quickly and incorporated immediate steps to stabilize the financial system. These measures were negotiated without full World Bank involvement, although they included components for which the World Bank was expected to take the lead in implementation. This led to coordination problems initially, further complicated by the large number of departments involved in both institutions. In response, the World Bank created its Special Financial Operations Unit to bolster its capacity to quickly field staff that can participate in the initial rounds of program negotiations in crisis countries. As a result of their efforts, early problems in coordination have been solved.

In addition to financial support, the IMF had to assign a large number of staff to the five countries discussed in this paper. This was particularly the case for the three crisis countries. During fiscal years 1998 and 1999, staff from the IMF's Monetary and Exchange Affairs (MAE) Department and headquarters-based consultants spent some 10 staff years in the field on missions to Indonesia, Korea, and Thailand. These visits were often made in parallel with or as part of Use of Fund Resources and Article IV missions. They were also done in conjunction with World Bank missions. Moreover, the IMF placed resident banking supervisors in Indonesia and Thailand and organized several expert visits to Korea. Participation of financial sector experts in missions to Malaysia and the Philippines has been less intense but has also required substantial IMF staff involvement, more recently as part of the IMF's Asia and Pacific Department and World Bank missions. In addition to mission-related work in Washington, MAE staff and Washington-based consultants have spent a considerable part of their time at IMF headquarters following events in all the countries, providing follow-up comments and assistance in implementation, and coordinating with other institutions. This is, of course, in addition to IMF staff resources that other IMF departments (notably the Asia and Pacific Department, or APD) had to commit to financial sector matters in the context of the IMF's day-to-day activities and surveillance work.

VIII   Conclusions and Lessons

The Asian experience with bank restructuring has already produced valuable lessons, many of which will evolve as the process continues. In particular, many "conclusions" at this time are actually interim assessments, as it will take several years before the restructuring of the financial and corporate sectors will be completed and the full economic implications of different measures become apparent.

More than any other recent financial crisis, the one in Asia has highlighted the linkages between financial sector soundness and macroeconomic stability. Highly leveraged corporate sectors with large amounts of unhedged foreign currency debt, much of which is short-term, and domestic bank borrowing, fed by large capital inflows during years of exceptional economic growth and exchange rate stability, created major vulnerabilities. The crisis highlights the danger that formally or informally pegged exchange rates may lull investors into ignoring currency risks (see Figure 8). Following the shocks to market expectations caused by exchange rate devaluations and widespread doubts about private sector solvency, the size and speed of the impact on the financial systems was unprecedented. Foreign banks cut their credit, asset prices collapsed, leading to major wealth losses, and real demand contracted sharply. The close integration of the Asian economies in world financial markets helped to spread the crisis to other countries in the region and to the rest of the world. Close attention should be paid to prudential supervision of foreign currency exposures and risks, especially when exchange rate regimes are inflexible.

Why did the financial sector crises take everyone by surprise? There were clear signals of overheating, such as prolonged rapid credit expansions, asset price inflation, and overcapacity in key sectors, although the underlying deterioration in banks' loan values and capital adequacy ratios were not yet reflected in their balance sheets. Meanwhile, the buildup of corporate indebtedness, unsustainable banking practices (such as directed, connected, and insider lending) and weaknesses in prudential regulation and supervision were known to policymakers

and market participants. The fact that all these factors were largely overlooked by most private sector and published official analyses—both at home and abroad—was probably related to the long-running success of those economies. In any event, greater disclosure of macroprudential and microinstitutional indicators and greater transparency of monetary and financial policies could have strengthened market discipline and policy effectiveness and could have helped to expose some vulnerabilities much earlier.

Compared with the three crisis countries, Malaysia and the Philippines had been pursuing policies before the crisis that clearly lessened the damage. Both countries, which had undertaken bank restructuring and structural reforms in the 1980s, avoided a full-blown crisis. Malaysia's traditional policies of limiting short-term foreign borrowing, encouraging foreign direct investment inflows, and relying on equity capital prevented the corporate sector from building up the large unhedged foreign exchange exposures and very high debt equity ratios that were so damaging in the crisis countries. These policies notwithstanding, Malaysia also faced substantial financial sector distress. In general, the crisis highlights the benefits of having developed money, bond, and equity markets. Developed capital markets would reduce corporate leverage and improve corporate governance; the reduced reliance on bank financing would make the system more resilient to shocks. The development of bond markets—especially for government bonds—would also facilitate financial sector restructuring.

The first priorities in the crisis countries were to stop excessive central bank credit expansion to insolvent institutions, stabilize the financial system, and prevent capital flight. To achieve this and to prevent bank runs, the governments needed to offer blanket guarantees for depositors and most creditors, close the worst institutions, and introduce credible macroeconomic stabilization and bank restructuring plans. These measures were successful in stopping the domestic deposit withdrawals, particularly after the credibility of the guarantees had been tested, but were less effective in securing rollover of foreign liabilities. To achieve the rollover, other measures,

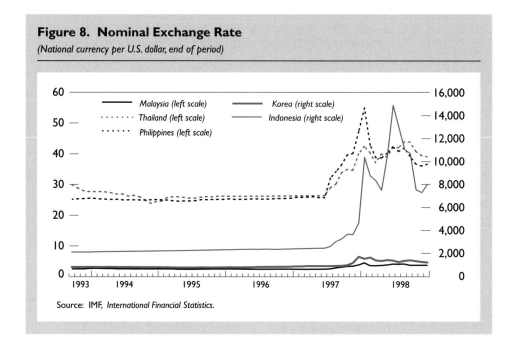

Figure 8. Nominal Exchange Rate

(National currency per U.S. dollar, end of period)

Source: IMF, *International Financial Statistics.*

such as the debt renegotiation in Korea, were needed. The experience of the crisis countries suggests that in a systemic crisis, a blanket guarantee, rather than a limited deposit guarantee, is needed to restore confidence in the financial system.

While closing the most insolvent institutions was considered necessary, it also became clear that any closing of financial institutions and sharing of losses with private sector creditors is an extremely difficult task to manage. Closing deeply insolvent institutions provides a way to cease central bank support, allows loss sharing with creditors, removes excess intermediation capacity, and frees resources to deal with remaining institutions. Decisions to close may have to rely on liquidity "triggers" until banks' loan-losses are recognized in their accounts. Any closing of financial institutions must be accompanied by a well-managed information campaign to support the policy, explain the reasons for bank closings, and reassure the public.

In all countries, except initially in Indonesia, the central banks were able to sterilize their liquidity support to individual banks, since deposits withdrawn from weak banks were largely deposited in other domestic banks perceived as being safer. To absorb excess liquidity of the latter and stem capital outflows, interest rate increases for short-term central bank instruments were necessary. This recycling was successful in all countries, except in Indonesia, where economic and political turmoil made the situation unmanageable during the first six months. Nonetheless, in all countries, exchange rates initially depreciated sharply due to concerns about credit-

worthiness and solvency of domestic counterparties and to uncertainties about policy implementation.

A slowdown in real credit growth to the private sector should not have come as a surprise. In addition to a sharp fall in credit demand, owing to overcapacity in the real sector and bleak short-term economic prospects, bankers became more cautious, as borrowers' creditworthiness deteriorated, reflecting in particular the large foreign exchange component of their debt. This slowdown seems to be more explained by structural factors than by an excessively tight monetary policy. Any policies to stimulate bank lending should be used cautiously so as not to worsen banks' conditions; for example, excessively low interest rate margins will be deterrents to new lending and further undermine banks' solvency and recapitalization. Lending cannot be expected to normalize until the corporate sector has regained its profitability and repayment capacity and banks' capital bases have been restored.

In broad terms, the strategies for systemic restructuring have sought to restore the financial systems to soundness as soon as possible. The process involves the introduction of the necessary legal, institutional and policy frameworks for dealing with nonviable financial institutions, strengthening viable ones, and resolving value impaired assets in the system. Systemic bank restructuring is a complex multiyear microeconomic process, which in the aggregate has major macroeconomic effects. No two situations are the same, and specific measures, pace, and effectiveness of implementation have varied between the different countries depending on the specifics of the problem, laws and institutions in place at the outset, and the sometimes strong preferences of the authorities for certain solutions. For example, there have been major differences in the ability of each government to endow official agencies involved in the restructuring with sufficient operational authority, financial independence, protection from lawsuits, and means to attract necessary expertise.

Key principles for the restructuring process in the three crisis countries have included strict criteria to identify viable and nonviable institutions and to remove existing owners from insolvent institutions. Private capital injections have been encouraged or required under binding memoranda of understanding schemes that also foster operational restructuring. To complement domestic equity investment in banks and to bring in international expertise, the three crisis countries liberalized their foreign ownership rules for the financial sector. To encourage new private equity investment, public solvency support also has been offered under strict conditions.

Successful implementation of systemic bank restructuring demands that national authorities take full responsibility of all the aspects of the program. Given the microeconomic nature of financial restructuring and the need for well-coordinated interplay between so many different government institutions, the process can be successful only if the authorities themselves take full control of the implementation process. However, because systemic banking crises occur very infrequently and require skills not readily available in most countries, access to international expertise can be particularly helpful. Thus, the IMF, the World Bank, and other international and bilateral agencies have provided advice and shared experiences from other countries that have dealt with similar problems. The institutions have also helped countries obtain the necessary expertise from the public and private sectors to assist in the restructuring.

A realistic valuation of financial institutions' assets is essential to measure net worth, yet extremely difficult in cases of severe corporate and financial distress. The valuation of nonperforming loans is particularly hampered by the lack of clear market values and continuously changing economic conditions. To better support the valuation process, all countries tightened their rules for loan classification, loss provisioning, income recognition, and collateral valuation, and have substantially strengthened their supervisory scrutiny of compliance with such rules by bankers and auditors. Asset valuation is a key element in computing banks' capital adequacy requirements, which have been the basis for their recapitalization plans. In this connection, all the countries seek to bring their capital adequacy requirements into full compliance with international standards by the end of the restructuring process. In doing so, banks have been given time, according to transparent rules, to gradually restore their severely eroded capital bases. Recent developments suggest that transparency in loss recognition practices has helped in the issuance of new private bank equity.

Management of nonperforming loans and other value-impaired bank assets is one of the most critical and complex aspects of bank restructuring. There is no single optimal strategy for all circumstances but rather a combination of options that may vary over time and for each bank, depending on factors such as the nature of the problem assets, their overall size and distribution, and legal and governance constraints. The strategy will need to consider the speed of disposition of the assets, whether or not to use a centralized process, which also involves ownership choices.

Countries have taken different views on the role of asset management companies. Indonesia, Korea, and Malaysia have opted for centralized public asset management companies that buy assets from private banks to help banks clear their balance sheets. Thailand has aggressively liquidated the impaired assets of closed institutions through a central agency but does not permit public sector purchases of impaired assets from private banks; the Thai authorities are instead encouraging each bank to establish its own asset management company. The key issue in asset purchases by an asset management company is realistic valuation, so as to ensure that it does not become a tool for the indirect bailout of existing shareholders, thus undermining the incentives for private sector recapitalization and proper governance of asset management companies and banks. The sale of banks' assets to an asset management company forces immediate recognition of the value of the loan. This may deter such sales in cases where banks have been carrying these loans at inflated values.

The use of vast amounts of public resources has been necessary to help restructure the financial system. This affects medium-term fiscal sustainability in the three crisis countries. An estimate of the exact cost of the crisis is not possible, as the costs are still emerging and the corporate debt restructuring process is far from completed. The outlays initially took the form of central bank liquidity support, but have been gradually identified as solvency support and been refinanced by public or publicly guaranteed debt. Only the carrying costs of the latter have been brought into the government budgets so far. The ultimate public sector costs will be reduced by proceeds from asset sales and bank privatizations. Moreover, more rapid and sustained economic growth as a result of a restructured, more efficient, and profitable financial system will yield additional tax revenue.

The problems in the financial sector also reflected profound problems in the corporate sectors. Solving the banking and the corporate sector crises therefore must go hand in hand. Resolving banking problems requires not only bank recapitalization, but also broad-based corporate debt restructuring. At the same time, resolving corporate sector turmoil, in turn requires properly functioning banks as a counterpart. Widespread corporate weaknesses and insolvencies are much more difficult and time-consuming to deal with than bank restructuring. Bankruptcy and other laws, which were either not in place at the onset of the crisis or inadequate, as well as judicial systems, are now being reformed to speed up corporate debt restructuring. Nevertheless, lags in corporate reform are slowing progress in bank restructuring.

Bank restructuring provides a key lever for corporate restructuring. Tighter and better enforced prudential regulations can induce the financial restructuring of corporations, especially those that are highly leveraged. Moreover, banks can play a lead role in inducing corporate restructuring, particularly if they have strong government support to do so, as is the case in Korea.

The IMF programs designed to deal with the problems of crisis countries in Asia have centered on structural reforms of the financial sectors since it was clear that macroeconomic measures alone would be insufficient. This represented a major departure from a traditional IMF-supported adjustment program. Program design and implementation allowed IMF staff to share with the authorities broad experiences from systemic crisis management in other countries. At the same time, the magnitude, depth, and local circumstances of each country required quick and innovative responses and a major deployment of IMF staff and experts in close cooperation with the World Bank. The structural components and conditionality of IMF- and World Bank-supported programs were clearly instrumental in implementing the authorities' restructuring programs.

The different country experiences have provided IMF staff with important lessons in actual crisis management. The crisis experiences have confirmed that all major elements of the IMF's *Toward a Framework for Financial Stability*, prepared in 1997 and published in 1998, remain valid (see Folkerts-Landau and Lindgren, 1998). The crisis has again highlighted the main vulnerabilities identified in that paper: problems of valuing bank loans (identified as "the Achilles' heel" of effective corporate governance, market discipline, and official oversight) and therefore banks' net worth; design of lender-of-last-resort facilities; deposit guarantee schemes and exit procedures; and importance of supervisory authority and capacity. Areas in which that paper could be expanded would be more in-depth analysis of the macroeconomic environment as a source of financial sector vulnerability and the relationship between the financial and real sectors.

Could the crisis have been prevented? In each country, alternative courses of policy that would have been preferable can be identified—but this is to give hindsight too much of a role. In the financial sector itself, more transparency of macro- and microeconomic data and policies clearly would have helped in bringing matters to a head earlier, which could have lessened the depth of the crisis. Policies to foster corporate governance and lower corporate leverage would also have helped. Better regulatory and supervisory frameworks would have helped, for example, in detecting and correcting problems such as excessive real estate lending and the proliferation of financial institutions. However, even if the Basel Core Principles (of April 1998) had been in place, bank supervisors probably would have been unable to take restrictive action, since the underlying problems were masked by the economic boom. For similar reasons, there was no way for fiscal policies to anticipate the size of the fiscal contingent liabilities building up in the financial systems. In particular, foreseeing the sudden and massive erosion of loan and asset values that took place once market sentiment changed and the exchange rates collapsed would have been very difficult.

Comprehensive reforms of legal, institutional, and administrative frameworks have been initiated with the aim of introducing international standards and best practices. Such reforms encompass modernization of financial sector laws and prudential regulations, including operational procedures for exit of problem banks. Reforms also include a strengthening of supervisory powers, procedures, and capabilities with the aim of bringing about better risk management in banks. Another key area of reform is new laws and procedures for corporate bankruptcy and governance.

The above reforms are facilitated by the broad-based international efforts under way to implement new standards, codes, core principles, and best practices. International initiatives have been undertaken to improve financial sector architecture, surveillance over national and international financial markets, dissemination of data, macroeconomic vulnerability indicators, and prudential regulations and supervision of international lenders. This last initiative, led by the Basel Committee on Banking Supervision, aims at revising, among others, solvency requirements and country risks.

National authorities may also draw other lessons from the crisis in terms of countercyclical prudential policies and more supportive macroeconomic policies. Banks' net worth, including capital and reserves, should be built up in times of economic booms so that a cushion is available to deal with inevitable downturns. Such prudential policies are often referred to as countercyclical, and could include a strengthening of requirements regarding liquid assets, collateral margins, capital adequacy ratios, and general loan-loss provisioning in good times—when the future bad loans are extended. It should also be stressed that prudential policies are not substitutes for a proper mix of macroeconomic policies.

The experience of the crisis countries illustrates once more the importance of prompt and decisive action to deal with banking problems, including pre-emptive bank restructuring actions, and the dangers of waiting for the situation to reverse itself. Preventive action, notably in prudential regulation and su-

pervision and in the form of more transparency, would have improved bank governance and market discipline and helped prevent weaknesses from building up. Early action also could have reduced the magnitude of the portfolio losses and the need for liquidity and solvency support. Conversely, once credible programs were put in place with broad domestic and international support, the crisis became manageable and provided a foundation for economic recovery: the scale and complexity of the problems would have made it difficult to address them without such support. This also suggests the importance of countries obtaining international assistance early in the process, in which the IMF and the World Bank play key roles.

Appendix I   Indonesia

In the decade prior to the emergence of the Asian crisis, Indonesia had undergone rapid development, with per capita income doubling from 1990 to 1997.[63] This resulted from a significant diversification of the economy away from a dependence on oil and gas to a wider export basket consisting of primary products, textiles, and light manufactures. Economic growth was supported by a stable macroeconomic environment, characterized by balanced budgets and low inflation policies geared to maintaining a stable real exchange rate.

Indonesia has a tradition of a liberal capital regime. Restrictions on both inflows and outflows were largely relaxed in the mid-1970s. Nevertheless, until the early 1990s capital inflows played only a minor role, given a relatively undeveloped financial system, while the stable macroeconomic environment avoided any large capital outflows.

Background

In the 1990s, Indonesia significantly liberalized its domestic economy but direct and indirect state influence still remained very important. In the financial area, less government control led to a significant increase in the number of banks, often associated with specific industrial groups. A stock exchange and other financial institutions complemented the system. These developments notwithstanding, state banks continued to play a major role in the system.

Macroeconomic Setting

Prior to the crisis, Indonesia had been struggling with significant capital inflows. Bank Indonesia had, on several occasions, widened the exchange rate band, each time leading to a maximum appreciation of the rupiah within the band. In response to the real appreciation of the currency, exports in late 1996 and early 1997 showed rapid signs of decline.

---

[63]This appendix draws on a draft by Charles Enoch and Olivier Frécaut.

The crisis in Indonesia was essentially triggered by contagion from Thailand, especially after Thailand floated its currency, the baht, in July 1997. Contagion occurred despite the fact that Indonesia had stronger macroeconomic fundamentals than Thailand, particularly as they pertained to exports and the fiscal balance. Following a widening of the rupiah's band in July, the currency was floated in August 1997. After a temporary reprieve, exchange market pressures heightened in September and October, by which time the rupiah had fallen by more than 30 percent since July, the fastest depreciation among the crisis countries. On November 5, 1997, the IMF approved a three-year Stand-By Arrangement with Indonesia, equivalent to $10 billion; additional financing was committed by other international financial institutions and contingent credit lines from other countries. The initial response to the program was positive, but it proved short-lived, and the exchange rate fell again precipitously in December 1997. A strengthened program was announced in January 1998 but political difficulties in the run-up to, and after, the presidential election led to severe economic disruption in the economy. In June, the rupiah hit an end-of-the-day low of 16,650 rupiah against the U.S. dollar.

In the aftermath of the May 1998 riots and the replacement of the President, the macroeconomic program was modified and a limited degree of macroeconomic stability was restored. The exchange rate recovered to 11,075 rupiah against the U.S. dollar by the end of August 1998, and has stabilized at about 8,000 rupiah per U.S. dollar since late 1998.

Characteristics of the Financial Sector

Rapid economic growth, a liberal capital account regime, and regulatory changes have all contributed to substantial development in Indonesia's banking sector. The main characteristics of the system at the outset of the crisis can be summarized as follows:

- *Size and concentration.* After relaxing bank entry, the number of banks increased from 111 in 1988 to 240 in 1994. (The financial system in Indonesia remains dominated by commercial banks; see Box 14.)[64] A 1994 increase of minimum capital requirements from 10 billion rupiah to 50 billion rupiah reduced the number of potential entrants, leaving the number of institutions almost constant until the crisis broke. The seven state banks had combined assets accounting for about 40 percent of the entire system, although their share of total bank lending declined markedly after liberalization.[65]

- *Ownership and entry.* Liberalization increased the attraction of the financial sector to commercial and industrial concerns, and many of Indonesia's large business conglomerates founded one or more banks. The 10 foreign banks that operated in Indonesia obtained licenses in the late 1960s. Since then and until 1999, the entry of foreign banks was limited through the requirement to form either joint ventures (with a maximum of 85 percent foreign ownership) or buy shares of domestic banks on the Stock Exchange where the maximum foreign holding was set at 49 percent.
- *Areas of business activities.* Domestic banks were required to direct 20 percent of credit to small-scale business projects, and foreign banks were required to lend 50 percent to export-oriented businesses, although these requirements were often not met.

Weaknesses in the Financial Sector

Several issues related to ownership and business practice made the Indonesian financial sector vulnerable to the shocks that were experienced in 1997.

Structural Vulnerabilities

- *Nontransparent ownership and portfolio problems.* Quantification of the extent of problem loans in Indonesia was difficult, given the large number of banks and the complex pattern of cross holdings of equity and loans, which impaired the transparency of reports.
- *Loan concentration in the real estate sector.* While difficult to detect in the data collected by Bank Indonesia before the crisis, there had been

a sharp increase in real estate and property-related lending, which increased to about 20 percent of total outstanding loans in early 1997. In Indonesia, the dangers of loan concentration were heightened by difficulties in seizing and realizing collateral.
- *Exposure of banks to market risks.* From 1988, Bank Indonesia regulated banks' activities in other financial areas and limited banks' direct involvement in leasing, venture capital, securities trading, and investment management. Banks were, however, permitted to pursue such activities through the formation of subsidiaries operating as nonbank financial institutions, and they made frequent use of this option.

Prudential Regulation and Supervision

In the late 1980s and the first half of the 1990s, Indonesia improved banking regulation and supervision. A comprehensive set of well-drafted and up-to-date prudential regulations was prepared and issued. An advanced version of the U.S.-inspired capital, asset, management, equity, and liquidity (CAMEL) rating system was put in place. All these regulations were frequently updated and improved. Yet shortcomings in the legal and regulatory framework remained, particularly in the areas of loan classification and establishment of an effective exit mechanism for failed banks. Even more important, enforcement of the regulations was a major problem, often owing to political interference.

Prudential regulation

- *Loan classification and provisioning.* Even when problem loans were identified, loan classification standards in Indonesia remained inadequate because it was easy to restructure loans to reduce the size of reported portfolio problems. Moreover, Indonesian standards allowed a bank to reclassify loans back to performing status as soon as one payment was made, irrespective of the anticipated future payment stream on the loan. Banking supervisors, while recognizing the drawbacks of these practices, had not focused thoroughly on the extent of loan restructuring as an additional indicator of banking sector soundness.
- *Bank exit.* No effective bank closure and exit regulation was in place. Instead, failed private banks were generally absorbed by Bank Indonesia. In late 1996, a bankruptcy law for banks was passed, but it was deficient because it granted important rights to shareholders in the liquidation process and foresaw a liquidation process lasting several years.

---

[64]This discussion excludes 9,200 rural banks, which are limited in the geographical area of operations, may only accept time and saving deposits and extend loans, and hold 1–2 percent of total banking assets. Minimum capital for rural banks is 50 million rupiah.

[65]Five state banks were included in a World Bank rehabilitation project, which at the time imposed limits on their asset growth.

Box 14. Indonesia: Outline of Steps Toward Bank Resolution

The process of resolving the banking crisis can be broken into nine steps.

Step 1. As of the end of June 1997, before the crisis, the Indonesian banking system consisted of the following categories:

	Number of Banks	Share of Assets (In percent, June 1997)
Private domestic banks	160	49.4
With foreign exchange (forex) license	80	43.9
Without forex license	80	5.5
Publicly owned banks	34	42.3
State-owned banks	7	39.8
Regional development banks	27	2.5
Joint ventures and foreign banks	44	8.3
Joint ventures	34	4.7
Branches of foreign banks	10	3.6
Banking system	238	100

Step 2. As part of the commitments included in the October 31, 1997, letter of intent, 50 banks identified as weak were subjected by Bank Indonesia to specific resolution measures, which included the closure of 16 private domestic banks:

	Number of Banks	Share of Assets (In percent, June 1997)
Private domestic banks	41	24.1
Closed (5 forex and 11 nonforex)	16	2.5
Other resolution measures (13 forex and 12 nonforex)	25	21.6
Publicly-owned domestic banks	8	10
State-owned banks	2	9.6
Regional development banks	6	0.4
Joint-ventures and foreign banks	1	0.2
Joint ventures	1	0.2
Branches of foreign banks	0	—
Total	50	34.3
Banking system (before the 16 closures)	238	100

Step 3. On February 14, 1998, the Indonesian Bank Restructuring Agency (IBRA) took over the surveillance of 54 banks, including 4 state banks subject to a restructuring plan under World Bank auspices, and 50 private and regional development banks that had borrowed from Bank Indonesia more than 200 percent of their capital, and had a capital adequacy ratio below 5 percent on adjusted end of December 1997 figures:

	Number of Banks	Share of Assets (In percent, June 1997)
Private domestic banks	37	11.2
Forex	22	10.8
Nonforex	15	0.4
Publicly-owned domestic banks	15	25.0
State-owned banks	4	24.7
Regional development banks	11	0.3
Joint ventures and foreign banks	2	0.5
Joint ventures	2	0.5
Branches of foreign banks	0	—
Total-BRA Banks	54	36.7
Total-Non-IBRA Banks	168	63.3
Banking system	222	100

Steps 4-A and 4-B. On April 4, 1998, IBRA took action against the 14 worst banks placed under its surveillance since February.

The seven largest borrowers from Bank Indonesia had borrowed more than 2 trillion rupiah each and accounted together for over 75 percent of the total Bank Indonesia liquidity support to the banking system. IBRA took control through suspending shareholders' rights and (apart from in the state bank) changing the management of the following banks. These were known as banks-taken-over (BTO).

Name	Category	Share of liabilities (In percent, June 1997)
Bank Umum National (BUN)	Forex	1.1
Bank Dagang Nasional Indonesia (BDNI)	Forex	3.4
Bank Modern	Forex	0.3
Bank Danamon	Forex	2.2
Bank Tiara Asia	Forex	0.5
PDFCI	Joint Venture	0.4
Bank Ekspor Impor Indonesia (EXIM)	State	7.7
Total		15.6

Seven small banks in a particularly critical condition had borrowed from Bank Indonesia more than 500 percent of their equity and 75 percent of their assets. These banks were frozen, equivalent to a closure, and their deposits transferred to designated state banks (BBO banks, or Bank Reku Operati, i.e., banks whose operations are frozen):

Name	Category	Share of Liabilities (In percent, June 1997)
Bank Surya	Forex	0.15
Bank Pelita	Forex	0.11
Bank Subentra	Forex	0.08
Bank Hokindo	Nonforex	0.01
Bank Istismarat	Nonforex	0.02
Deka Bank	Nonforex	0.01
Centris International Bank	Nonforex	0.02
Total		0.40

As a result, the total number of active banks in Indonesia was reduced from 222 to 215, of which 47 were under IBRA's, and 168 under Bank Indonesia's surveillance.

Step 5. On May 29, 1998, following relentless runs that led Bank Indonesia to provide it with 32 trillion rupiah of liquidity support, Bank Central Asia, the largest domestic private bank (12.0 percent of the liabilities of the banking sector) was taken over by IBRA, the owners' rights were suspended, and the management replaced, and Bank Central Asia became the eighth BTO bank.

The number of IBRA banks went from 54 to 55 (40 active, 8 BTO, and 7 frozen), but was shortly thereafter reduced to 53 when 2 nonforex IBRA banks were merged with another IBRA bank.

During the same period, two non-IBRA private domestic banks (one forex and one nonforex) were merged with other non-IBRA banks. At that stage, the distribution of banks was therefore as follows:

	Number of Banks	Share of Assets (In percent, June 1997)
Private domestic banks	127	23.1
Forex	68	21.7
Nonforex	59	1.5
Publicly-owned domestic banks	41	67.5
State-owned banks	7	44.6
Regional development banks	27	1.9
IBRA banks (BTO)	7	21.0
Joint ventures and foreign banks	43	9.4
Joint ventures	33	4.7
Branches of foreign banks	10	4.7
Total active banks	211	100

Step 6. On August 21, 1998, based on the results of portfolio reviews, the authorities announced that three of the banks taken over by IBRA on April 4 (Step 4-A), namely Bank Umum Nasional, Bank Dagang Nasional Indonesia, and Bank Modern would be frozen, and their deposits transferred to designated state banks. The number of active banks was to be reduced to 208. Danamon was to be recapitalized by the government to serve as a bridge bank, PDFCI and Bank Tiara Asia were to be given a final opportunity for recapitalization by their owners, and negotiations began with the owners of Bank Central Asia to reacquire their bank.

Step 7. On September 30, the authorities announced the intent to merge four banks (Bumi Daya, Bank Pembangunan Indonesia, or BAPINDO, BRI, and EXIM) into the newly formed Bank Mandiri. They also announced a plan for the recapitalization of the state banks.

Step 8. In the October 19, 1998 Supplementary Memorandum of Economic and Financial Policy, the authorities announced their intention to commence the liquidation of the 10 IBRA frozen banks (Steps 4-B and 6). The distribution of surveillance responsibilities for the 208 active banks changed again, as only the BTO and frozen banks remained under IBRA's responsibility, while 11 other banks were returned to Bank Indonesia for supervisory purposes (in advance of the prospective restructuring of the state banks).

Step 9. On March 13, 1999, the government announced the results of the private recapitalization program; 74 banks, comprising 6 percent of total banking sector assets, had over 4 percent capital adequacy requirement and were categorized as "A" banks. Nine banks, comprising 12 percent of liabilities, had capital adequacy requirements between 4 percent and –25 percent, and were deemed eligible for recapitalization; seven banks, comprising 4 percent of liabilities, were taken over by IBRA; and 38 banks, comprising 5 percent of liabilities, were closed, including 17 banks with capital adequacy requirements worse than –25 percent (the "C" category banks). After these measures, the breakdown of the banking sector was as follows:

	Number of Banks	Share of Assets (In percent, June 1997)
Private domestic banks	83	17.9
Forex	30	4.8
Nonforex	44	1.1
Eligible for recapitalization	9	12.0
Publicly-owned domestic banks	45	71.8
State-owned banks	7	50.3
Regional development banks	27	2.1
IBRA banks (BTO)	11	19.3
Joint ventures and foreign banks	40	10.3
Joint ventures	30	5.1
Branches of foreign banks	10	5.2
Total active banks	168	100

Prudential supervision

Despite the improvements in the supervisory framework, serious implementation shortcomings remained. These included:

- *Substantial forbearance.* Violations of prudential rules were not appropriately sanctioned and noncompliance was widespread.
- *Ineffective on-site supervision.* Onsite inspections in Indonesia yielded limited additional insight into the actual number of problem loans, in contrast with the experience in other countries, where these inspections usually found a much higher number of nonperforming loans than reported by banks.
- *Insolvent banks remained in the system.* Given the problems with bank closure, several known insolvent banks remained open. While the combined overall negative net worth of insolvent banks remained relatively small (about 0.5 percent of GDP in 1996), the situation created moral hazard problems.

Impact of the Crisis on Bank Performance and Initial Resolution Measures

The following provides a chronology of the developments in the Indonesian banking crisis and summarizes the initial reactions.

From a Limited to a Systemic Banking Crisis: October–December 1997

When Indonesia requested IMF assistance in early October 1997, teams from the IMF, the World Bank, and the Asian Development Bank worked jointly to review the condition of the banking sector to provide support on financial sector issues. Based on data made available by Bank Indonesia, the financial condition of 92 of the 238 banks, representing 85 percent of the assets of the banking system, was evaluated. The depreciation of the rupiah, combined with a sharp shift in market sentiment, had already made a serious impact on the banking sector. At that stage, however, the banking sector did not show the characteristics of a systemic banking crisis despite deposit withdrawals from some small banks. State-owned banks' weaknesses appeared manageable as part of the fiscal adjustment, and most major private banks still posted comfortable cushions of positive equity.

In the framework of the overall program, aiming at a swift macroeconomic recovery, the IMF and the Indonesian authorities agreed on a comprehensive bank resolution package consisting of:

- intensified supervision, including frequent and detailed reviews, in addition to daily monitoring of key elements like liquidity and foreign exchange exposure for six of the country's largest private banks (market share: 18.0 percent) in which some critical weaknesses had been identified;
- rehabilitation plans, based on memoranda of understanding or cease-and-desist orders for seven small private banks (market share: 0.7 percent) in which serious weaknesses, including undercapitalization, had also been identified;
- conservatorship for three small, severely undercapitalized private banks (market share: 0.1 percent), and for six insolvent regional development banks (market share: 0.4 percent), pending the results of discussions with the regional government owners;
- transfer of the performing assets for two insolvent state-owned banks (market share: 9.6 percent) to a third state-owned bank; merger of the two insolvent banks, and transformation of the resulting entity into an asset recovery agency;
- definition and implementation of rehabilitation plans for 10 insolvent private banks (market share: 3.0 percent) that had benefited from a Bank Indonesia-sponsored and legally binding rescue package prior to the crisis, accelerating their return to solvency; and
- immediate closure of 16 small and deeply insolvent private banks (market share: 2.5 percent), with protection limited to small depositors.

In total, the resolution package announced to the public included 50 banks, representing 34.3 percent of the banking system. This package included the closure of the 16 small private banks. Since the remaining 34 banks were not identified, however, this created uncertainty among the public regarding the fate of all other banks. In the announcement, Bank Indonesia indicated its readiness to provide protection against runs through liquidity support for all banks that remained open, while a comprehensive action plan to improve the institutional, legal, and regulatory framework was set in motion.

After a short-lived positive reaction to the recovery program, and an appreciation of the rupiah, the environment rapidly began to deteriorate again. By early December, a number of elements had combined to reduce public confidence in the banking sector:

- the depreciation of the rupiah, high interest rates, and a slowdown in the economy took an increasing toll on bank profitability and soundness;
- rumors about the President's health and his last minute cancellation of a high-profile trip abroad created an atmosphere of political instability;

- the fast deterioration of the macroeconomic situation in Korea added to the uncertainty; and
- the developments regarding Alfa Bank were viewed as a sign that the authorities were not genuinely determined to implement the program as agreed with the IMF.[66]

The deposit runs multiplied amid rumors that a new wave of bank closures was under preparation, and the segmentation of the interbank market intensified. By mid-December 1997, 154 banks representing half of the total assets of the system had faced, to varying degrees, some erosion of their deposit base. During December 1997, Bank Indonesia's liquidity support increased from 13 trillion rupiah to 31 trillion rupiah, equivalent to 5 percent of GDP. Insofar as the liquidity support, paid in rupiah, was needed by banks to meet reductions in dollar deposits, in effect it served to fuel capital flight and, thus, the continuing depreciation of the exchange rate. In contrast to other crisis countries, efforts at sterilization were not successful, reflecting a loss of monetary control by Bank Indonesia.

Stabilizing the Banking Sector: January–February 1998

During January 1998, a sudden and deep deterioration in the economic environment took place, with the rupiah heading into a free fall. The rate fell from 4,600 rupiah per U.S. dollar at the end of December 1997 to 15,000 rupiah per U.S. dollar in late January 1998, with some trades even at 17,000 rupiah. The Indonesian authorities signed a letter of intent with the IMF on January 15, 1998, but continued evident failure to live up to commitments by the Indonesian authorities led to further exchange rate depreciation, notwithstanding renewed discussions to bolster the commitments made in the January 1998 letter of intent. When it became impossible for Indonesia to present a credible recovery program to the IMF, the banking sector problems turned into a full-fledged systemic crisis, with liquidity support from Bank Indonesia exceeding over 60 trillion rupiah (about 6 percent of 1998 GDP), risk of hyperinflation, and complete financial sector "meltdown."

On January 27, 1998, a new financial sector strategy was introduced, with the authorities' immediate priority being to avoid a financial collapse and to stabilize the banking sector. The government announced a three-point emergency plan. First, all depositors and creditors of all domestic banks were, henceforth, to be completely protected.[67] Second, IBRA was established for a period of five years, under the auspices of the ministry of finance, to take over and rehabilitate weak banks and manage the nonperforming assets of intervened banks. Third, a framework for handling corporate restructuring was proposed. The impact of the announcement was immediate, with the exchange rate recovering to 12,000 rupiah per U.S. dollar and appreciating further in subsequent days. Attempts were made to place restrictions on banks' activities to mitigate the moral hazard effects of the blanket guarantee; for instance, deposit rates were capped at a specific premium above the levels being offered by the best-run banks.

In the following two months, efforts were made to reestablish monetary control by rationalizing Bank Indonesia liquidity facilities and by developing effective penalties to deter banks from seeking access to these facilities. To better assert the authorities' control, surveillance over 54 banks (comprising 36.7 percent of the banking sector; see Box 14, Step 3) that had borrowed heavily from Bank Indonesia was transferred to IBRA on February 14. This included four state-owned banks (BAPINDO, Bank Bumi Daya, BDNI, and Bank Exim), accounting for 24.7 percent of the liabilities of the banking sector. IBRA examiners were placed in those banks, and the banks were required to sign memoranda of understanding setting out the strengthened supervision under which they would operate.

While this initial operation was carried out relatively smoothly, its impact was much reduced by the refusal of the President to publicize it lest it trigger a renewal of runs. As a result, the initial workings of IBRA were not apparent to the public, there was confusion as to the authorities' intentions, and the momentum generated by the January 27 announcements was largely lost. Even worse followed when, in late February, the President dismissed the head of IBRA, at that time a highly respected finance ministry official, and some of the staff seconded into IBRA were returned to Bank Indonesia. The government itself drifted through the period up to the presidential election of 1998 and a prolonged debate ensued over the possible introduction of a currency board arrangement. Liquidity support to the banking system continued to increase, largely to meet continuing deposit withdrawals but also in the face of withdrawals of credit lines to domestic banks, as

---

[66]The President's son, whose Bank Andromeda had been closed on November 1, was allowed to take over the small Alfa Bank, which was immediately granted a foreign exchange license by Bank Indonesia, and to transfer into it most of his former activities, effectively reopening his former bank under a new name.

[67]The blanket guarantee was to last a minimum of two years, and at least six months' notice would be given before its termination. Subsequently, the guarantee was retroactively applied to the 16 closed banks and thereafter to the 9,200 rural banks.

well as emerging losses in derivatives businesses in a few banks, including one state bank with more than 20 trillion rupiah (2 percent of GDP) of such losses. Altogether, by that time, liquidity support to banks stood at more than 60 trillion rupiah (6 percent of GDP).

First Resolution Initiatives and New Shock: March–May 1998

The ensuing three months saw the authorities taking their first initiatives to resolve ailing banks and then facing a major new shock. With monetary conditions progressively being brought under control, the main focus turned to establishing the necessary infrastructure for handling the banking crisis: making IBRA operational, preparing the legal framework, obtaining better information on the financial condition of the banks, and beginning to take action.

In early March 1998, Bank Indonesia announced the redesign of its liquidity support facilities. Until then, support had been provided through several windows—with the deterrent to usage, in theory, being highly punitive interest rates. Virtually no banks, however, were actually paying interest, which was therefore routinely capitalized, causing a rapid further expansion in outstanding liquidity support. The new system involved a single liquidity facility with interest rates, generally only a small margin above market rates. The new focus was on nonmarket sanctions; any bank with borrowings outstanding for more than a week would have a special Bank Indonesia inspection, which would produce a report within a further week, increase restrictions on the bank's activities, and culminate in possible transfer to IBRA.

By late March 1998, the new IBRA management team was ready for more substantive intervention into the most critical of IBRA banks. On April 4, in its first major public action, IBRA took over the seven banks (Box 14, Step 4, part A) that had each borrowed more than 2 trillion rupiah (all but two of these had borrowed more than 5 trillion rupiah each, and two of them over 20 trillion rupiah); together they accounted for about 72 percent of total Bank Indonesia liquidity support to the banking system. The focus at this stage was on liquidity, rather than solvency, to determine which banks should be intervened. This was partly because, in the absence of reliable data on the solvency condition of the banks, liquidity criteria could serve as a proxy, and partly because of the urgent need to tackle the provision of Bank Indonesia liquidity support itself in order to stabilize monetary conditions.

For the six private banks among them, owners were suspended and managements removed; new management was put in place through "twinning" arrangements with designated state banks.[68] At the same time, seven smaller banks (Box 14, Step 4, part B), comprising 0.4 percent of the banking system, which had each borrowed more than 500 percent of their capital, were closed; all deposits were transferred over that weekend into a designated state bank, Bank Negara Indonesia. Great efforts were made to ensure uniform application of objective criteria in the choice of both sets of banks, and there was an intensive and professional public relations campaign over the weekend to explain the moves to the public. As a result, the moves were received favorably in the markets; there were sporadic runs on a few of the acquired banks, but these diminished. These actions were a major step to demonstrate the authorities' commitment toward bank resolution and to bring a revised IMF-supported program to the IMF's Executive Board for consideration in late April.

The riots in mid-May of 1998 led to a depreciation of the recently stabilized rupiah and a further loss of confidence by both domestic and foreign investors. In the aftermath of the riots, there were massive runs on Bank Central Asia, the largest private bank, which accounted for 12 percent of total banking sector liabilities. Given the circumstances, support was effected relatively smoothly. Bank Indonesia, in conjunction with two of the state banks, supplied over 30 trillion rupiah in cash to Bank Central Asia over the week following May 16 as deposits were withdrawn. On May 29, Bank Central Asia was brought under the auspices of IBRA, the owners' rights were suspended, and an outside management team introduced. By the end of the month, runs on Bank Central Asia had decreased.

The specific nature of the attacks against Bank Central Asia was especially devastating to confidence in the banking sector, with many viewing the run on the bank as politically inspired.[69] In this environment, other bankers sought to maximize their immediate liquidity to protect themselves in the event of runs. The stock of vault cash increased, intermediation declined even further, and interbank markets became more segmented. With interest rates rising in the face of uncertainty, banks bid up deposit rates to levels substantially above those that they were able to charge their borrowers. The sizable negative interest spread across much of the banking sector caused

---

[68]In the seventh bank, the state-owned Bank Exim, part of the management team was replaced. The bank now has become part of the new Bank Mandiri.

[69]Seventy percent of Bank Central Asia was owned by the Salim Group, the largest conglomerate in the country, and associated with the Suharto government. Thirty percent of the bank was owned by two children of the then President.

a continuing erosion of the capital base of the affected banks. Nevertheless, liquidity support from Bank Indonesia—apart from that to Bank Central Asia—remained limited, and Bank Indonesia was increasingly successful in stabilizing monetary conditions in line with commitments under the IMF-supported program. By mid-July 1998, Bank Indonesia also reintroduced market-based monetary management—with the start of auctions of one-month central bank bills—to enhance monetary control, and thus helping to redistribute liquidity in the segmented interbank market (three-month auctions of central bank bills were started in October 1998).

Meanwhile, the bank restructuring process was given a fresh impetus. A third head of IBRA had been appointed, a finance ministry official with previous experience in the banking sector. Continuity in the restructuring process was assured with the appointment of the first head of IBRA as finance minister in the new government. The new team needed to ascertain the true condition of the banks in order to undertake appropriate remedial action. The banks' own reported figures were deeply unreliable, with many banks still posting profits in early 1998 on the basis of unrealized foreign exchange valuation gains and lack of recognition of deterioration in their loan portfolios. In March 1998, Bank Indonesia had announced new provisioning and classification guidelines, broadly in line with international standards, but application was very patchy, in part because of lack of expertise both at Bank Indonesia and in the banks.

International auditors were contracted—financed by the World Bank in the case of the 55 IBRA banks, and by the Asian Development Bank in the case of the major non-IBRA banks—to conduct portfolio reviews on international accounting standards by using the new classification and provisioning rules.[70] As these were completed, they confirmed the picture of deep and pervasive problems.

Toward a Comprehensive Resolution Strategy

Portfolio Review

Action toward the resolution of ailing banks resumed when audit results became available. In June 1998, the results of the portfolio reviews of the condition of the six private banks included in the seven largest borrowers of Bank Indonesia resources (Box 14, Step 4, part A) showed that they had nonperforming loans equivalent to at least 55 percent of total loans (over 90 percent in one large bank), and all the banks were proven to be deeply insolvent.[71] For most of these banks the loan portfolios were dominated by connected lending. In July 1998, four of the six banks were formally declared insolvent. On August 21, a resolution strategy was announced for these six banks. Three were "frozen" (Box 14, Step 6), while a rehabilitation program was defined for the other three. One bank, Danamon, the second largest private bank in terms of number of depositors before the crisis, was to be recapitalized and used as a "bridge" bank to receive deposits and assets from some of the closed banks. For the two remaining banks, the former owners would be given a last opportunity to clear their insolvencies; otherwise they would be merged into Danamon or closed. The process served also to highlight deficiencies in the legal framework under which IBRA had been operating, with recalcitrant shareholders in the remaining two banks able to hold up the insolvency declarations in those banks. Ensuring proper powers for IBRA to assume control of insolvent banks was one of the most important objectives of the amendments to the banking law prepared at the time.

By early August 1998, the results of the portfolio reviews for a group of 16 large banks, all of them non-IBRA except for Bank Central Asia, were becoming available. These showed that the banks were, in general, clearly different from IBRA banks, in terms of quality of risk controls, compliance with prudential norms, and overall quality of management. Nevertheless, the financial condition of these banks, too, was shown to be very weak, with many of the banks insolvent. Given that many of these banks would have been expected to be among the strongest in the country, these reviews confirmed the deep insolvency of the banking system as a whole.

Legal and Supervisory Preparations

In October 1998, the parliament passed amendments to the banking law that modified previous requirements regarding bank secrecy and ended restrictions on foreign ownership of banks. These amendments also enabled IBRA to operate effectively—for instance to be able to transfer assets and to foreclose against a nonperforming debtor.

Consistent with program commitments, substantial progress has also been achieved in reviewing

---

[70]Portfolio reviews on a similar basis were conducted by Bank Indonesia supervisors themselves in the case of the smaller, non-foreign exchange banks.

[71]Results of these initial reviews were quickly leaked to the press, causing consternation among the public. Security procedures, and other aspects of conducting the reviews, were tightened substantially in the light of experience with this first "wave."

and strengthening the prudential and regulatory framework on a number of critically important issues, as follows:

- *Loan classification, loan provisioning, and the treatment of debt restructuring operations.* These three new regulations became effective as of the end of December 1998. Five loan categories are defined, namely, pass, special mention, substandard, doubtful, and loss, with respective provisioning of 1 percent, 5 percent, 15 percent, 50 percent, and 100 percent.
- *Liquidity management.* Banks are now required to submit a liquidity report twice monthly for their global consolidated operations. The report comprises a foreign currency liquidity profile, and a combined rupiah and foreign currency profile. The liquidity report collects data in weekly maturity bands for four weeks and for the next two-month period. The report includes a section outlining the efforts the bank intends to take to cover any liquidity shortfall or absorb any liquidity surplus.
- *Foreign exchange exposure.* The regulation has been broadly satisfactory but there are certain shortcomings regarding implementation of the regulation. For example, Bank Indonesia may (rather than must) impose administrative sanctions on banks that do not comply with the limits for foreign exchange exposure.
- *Connected lending.* The newly published regulations tighten the rules in this field where the most widespread and damaging abuses took place in the period leading to the crisis, by and large in line with international best practices.
- *Capital adequacy.* The required capital adequacy level has been temporarily lowered to 4 percent. The new regulation also ensures that banks can compute as supplementary capital (Tier 2) only general reserves for possible earning asset losses up to a maximum of 1.25 percent of total risk-weighted assets, whereas the previous regulation allowed banks to count as Tier 2 both general and specific loan-loss provision. The regulation will be reviewed by the end of 1999 to evaluate setting the date for banks to comply again with a minimum capital adequacy requirement of 8 percent.
- *Disclosure of financial statements.* Banks are now required to publish their financial statements quarterly, beginning April 1999.

IBRA conducted forensic type audits to identify possible irregularities and to examine the compliance with legal requirements of the 14 banks then under its control. On August 21, 1998, the government announced that former owners of 10 of the banks that had been out of compliance with legal requirements had one month to pay back the liquidity support Bank Indonesia had provided, or be subject to further penalties. By late September, about 200 trillion rupiah of assets, at the owners' valuation, had been pledged from several of these owners as well as about 1 trillion rupiah in cash. IBRA's advisors valued the assets at 92.8 trillion rupiah, and IBRA tentatively announced full settlement with owners of three of the banks, including Bank Central Asia. These agreements, however, were not accepted by the government, which sought a greater up front contribution of cash. After protracted negotiations, the owners agreed to settle their obligations within four years, but that assets representing these obligations would be transferred to IBRA to be placed into a holding company; it was intended that 27 percent of the obligations would be realized in the first year. With Bank Central Asia arriving at the first such agreement, other former owners reached similar agreements quickly. In mid-1999, however, owners of three banks were deemed not to be negotiating seriously, and in fact, IBRA was preparing to take legal action against them.

Strategy for State Banks

In late August 1998 the authorities announced that the four state banks (including Bank Exim) under IBRA's auspices would be merged into a single new bank, Bank Mandiri, under a management and operational restructuring contract with a major international bank. The corporate business of a fifth, non-IBRA state bank, Bank Rakyat Indonesia (BRI), was also considered to be merged into this bank. Bank Mandiri would start with 30 percent of the assets of the banking sector. Although this share might decline as part of the restructuring, Mandiri would still be, by some margin, the largest bank in the country.

On September 30, 1998, Mandiri was established as holder of 100 percent of the shares of the four component banks. On February 12, 1999, a voluntary severance scheme was offered to the headquarters staff of the four component banks as a prelude to integrating their functions, and plans were finalized for centralizing two critical functions—treasury and credit assessment. The bad loans from the component banks were transferred to the asset management unit at the end of March 1999, and performing loans were progressively transferred from the component banks into Bank Mandiri.

Meanwhile, the portfolio reviews confirmed that the three remaining state banks—Bank Negara Indonesia, BRI, and BTN—were also deeply insolvent. The government announced plans to recapitalize them, and in April 1999 presented a blueprint for the restructurings. Bank Negara Indonesia is likely to be the second largest bank in the country, with about 15 percent of the sector. Meanwhile, the government had also announced plans to recapitalize the 27 regional development banks, which together made up 2 percent of the banking sector.

Bank Mandiri has made solid progress in implementing its restructuring plan, and is preparing to almost halve its staff and close branches. Plans to enhance loan recoveries have been prepared. A merger of its four component banks is scheduled; capitalization of the bank is envisaged to be completed by the end of the year. Privatization is scheduled to begin within two years.

Meanwhile, the other state banks are in the process of finalizing blueprints for their restructuring. Recapitalization is envisaged to take place between September 1999 and March 2000. Privatization of the largest of these banks, Bank Negara Indonesia, is expected in 2002. IBRA announced the resolution strategy for the banks it has taken over. One small bank will be merged into Bank Central Asia, and eight banks into Danamon. Bank Central Asia and the "B" bank whose owners were unable to provide their share of the recapitalization needs are expected to be sold by the end of 1999. At that stage, therefore, there will be only one IBRA bank (Danamon), which will serve as a "bridge bank" to wind down the activities of the banks brought under its control.

Strategy for Private Banks

On September 30, 1998, on behalf of the government, Bank Indonesia announced a plan for the joint recapitalization of those remaining private banks that met certain specified conditions. The objective of this plan was to retain a residual private banking sector from among the "best" private banks, recognizing that given the economic turmoil that has affected Indonesia, even well-run banks would likely have run into serious difficulties. Moreover, the plan was designed to foster burden sharing between the private sector and the government regarding the cost of resolving these banks. The details are as follows:

- For those banks that had capital adequacy ratios between negative 25 percent and 4 percent, business plans that demonstrated medium-term viability, and owners deemed to be "fit and proper," the government indicated its willingness to contribute up to four rupiah for every rupiah contributed by those owners to restore a bank to having a capital adequacy ratio of 4 percent—the minimum capital adequacy requirement for the end of December 1998. Owners' contributions would generally be in cash, while those of the government would be in bonds.
- The government announced that it would obtain its equity stake through preference shares that would be convertible into ordinary shares in either of two situations—if the bank failed to comply with the targets of its own business plan, or after a period of three years. During the three-year period, the owners would be able to reacquire their shares in the bank by repaying the government's contribution (in effect, the contribution would have been a loan), either for their own account or for an outside investor. At the end of the three years, the government would seek an independent valuation of the bank, and the owners would have the first option to buy back the government's shares. Otherwise, the government would sell its shares within a specified period. To encourage owners to put in new capital, the government pledged to allow owners to retain day-to-day control of banks.
- In addition, once the joint recapitalization was agreed upon, all category 5 loans (i.e., those loans classified as "loss") were to be transferred at a zero price to the asset management unit, which would enter into a contract for the recovery of the loans with the originating bank. At their discretion, the banks could also transfer category 4 loans (those classified as "doubtful") at zero price to the asset management unit, for handling on the same basis as the category 5 loans. Any recoveries from such loans would be used immediately to buy back the government's preference shares, thus giving the government the prospect of an early return of its financial infusion, and reducing the amount to be paid by the owners to reacquire full control of their bank.

In December 1998, the plan was threatened to be reversed when the President announced instead a strategy of forced mergers. With the uncertainty in the markets, as well as the worst rioting since May 1998, leading to renewed depreciation of the rupiah (from about 7,500 rupiah to the U.S. dollar to 9,000 rupiah per U.S. dollar), the private bank recapitalization plan was finally reaffirmed. In February 1999, Parliament passed a budget that included 34 trillion rupiah for bank restructuring (17 trillion rupiah net of expected recoveries).

By that time, work on assessing business plans—the fitness and propriety of owners and managers and availability of capital infusions—had been completed, and bank closures were widely regarded as imminent. Indeed, ministers had made it clear that banks that failed the tests for the recapitalization plan would be closed on February 26, 1999. However, intense lobbying from owners of banks that realized that they were in danger of being closed succeeded in postponing the government-scheduled interventions at the last minute. The pub-

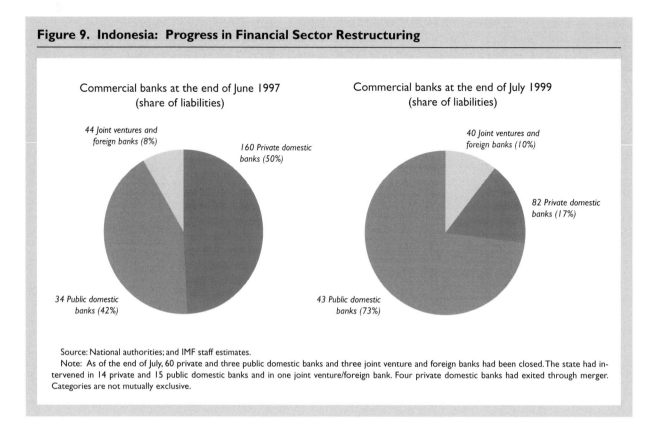

Figure 9. Indonesia: Progress in Financial Sector Restructuring

Commercial banks at the end of June 1997
(share of liabilities)

44 Joint ventures and
foreign banks (8%)

160 Private domestic
banks (50%)

34 Public domestic
banks (42%)

Commercial banks at the end of July 1999
(share of liabilities)

40 Joint ventures and
foreign banks (10%)

82 Private domestic
banks (17%)

43 Public domestic
banks (73%)

Source: National authorities; and IMF staff estimates.
Note: As of the end of July, 60 private and three public domestic banks and three joint venture and foreign banks had been closed. The state had intervened in 14 private and 15 public domestic banks and in one joint venture/foreign bank. Four private domestic banks had exited through merger. Categories are not mutually exclusive.

lic recognized the cause of the postponement, and amid clear indications of government disarray the rupiah fell another 10 percent, to almost 10,000 per the U.S. dollar.

On March 13, 1999, the government announced the closure of 38 banks (comprising 5 percent of the banking sector) and the takeover by IBRA of seven others (comprising 2 percent of the sector). Nine banks (or 10 percent of the banking sector) were deemed eligible for recapitalization under approved business contracts. The banks subsequently provided their share of capital by April 21. At the time, 73 banks (5 percent of the banking sector) had capital adequacy ratios of at least 4 percent and, hence, did not need government support. Although the terms of the original recapitalization plan were thus broadly reaffirmed, the government did not explicitly restate its earlier commitment to leave the day-to-day running of the banks in the hands of the owners.

The closures and takeovers were handled efficiently by Bank Indonesia and IBRA, although the agencies had difficulty transferring the deposits to designated recipient banks over the weekend of March 13, since staff in a number of banks denied them access in order to increase their bargaining power for higher severance payments. IBRA undertook to pay twice the legal minimum, and indicated

that severed staff should negotiate with the former owners for anything more. Although over the following weeks there were public disturbances by employees of the closed banks, Bank Indonesia/IBRA gradually achieved access to the remaining branches of the banks.

The March 13, 1999 announcements indicated also that the "A" category banks would be subject to review regarding the fitness and propriety of their owners and managers and, for some of them, the sources of their capital infusions. The sources of capital were verified by April 21. However, one-third of the owners, managers, and commissioners failed the "fit and proper" test. These commissioners and managers were required to be replaced immediately and failed owners themselves were given up to 90 days to divest their holdings.

Of the nine banks eligible for recapitalization under the government's plan, owners of seven banks supplied their share of the necessary additional capital in advance of the April 20 deadline. IBRA became involved in intense discussions as the deadline approached to resolve the situation of the remaining two banks. Ultimately, one of these banks (holding about 1 percent of total bank assets) was acquired by a major foreign bank, the largest such acquisition since the banking crisis began; for the other—discussions on which were hampered by the absence of a controlling shareholder—no sources of capital could be found in time, and the bank was taken over by IBRA.

Over the following month, IBRA negotiated performance contracts and memoranda of understanding with the managements of the eight remaining banks. The government had decided that it wished to hold its shares in these banks as ordinary stock, rather than convertible preference shares, but these memoranda of understanding provided essentially the same protection to the owners of the banks—that is, the owners retained the day-to-day control of the banks, and various areas of the government retained the right to become involved if necessary. Meanwhile, updated audits provided revised figures for the banks' insolvency, indicating capital needs almost double the amount earlier estimated.

At the end of May 1999, the owners of the banks provided their share of the extra capital requirement, and the government issued bonds to provide its share of the necessary recapitalization.[72] In the case of the listed banks, a rights issue underwritten of up to 80 percent by the government served to reduce need for public funds; for the largest recapitalized bank, this issue was particularly successful in attracting new private investment. The government now owns between 60 and 80 percent of the stock of these banks; at the end of three years independent valuations of these banks will be conducted, and the owners will be given the right of first refusal to buy back the government's shares. If the owners decide not to purchase the shares, the gov-

ernment will sell its shares over the following year. In the meantime, the government can only dilute its shareholding with the concurrence of the owners. The government's share will also decline during the three years, representing the loan losses realized that will be subsequently transferred to IBRA. During this period, the owners may themselves buy back the government's shares, at the price the government paid plus interest. With the prices of these banks shares now rising strongly, it appears that the owners of at least one of the banks are already seeking to buy back the government's shares. Thus, the recapitalization program has saved these banks, and the government seems likely to get back at least a share of its investment sooner than originally envisaged.

State of Restructuring Efforts

The Indonesian banking sector has been consolidated significantly in the last two years (Figure 9). Since mid-1997, the number of private domestic banks has been nearly halved through closures or state takeovers. Reflecting this consolidation, banks under state control now hold about 70 percent of liabilities, compared to 40 percent before the crisis.

Public Cost of Financial Sector Restructuring

As of mid-1999, the public contribution to financial sector restructuring has been equal to 51 percent of GDP (Table 15). The largest share of this has been used to recapitalize banks and provide liquidity support. The expected budgetary cost of bank restructuring (i.e., the interest cost on the government bonds) in the 1999/2000 fiscal year is 34 trillion rupiah or 3 percent of GDP; half of this is to come from recov-

---

[72]Except for the bank being taken over by the foreign bank, where the capital infusion will follow once the foreign bank has completed its due diligence.

eries, mainly from shareholder settlements. IBRA has been investigating all failed banks (those closed and those taken over) to see if there were violations of insider lending limits, and, if so, will pursue the former owners of these banks to provide assets as compensation for these violations. Agreements have already been reached with the former shareholders of eight such banks, and negotiations with several more are in progress. Two of these agreements have so far resulted in assets being transferred from two of these banks to holding companies under the joint control of IBRA and the former owners. Sales from these assets are likely to begin in the coming months, with over 12 trillion rupiah expected by March 2000.

Meanwhile the state and IBRA have intensified their loan recovery efforts. Each institution has published the names of their largest debtors and invited them to begin negotiations. IBRA aimed at classifying all debtors into four categories by the end of August 1999, depending on their degree of cooperation and business viability. IBRA hoped to adopt a strategy for each debtor based upon its classification. Noncooperating debtors will be widely publicized. An interdepartmental committee has been established to coordinate the preparation of a database on the debtors, and to facilitate the establishment of a joint-creditor negotiating position, with the debtors under a lead creditor institution.

Appendix II   Korea

Korea, a largely industrialized country and member of the Organization for Economic Cooperation and Development (OECD), was initially thought immune from the financial sector problems in its less developed neighboring countries.[73] Nevertheless, by late 1997, structural similarities and the forces of contagion contributed to the extension of the crisis to the Korean economy.

Background

Korea's exchange rate remained broadly stable through October 1997. However, the high level of short-term debt and the low level of usable international reserves made the economy increasingly vulnerable to shifts in market sentiment. While macroeconomic fundamentals continued to be favorable, the growing awareness of problems in the financial sector and in industrial groups (chaebols) increasingly led to the difficulties for the banks in rolling over their short-term borrowing. Declining rollover rates brought this ratio down to less than half at the end of 1997. International reserves decreased from the equivalent of 2.6 months of imports in 1993 to two months in 1996, and—with the onset of the crisis—dropped to 0.6 months in 1997. Korea widened the exchange rate band on November 17, 1997; the won fell sharply, and the Bank of Korea had to provide large amounts of foreign exchange for Korean banks to honor their overseas commitments.

On December 4, 1997, Korea entered into a three-year Stand-By Arrangement with the IMF, amounting to $21 billion, augmented by arrangements with the World Bank and the Asian Development Bank. Several countries pledged additional $22 billion as a second line of defense. Agreement on the program—which also included far-reaching steps toward financial sector rehabilitation—initially failed to increase rollover rates of short-term foreign debt, and the won fell further. However, the combination of an agreement with private foreign bank creditors on a voluntary rescheduling of short-term debt (concluded by the end of January 1998) and a rephasing of the IMF arrangement to allow an advancement of drawings succeeded in alleviating short-term foreign exchange pressures and permitted stabilization to begin. Progress in stabilization allowed a gradual reduction in interest rates, now standing at below pre-crisis levels. The won, which had depreciated close to 2,000 won per U.S. dollar, has stabilized in the range of 1,200 won per U.S. dollar. Useable reserves have increased to $52 billion as of mid-1999. Growth is now expected to be about 9 percent in 1999.

Macroeconomic Setting

Prior to the crisis, Korea's macroeconomic performance was generally praised, with GDP growing at an average rate of 8 percent in 1994–97. An increase in investment and exports fueled the growth. Unemployment remained low, averaging slightly above 2 percent during the period, and inflation was stable at about 5 percent. The fiscal position appeared to be strong, and public debt was below 11 percent of GDP, of which only about one-fifth was foreign debt. Developments in the external sector followed closely the evolution of the yen, which in 1995–96 led to a widening of the current account deficit to the equivalent of almost 5 percent of GDP in 1996 and which declined the next year to 2 percent. This external deficit was financed by private capital inflows. The ratio of total external debt to GDP increased significantly from 20 percent of GDP in 1993 to 33 percent in 1996 and to 35 percent in 1997. At the same time, the proportion of short-term debt to total debt increased, amounting to about two-thirds of total debt in 1996.

Characteristics of the Financial Sector

The Korean financial system was unusual among emerging markets for its diversity. It comprised private commercial banks, a number of government-owned specialized and development banks, and a

---

[73]This appendix draws on Baliño and Ubide (1999) and on contributions from Peter Hayward and Leslie Teo.

wide variety of very sizable nonbank financial institutions. These institutions were closely interlinked. In particular, commercial banks had significant off-balance sheet exposures to nonbank financial institutions through their holdings or guarantees of commercial paper and corporate bonds underwritten by merchant banks.

Commercial banks accounted for just over half the assets of the financial system. As of September 1997, the sector comprised 16 nationwide banks, 10 regional banks, and 52 foreign banks. The top eight banks accounted for about two-thirds of commercial bank assets (excluding trust accounts). Regional banks were established to develop specific regions, particularly to foster the growth of small- and medium-sized enterprises. Foreign banks have been allowed to open branches since 1967, although their market share remained very small. Commercial banks were supervised by the Office of Banking Supervision at the Bank of Korea.[74] Commercial banks also operated trust accounts that were separately accounted for but were managed like the rest of their banking business.[75] Trust accounts had grown rapidly in recent years (they accounted for close to 40 percent of total commercial bank assets as of the end of 1997), largely because they had been less regulated and had been able to offer higher interest rates than regular commercial bank business.

Specialized and development banks were established in the 1950s and 1960s to provide funds to specific strategic sectors.[76] They accounted for about 17 percent of financial system assets. Although specialized banks could borrow from the government, deposits constituted their main source of funding. Funding for development banks, which are wholly government-owned, came mainly from bonds issued domestically and abroad.[77] The Korean Development Bank, the largest development bank, was established in 1954 to supply long-term credit to major industries. Its assets were heavily concentrated in lending to large corporations, mainly financing fixed investment (including infrastructure projects). These banks were traditionally not subject to the same prudential standards and supervision as commercial banks, and were overseen by the ministry of finance and economy.

Meanwhile, nonbank financial institutions comprised 30 percent of financial system assets at the end of 1997 and consisted of three types of institutions: investment companies, savings institutions, and insurance companies. Of these, investment institutions, which consisted of merchant banks, investment trust companies, and securities companies, were the largest in terms of assets, followed closely by savings institutions. Many nonbank financial institutions were predominantly owned, directly or indirectly, by chaebols and other large shareholders. They were used to finance activities within the chaebol group, and became an increasingly important source for intermediating chaebol notes and other paper. Nonbank financial institutions and trust accounts at commercial banks provided a means to circumvent restrictions on commercial bank intermediation.

Precrisis Weaknesses in the Financial System

Structural Vulnerabilities

During the 1960s and 1970s, Korea embarked on an outward-oriented industrialization strategy spearheaded by the chaebols, which were supported by preferential access to subsidized credit (so-called policy loans).[78] Interest rates were administered, financial innovation was restricted, and competition in the banking system was limited. These government policies resulted in a tightly controlled, government-administered financial system characterized by chronic excess demand for credit.

Since the mid-1970s the government took steps—including the granting of tax preferences—to develop capital markets and thus to reduce corporate reliance on bank borrowing. A program of gradual domestic financial sector reform was introduced in the early 1980s, including bank privatization and deregulation of banks' activities, abolition of credit controls, introduction of new financial instruments, granting of greater business opportunities to the nonbank financial institutions, and partial interest rate

---

[74]The banks' trust account business and leasing affiliates were not under the supervision of the Office of Banking Supervision.

[75]In 1970, the trust business was assigned exclusively to Korea Trust Bank, which merged with Seoul Bank in 1976. By the end of 1995, all deposit money banks and development institutions, with the exception of the Korea Export-Import Bank (KEXIM) and foreign banks, were allowed to engage in trust businesses.

[76]There are four specialized banks—the Industrial Bank of Korea and three other banks centered on agricultural, fisheries, and livestock cooperatives. Development banks comprise the Korean Development Bank, KEXIM, and the Long-Term Credit Bank.

[77]Although those bonds did not carry a formal government guarantee, the government was legally obliged to ensure that the banks were always in a position to meet their liabilities when they fell due.

[78]The National Investment Fund was created in 1974 for this purpose, and was funded by the compulsory deposit of savings from pensions, savings and postal savings accounts, and by other purchasers of National Investment Fund bonds, such as life insurers.

deregulation. At the same time, many controls remained, particularly on commercial bank lending and interest rates. In an effort to reduce the reliance of the chaebols on bank borrowing, the government tightened the credit control system by setting a ceiling on the share of bank credit to chaebols. In addition, banks were required to meet minimum credit targets (initially set at one-third of new lending) for small- and medium-sized enterprises.

Beginning in the early 1980s, government involvement in bank lending decisions was gradually reduced, but banks developed few skills in credit analysis or risk management. Lending decisions were still largely based on the availability of collateral rather than on an assessment of risk and future repayment capacity. Because of their large exposures and inadequate capitalization, banks were generally in a weak position relative to their chaebol clients. Reflecting the history of directed lending, banks did not insist on, or receive, full financial information from chaebols. In addition, basic accounting, auditing, and disclosure practices were significantly below international best practice (for example, consolidated accounting or marking to market were mostly absent in Korea). Furthermore, the strong role of banks in the bond market, along with the bonds' relative illiquidity and the lack of transparency in the equity market (due to lax disclosure standards), impeded the capital markets' role in ensuring sound corporate governance. Meanwhile, the banks were rapidly expanding their foreign operations and becoming subject to significant liquidity risk; failure to manage this risk was a probable cause of the crisis.

The high leverage ratios of the chaebols and their low profitability made them very vulnerable to any shock to their cash flow.[79] The health of the banking system, in turn, was extremely dependent on the viability of the chaebols. Banks were highly exposed to them, both directly through loans and discounts, and indirectly through the guarantee of corporate bonds and commercial paper.[80]

A large portion of the foreign borrowing by banks, particularly by merchant banks, was undertaken through overseas subsidiaries and foreign branches.[81] Several factors explain the reliance on short-term capital inflows:

- The capital account had been only partially liberalized, with intermediation through domestic banks favored over foreign direct investment and direct corporate borrowing.[82] Restrictions against short-term foreign borrowing by financial institutions were relaxed, while limits on long-term borrowing and foreign participation in domestic equity and bond markets were retained, encouraging the development of large maturity mismatches in banks' balance sheets. At the end of December 1997 short-term assets covered only about half of short-term liabilities in commercial banks, and 25 percent in merchant banks, despite the introduction of a required minimum ratio of 70 percent.
- Increased access to trade credits and deregulation permitted the use of trade credits for working capital. There was a seven-fold increase in trade credits during 1994–96, only partly accounted for by the rapid growth in trade volume.
- The substantial nominal interest differential in favor of dollar and yen borrowing was reinforced by the expectation of a stable exchange rate resulting from the won's managed peg to the dollar. In addition, the short-term risk premium was lower than for longer maturities, and short-term funds could be raised relatively easily in international money markets.[83] Thus, domestic banks relied on external short-term funds to finance long-term domestic investments.

Weaknesses in Prudential Regulation and Supervision

Prudential regulations and, especially, supervision were not strengthened when the banks were granted greater independence in lending decisions and when domestic financial markets and the capital account

---

[79]The debt ratio of most chaebols exceeded 400 percent during the 1990s, compared with an average of 210 percent in Japan, 150 percent in the United States, and 90 percent in Taiwan, Province of China. Low profits decreased their ability to service this debt; operating cashflow as a percentage of interest payments was only 80 percent in 1996.

[80]At the end of 1997, the 30 largest chaebols accounted for half, and the five largest chaebols for one-third, of the corporate debt outstanding. The top 30 chaebols were responsible for about 30 percent and the top five chaebols for about 18 percent of commercial bank loans at the end of 1997.

[81]Foreign liabilities of domestic financial institutions, including those of overseas subsidiaries and foreign branches, increased from $40 billion at the end of 1993 to $160 billion by the end of September 1997.

[82]There were restrictions on issuance of securities abroad—only corporations that had obtained an international credit rating of BBB and above could undertake such issuance—and on contracting loans at spreads higher than 100 basis points over LIBOR. These regulations strengthened the role of the major Korean banks (whose ratings benefited from implicit government support) as the conduits of external finance to domestic corporations.

[83]International interbank lending to Korea of about $15 billion in 1994 and about $25 billion in 1995–96, to reach a total of $108.5 billion at the end of 1996. Of this amount, about 70 percent had a maturity of less than a year.

were liberalized. A reform plan included several proposals to bring prudential regulations closer to international standards. Commercial banks were required to reach a minimum of 8 percent capital adequacy ratio by the end of 1995. In 1995, the Office of Banking Supervision introduced a reporting system based on the CAMEL framework, designed to give early warning of problems. In addition, the government introduced, effective January 1997, a deposit insurance scheme funded by the financial institutions. The scheme provided full coverage for all insured deposits, up to 20 million won per individual depositor. Despite these reforms, several aspects of the Korean supervisory and regulatory framework diminished the effect of these improvements.

Supervision was fragmented. Commercial banks were under the direct authority of the monetary board (the governing body of the Bank of Korea) and the Office of Banking Supervision. However, specialized banks and nonbank financial institutions were under the authority of the ministry of finance and economy, although the ministry delegated on-site examination of some nonbank financial institutions to the Office of Banking Supervision. This lack of a unified system of supervision and regulation, together with the weak supervision performed by the ministry on nonbank financial institutions, created conditions favorable to regulatory arbitrage and high-risk practices, especially among commercial banks' trust business and merchant banks. In addition, the supervisory authority had the power to waive requirements, which not only facilitated forbearance but also made enforcement nontransparent.[84]

Standards for loan classification and loan-loss provisioning were rather lax. Nonperforming loans were defined as loans that had been in arrears for six months or more. Published data on bad loans only included those nonperforming loans not covered by collateral.[85] The classification system was based on the loan's servicing record and the availability of collateral without regard to the borrower's future capacity to repay. Provisions were based on credit classification and consisted of 0.5 percent of "normal" credits, 1 percent of "precautionary" credits, 20 percent of "substandard" credits, and 100 percent of "doubtful" and estimated "loss" credits. However, the minimum provisioning requirements were to be phased in over a number of years ending at the end of 1998. Losses were not expected to exceed 2 per-

cent of total loans, and any excess provisioning over 2 percent was not tax deductible. As a result of these regulations, aggregate provisions were still under 2 percent at the end of 1997.

Provisioning rules and accounting standards for securities holdings also fell short of international best practice. Banks' books recorded securities at cost: mark-to-market accounting was not fully applied. Meanwhile, the banks had large unrecorded losses arising from their equity holdings during a period of declining market prices. Furthermore, there was no consolidation of statements encompassing a parent bank and its subsidiaries.

The lax limitations on risk concentration facilitated the highly leveraged corporate finance structure of Korean conglomerates. A 1991 revision of the General Banking Act set the limit for single borrowers at 20 percent of a bank's capital for loans and 40 percent for guarantees, with a very generous grandfathering clause and a phase-in period of three years. The grandfathering arrangements were extended in 1994 and 1997. Limits on lending to big conglomerates were set bank-by-bank under the "basket control system," under which the shares of loans to the top 5 and 30 business groups relative to total loans of the bank should not exceed the ratios set by the Office of Banking Supervision. These limits were tightened in August 1997; they limited lending to a single chaebol (including guarantees) to 45 percent of banks' capital for commercial banks and 150 percent for merchant banks. Not only were these tighter regulations still lax in comparison to those in other OECD countries but many banks continued to breach them.

Restoring the Soundness of the Financial Sector

Emergency Measures

From the late summer of 1997, international creditors began to reduce their exposure to Korean financial institutions and to withdraw their short-term credit lines. The devaluation of the Thai baht in July 1997, the subsequent contagion to other regional currencies, and the crash of the Hong Kong stock market in late October 1997 sent shock waves to the Korean financial system. Market confidence dropped sharply and rating agencies downgraded Korea's sovereign status.

In August 1997, the Korean authorities announced that they would ensure that Korean financial institutions would meet their foreign liabilities. Nonetheless, the withdrawal of foreign credit lines intensified in the ensuing weeks. Faced with increasing difficulties in meeting their short-term foreign oblig-

---

[84]Supervisors sometimes allowed only partial application of regulations, such as provisioning requirements, to avoid weakening banks' earning reports.

[85]Nonperforming loans, as a percentage of total loans, were only 0.8 percent in 1996; however, if "substandard" loans were included, the figure, even using Korean definitions, would have been 4.1 percent.

ations, banks turned to the Bank of Korea for foreign exchange liquidity support.

Meanwhile, the government had deliberately stepped back from direct intervention and did not bail out failing chaebols. From the beginning of 1997, an unprecedented number of the highly leveraged chaebols went into bankruptcy, dragged down by excessive investment, declining profits, and a substantial debt burden. By the end of November, six of the top 30 chaebols had filed for court protection; a seventh went into bankruptcy in December. These large bankruptcies, together with rising bankruptcies among small- and medium-sized enterprises, further damaged the asset quality of financial institutions.

By the fall of 1997, the balance sheets of Korean financial institutions had deteriorated severely. The share of nonperforming loans in total assets of commercial banks had increased by about 70 percent between December 1996 and September 1997 and amounted to about 80 percent of banks' capital.[86] As a result, the net worth of many financial institutions fell perilously low, and a significant shortfall in capital adequacy emerged.[87] Of the 26 commercial banks, 14 had capital adequacy requirements below 8 percent, of which two were deemed to be technically insolvent (with zero or negative capital). In addition, 28 of the 30 merchant banks had capital adequacy requirements below 8 percent and 12 were deemed technically insolvent.

During November and December 1997, the Bank of Korea placed some $23 billion of official reserves in deposit at foreign branches and subsidiaries of domestic financial institutions, which the banks used to repay their short-term debt that they could not rollover. The Bank of Korea's usable official reserves were thus quickly depleted. On November 19, the government attempted to calm markets by announcing a reform package that included a widening of the daily exchange rate band to +/– 10 percent (from +/– 2¼ percent) and measures to purchase nonperforming loans. Market concerns remained,

however, and during the last week of November the depletion of international reserves intensified to some $1 billion to $2 billion a day, driving usable reserves to only $5 billion by the end of the month.

To maintain public confidence in the banking system, in mid-November 1997, the government guaranteed all deposits of financial institutions until the end of 2000, and announced that it would provide temporary liquidity support to banks when needed. Strengthening the financial sector was a key component of the IMF-supported program adopted in December 1997.

Institutional Changes

The government also completed important reforms of the institutional arrangements, which had been recommended by the Presidential Commission on Financial Reform earlier in 1997. Many of these reforms became part of the IMF-supported program. These reforms included:

- Laws passed in December 1997 significantly strengthened the independence of the Bank of Korea; consolidated all financial sector supervision (for commercial banks, merchant banks, insurance companies, securities firms, and other nonbank financial institutions) in a single Financial Supervisory Commission separate from the government; and merged all deposit insurance protection agencies into the Korea Deposit Insurance Corporation (KDIC), a new agency. The new supervisory agency was established in two stages to give time for the necessary preparation and not to detract unnecessarily from the management of the crisis. The Commission itself was established in April 1998, and the various supervisory bodies fell under its control as of that date. However, the full unification of supervisors, as the Financial Supervisory Service (FSS), with concomitant and extensive management and structural changes, took place only as of January 1, 1999. In April 1999, the operational autonomy of the Financial Supervisory Commission was strengthened with the passage of legislation to grant it the power to license and de-license financial institutions, as well as to supervise specialized and development banks.

- In early 1998, the government established a Financial Restructuring Unit within the Financial Supervisory Commission to oversee and coordinate the restructuring of the financial sector. A similar unit was also set up to spearhead the government's efforts to restructure the financial position of the weaker chaebols. The KDIC was provided with powers and funds to pay back deposits in failed institutions and, if necessary, to also provide recapitalization funds to banks.

---

[86]Nonperforming loans are a lagging indicator of the soundness of the banking sector, especially when loans are only classified as nonperforming after having been in arrears six months, rather than the usual three months. A more valid measure is the ratio of dishonored bills and checks, which more than doubled during the same period and increased fivefold in the last quarter of 1997.

[87]One measure of balance sheet deterioration is the shortfall in capital adequacy represented by the amount of funding needed to bring a bank's ratio of capital to risk-weighted assets to the minimum of 8 percent recommended by the Basel Committee for Banking Supervision. Estimates based on the end of September 1997 balance sheet data showed, under Korean provisioning and loan classification rules, a shortfall of some 11.3 trillion won (3.0 percent of 1997 GDP) for commercial banks, merchant banks, development, and specialized banks.

Box 15. Korea: KAMCO Operations

The Korean Asset Management Corporation (KAMCO) was established in 1962 to collect nonperforming loans for banks. In November 1997, legislation was passed to create a new fund under KAMCO, supported by contributions from financial institutions and government guaranteed bond issues. This KAMCO-administered fund was given the mandate to purchase impaired loans from all financial institutions covered by a deposit guarantee.

On August 10, 1998, a major reorganization of KAMCO as a "bad bank" was completed with a view to strengthening its asset management and disposition capabilities. KAMCO adopted a structure similar to the U.S. Resolution Trust Company, providing additional business functions such as workout programs for nonperforming loans and more efficient asset disposal. To enhance the transparency and the efficiency of its operations, KAMCO has its accounts audited semiannually and publishes the results.

As of mid-June 1999, KAMCO has purchased assets with a face value of 46 trillion won (11 percent of GDP). Its purchases comprise two categories of assets: (1) "general" assets of companies currently operating and (2) "special" assets, which correspond to cases that are currently in court receivership and account for 70 percent of the total portfolio. Only 20 percent of these special assets have been finally resolved by the courts. Until recently, KAMCO only purchased won-denominated assets, owing to lack of funding capacity in foreign exchange. To overcome this deficiency, KAMCO for the first time issued U.S. dollar denominated bonds in late December 1998 for $513 million to purchase foreign currency denominated assets from commercial banks.

For the purchase of nonperforming loans, KAMCO pays 45 percent of the book value of the underlying collateral, which is the average price obtained in auctions of similar collateral in the market. For unsecured loans, the price is set at 3 percent. The prices for the ordinary nonperforming loans are final. However, most of the loans purchased so far have been special loans and for these types of loans, KAMCO pays 45 percent of the face value of the loans; but once a court ordered repayment schedule is implemented, the price of the purchase is readjusted to reflect the present value of the settlement.

KAMCO's sale strategy is to dispose of nonperforming loans in the fastest way possible, but in a manner that maximizes recovery value. KAMCO has used four methods to collect on its assets: it has sold nonperforming loans to international investors, foreclosed and sold underlying collateral; sold nonperforming loans in a public auction; and collected on loans. As of June 1999, KAMCO had recovered—through sales and collections—about 9 trillion won from loans with a face value of 17 trillion won. Details on these operations are provided in the table below.

Disposition and Sale of KAMCO's Assets
(In trillions of won, as of June 1999)

Disposition/Sale	Face Amount	Price Paid by KAMCO	Amount Recovered by KAMCO
International sale	2.9	1.1	1.2
Foreclosure auction	2.1	1.0	1.0
Public sale	0.2	0.1	0.1
Collection	11.3	5.9	6.5
Total	16.5	8.1	8.8

Source: KAMCO

• A bridge bank (Hanaerum Merchant Bank) was created at the end of December 1997 to take over the assets and liabilities of closed merchant banks. The role of the Korean Asset Management Corporation (KAMCO) was expanded to enable it to purchase impaired assets from all financial institutions (Box 15).

A Bank Restructuring Plan

As part of the financial sector restructuring program, the authorities examined financial institutions to determine their solvency; several groups of institutions were also subject to external diagnostic reviews. Based on these examinations, the Financial Supervisory Commission required weak institutions to submit rehabilitation plans that had to be approved by evaluation committees set up by the Financial Supervisory Commission. These plans specified how the affected institutions would raise capital and operationally restructure to improve profitability. Institutions whose plans were approved signed memoranda of understanding with the Financial Supervisory Commission promising to meet targets set forth in their rehabilitation plans. For institutions whose plans were not approved, the Financial Supervisory Commission developed and implemented several exit strategies.

The government undertook to commit public resources for bank recapitalization only under limited circumstances. After June 30, 1998, public resources—through subscription of capital instruments and nonperforming loan purchases—could only be committed in the context of approved recapitalization plans, and on the condition that adequate contributions be made by shareholders and other stakeholders (exceptions would be made only under well-specified conditions).

The program was implemented in stages, starting with the most serious problems—the clearly insolvent merchant banks. Simultaneously, the government announced a timetable for merchant banks and commercial banks to be evaluated, and to attain minimum capital adequacy requirements. From mid-1998, steps were taken to restructure the remaining nonbank financial institutions, in particular, investment trust companies and life insurance companies. Measures were adopted to strengthen prudential regulations and supervision, particularly in the areas of loan classification and provisioning, foreign exchange liquidity, large exposures, and connected lending.

Merchant banks

In mid-December 1997, at the height of the crisis, the government announced the suspension of 14 merchant banks, of which 10 were closed the following January. The bridge bank, Hanaerum Merchant Bank, took over and liquidated their assets.[88] The remaining 20 merchant banks were required to submit rehabilitation plans that demonstrated the ability to gradually strengthen their capital adequacy requirements. On the basis of these plans, four merchant banks were closed by the end of April, 1998. The remaining 16 merchant banks were required to meet capital adequacy requirements of 6 percent by the end of June 1998 and 8 percent by the end of June 1999. In July and August 1998, the Financial Supervisory Commission conducted examinations to ensure that merchant banks were complying with their plans. As a result of these examinations, two more banks were closed. Subsequently, two merchant banks announced mergers with commercial banks and one more was closed in June 1999, leaving a total of 11 merchant banks.

The government has not directly committed resources to recapitalize merchant banks in view of their small size and the fact that many are owned by chaebols. Rather, these remaining merchant banks have raised significant amounts of capital from current owners between the end of December 1997 and the end of June 1999, with capital increasing from 0.4 trillion won to 2.5 trillion won.

Commercial banks

In December 1997, the government took over two large commercial banks, Korea First Bank and Seoul Bank, which were technically insolvent. Given their systemic importance, the government recapitalized them, and following the approval of requisite legislation, wrote down the equity of existing shareholders by a factor of about 8:1 and removed managers responsible for the losses. The government and the KDIC injected capital, acquiring a stake of about 94 percent in each bank. Since March 1998 the banks have been prepared for privatization with the help of foreign advisors; memoranda of understanding to sell them have been signed with Newbridge Capital and HSBC (in late 1998 and early 1999), but the deals have yet to be finalized (Box 16).

In early 1998, 12 commercial banks that did not meet the minimum capital adequacy requirement of 8 percent at the end of 1997 were required to submit recapitalization plans, which the Financial Supervisory Commission evaluated with the help of internationally recognized accounting firms. On June 29, 1998 the Financial Supervisory Commission announced the decisions on the recapitalization plans. Five small- to medium-sized banks were closed, with their assets and liabilities transferred to five stronger banks in purchase and assumption operations.[89] Four large banks and three small banks received conditional approval for their rehabilitation plans and were requested to submit revised plans by the end of July 1998.[90] The three small banks will not be allowed to engage in foreign exchange business. In any event, the resubmitted plans were approved at the end of 1998: five of these banks have merged (with public financial support) to create two new banks, one has been recapitalized with funds from the Bank of Korea and a foreign bank, and the remaining small bank has raised capital from current owners (this capital was matched with public funds).

---

[88]The bridge bank was financed by the KDIC. In January, it took over the deposits of the suspended merchant banks along with most of their performing assets. After a due diligence process, the value of assets and liabilities transferred was set at 8.7 trillion won and 12.1 trillion won, respectively. Shortly after intervention, depositors were offered cash reimbursement, with households being compensated first, followed by enterprises and financial institutions. As of the end of June 1999, 99 percent of private and institutional depositors had been repaid, as well as all financial institutions' call money deposits, for a total amount of 9.7 trillion won. A further 4.4 trillion won remains to be repaid, mainly deposits of financial institutions.

[89]The five closed banks had capital adequacy requirements between –4 percent and –11 percent at the end of March and a negative net worth totaling 920 billion won (representing 7 percent of total assets of the banking sector).

[90]One small bank was given conditional approval despite receiving a negative evaluation from the Evaluation Committee because the Korean legislation did not allow for the closure of a bank with positive net worth. This legislation was amended in August 1998.

Box 16. Korea: Mergers and Foreign Investment in the Financial Sector

Mergers of financial institutions and foreign investment have been important elements in the changing financial structure in Korea. A number of mergers among the stronger banks have taken place, supported by purchases of impaired assets by KAMCO. These include the merger between Kookmin Bank and Long-Term Credit Bank, and between Hana Bank and Boram Bank, both announced in September 1998. Each merger was supported by about 300 billion won in nonperforming loan sales to KAMCO.

Weaker banks were also encouraged to merge with government support in the form of nonperforming loan purchases and capital injection. These include the Commercial Bank of Korea and Hanil Bank, which merged in September 1998 to form Hanvit Bank; Cho Hung Bank, Kangwon Bank, Hyundai Merchant Bank, and Chungbuk Bank, which announced their plans to merge into one bank in early 1999. The government has become the largest shareholder in both banks, although it intends to reduce its shareholdings by 2002, possibly by selling stakes to strategic foreign investors. In both mergers, memoranda of understanding were signed by management, specifying targets on profitability, management, and operational restructuring.

Foreign investment is also an important element in the recapitalization of the Korean banking sector. In June 1998, the International Finance Corporation invested $152 million in Hana Bank and $25 million in KLTCB. Germany's Commerzbank invested $249 million in Korea Exchange Bank, acquiring a stake of 30 percent, mainly by converting existing credits to this bank into equity. In December 1998 a U.S. consortium agreed, subject to due diligence, to purchase a 51 percent stake in Korea First Bank. In February 1999, HSBC Holdings similarly agreed to purchase a 70 percent stake in Seoul Bank. Conclusion of the deals is pending, with ongoing negotiations focusing on the evaluation and treatment of the nonperforming loans. In April 1999, Goldman Sachs announced that it would invest $500 million to acquire a 17 percent stake in Kookmin Bank. In the same month, Shinhan raised $400 million through global depository receipts. Most recently, ING Group acquired a 10 percent stake in Housing and Commercial Bank for about $280 million, while New York Life and the International Finance Corporation signed memoranda of understanding to purchase a two-thirds stake in Kookmin Life Insurance for $105 million.

All of these banks have signed memoranda of understanding with the Financial Supervisory Commission undertaking to meet recapitalization and restructuring targets, such as branch closures.

The government has provided about 30 trillion won (7 percent of GDP) to support commercial banks. About 50 percent of this amount has been used by KAMCO to purchase nonperforming loans, while the other half has facilitated mergers and the purchase and assumption operations. Government recapitalization of banks has been conditional on a writedown of current owners and management changes. As a result of the restructuring, the government now owns shares in 11 out of the 17 remaining banks; its ownership exceeds 90 percent in 4 large banks (Table 16).

Financial consolidation was helped by mergers and foreign investment. In September 1998 four relatively strong banks merged into two new entities, each undertaking facilitated by some KAMCO purchases of nonperforming loans. In the case of two rounds of mergers among much weaker partners, announced in September 1998 and early 1999, government involvement in loan purchases and capital injection amounted to a total of more than 8 trillion won and led to the effective nationalization of the two new banks. Foreign investment of about $1 billion has been announced, and several other significant undertakings are in advanced stages of preparation.

In the summer of 1998, banks not undercapitalized at the end of 1997 were also subject to diagnostic reviews. As a result of these reviews and the Financial Supervisory Commission's own appraisals, three small banks were subject to prompt corrective action procedures and were required to raise additional capital.

Other financial institutions

The government has also recapitalized the specialized and development banks, whose portfolios had deteriorated significantly, and made them subject to regulations in line with those applied to commercial banks. In the case of the Industrial Bank of Korea, these moves effectively reversed the process of privatization that had begun before the crisis. Recapitalization was done by buying equity in the banks and paying for it with government shares in public enterprises. A total of more than 9 trillion won has been injected into these banks.

Once the strategy for commercial and merchant bank restructuring was in place, the authorities targeted the restructuring of other financial institutions whose soundness had deteriorated significantly because of the severity of the crisis and inadequate supervision. At the end of March 1998, the Financial Supervisory Commission estimated that this sector had about 30 trillion won in nonperforming loans,

Table 16. Korea: Government Ownership of Commercial Banks

	Percent of Shares at the End of May 1999
Hanvit	94.8
Cho Hung	91.8
Seoul	93.8
Korea First	93.8
Korea Exchange	29.5
Peace[1]	42.3
Kookmin[1]	14.5
Korea Housing & Commercial[1]	39.9
Shinhan[1]	20.1
KorAm[1]	34.7
Hana[1]	46.2

Source: Financial Supervisory Commission (FSC).
[1]Preferred shares.

about 7 percent of those institutions' total assets (and almost equal to nonperforming loans in commercial banks). In June 1998 the Financial Supervisory Commission announced a restructuring plan for life insurance companies, investment trust companies, leasing companies, and securities companies.

The restructuring program for life insurance companies began with diagnostic reviews of 18 "weak" life insurance companies by the Financial Supervisory Commission. As a result, four companies were closed through purchase and assumption-type operations, seven were required to submit rehabilitation plans, while the remaining seven were required to sign memoranda of understanding with the Financial Supervisory Commission undertaking to meet explicit restructuring objectives. In 1999, six of these companies (having failed to implement their plans) were put up for sale by the Financial Supervisory Commission. To strengthen the supervision and regulation of life insurance companies, the Financial Supervisory Commission revised the solvency margin regulation in April 1999, making it consistent with the European Union standard. Accounting rules and loan classification standards were also brought in line with those applying to commercial banks.

In mid-1998, the Financial Supervisory Commission revoked the licenses of two investment trust companies, and the six remaining were placed under management improvement orders and required to submit rehabilitation plans and raise new capital from owners and reduce their indirect borrowings from trust assets.[91] Measures to reform the sector in-

clude the requirement that all funds established after mid-November 1998 be marked-to-market; further, all funds have to be marked-to-market by mid-2000. Ten out of 25 leasing companies were closed and their businesses transferred to a bridge leasing company. Several securities companies were also closed, and regulations were issued to assure full segregation of proprietary and customer accounts, which had been a problem.

The Financial Supervisory Commission also took steps to bring the regulation of mutual savings companies and credit unions into line with that of the commercial banks. These companies were required in January 1999 to meet capital adequacy requirements calculated on the same basis as commercial banks. Companies that failed to meet minimum thresholds have been subject to prompt corrective action rules—resulting in the closure of 19 mutual savings and 40 credit unions.

The Korean financial sector has thus been significantly consolidated (Figure 10). Since December 1997, 9 out of 26 commercial banks and 19 out of 30 merchant banks have been either closed or merged. Moreover, a substantial recapitalization effort has taken place, including through foreign capital.

As of mid-1999, the government has spent close to 47 trillion won (11 percent of GDP) to recapitalize financial institutions and purchase nonperforming loans (Table 17). The budgetary cost, that is, interest on bonds issued to financed restructuring, is close to 2 percent of GDP. An additional amount of 16 trillion won (4 percent of GDP) in asset swaps has also been spent to recapitalize government-owned, specialized, and development banks.

Corporate restructuring

The process of reconstructing the financial sector was accompanied by measures to rehabilitate the finances of many of the chaebols. A number of the larger firms were dealt with by a modified version of the "London Approach."[92] This has involved setting

---

[91]One ITC subsequently converted into an investment trust management company.

[92]The "London Approach" is a framework for voluntary workouts between creditors (banks) and borrowers (corporations). The approach involved establishing a corporate restructuring agreement, signed by financial institutions, under which they agreed to follow specific procedures for debt workouts and to subject themselves to binding arbitration by a private agency, especially set up for the purpose, called the Corporate Restructuring Coordinate Committee (CRCC). These procedures included the creation of creditor committees to deal with the restructuring of individual corporations or conglomerates. Lead banks or groups of institutions holding more than 25 percent of a corporation's debt were able to call a creditors' committee meeting. An automatic standstill on debt payments applied while the committee negotiated. Upon agreement among banks, the lead bank negotiated with the debtor corporation. In all cases, arbitration by the CRCC has been available to seek to resolve bottlenecks in the negotiations.

Figure 10. Korea: Progress in Financial Sector Restructuring

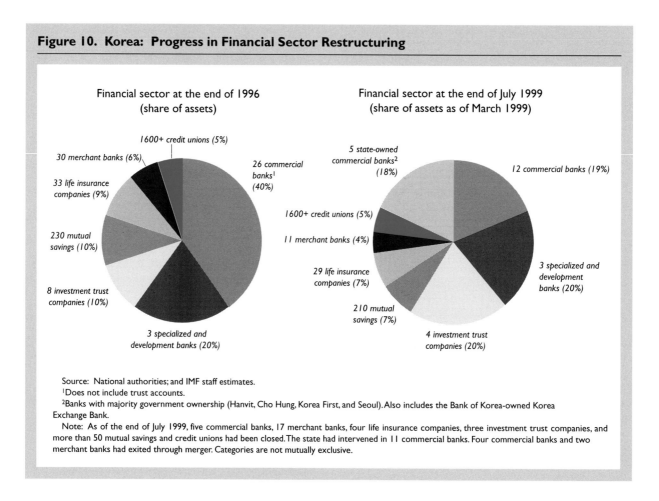

Financial sector at the end of 1996
(share of assets)

1600+ credit unions (5%)

30 merchant banks (6%)

33 life insurance companies (9%)

230 mutual savings (10%)

8 investment trust companies (10%)

3 specialized and development banks (20%)

26 commercial banks[1] (40%)

Financial sector at the end of July 1999
(share of assets as of March 1999)

5 state-owned commercial banks[2] (18%)

1600+ credit unions (5%)

11 merchant banks (4%)

29 life insurance companies (7%)

210 mutual savings (7%)

4 investment trust companies (20%)

12 commercial banks (19%)

3 specialized and development banks (20%)

Source: National authorities; and IMF staff estimates.

[1]Does not include trust accounts.

[2]Banks with majority government ownership (Hanvit, Cho Hung, Korea First, and Seoul). Also includes the Bank of Korea-owned Korea Exchange Bank.

Note: As of the end of July 1999, five commercial banks, 17 merchant banks, four life insurance companies, three investment trust companies, and more than 50 mutual savings and credit unions had been closed. The state had intervened in 11 commercial banks. Four commercial banks and two merchant banks had exited through merger. Categories are not mutually exclusive.

up debt workout units within banks and voluntary creditor committees (including banks and other creditors). These arrangements are expected to contribute to strengthening credit analysis and risk management capacity within domestic banks. Debt workouts often involved rescheduling, interest rate reduction, and debt forgiveness, as well as swaps of bank debt for equity or convertible bonds. In the case of small- and medium-sized enterprises, banks were encouraged to roll over debt until the viability of such firms could be better assessed in the light of the performance of the economy. The largest five chaebols are proving a less tractable problem, and it may not be clear for some time to what extent further value adjustments to bank claims are necessary in these cases. The entire process will not be concluded for some time and, in the meantime, the need for further restructuring in the financial sector, including the provision of more government funds, may be needed.

Banks have provided some of the impetus for corporations to restructure. One reason for this is because measures to strengthen prudential regulations and supervision, including limits on large exposures

and connected lending, require banks to reduce their exposures to corporations. Another reason is the role of government-owned banks (commercial or development), which are better able to pressure large chaebols into restructuring.

Strengthening the Banking Environment

To prevent the recurrence of banking system problems, the financial reform strategy calls for improving the supervision and management of banks. The main elements comprise a shift to consolidated bank supervision and a strengthening of prudential regulations and supervision; the liberalizing of restrictions on foreign ownership and management of banks; and a strengthening of the banks' credit evaluation and risk management capabilities.

As noted earlier, the Financial Supervisory Commission is responsible for the supervision and prudential regulation of all financial institutions. Regulations are being phased in to bring merchant banks and other financial institutions under the supervisory

Table 17. Korea: Public Cost for Financial Sector Restructuring
(as of mid-1999)

	Percent of GDP	Billions of U.S. Dollars
Recapitalization including outlays for deposit guarantee	6	22
Purchases of nonperforming loans or capital for asset management company	5	17
Interest cost (on budget)	2	7
Total	13	46
Memo item: Asset swaps	4	16

Source: National authorities; and IMF staff estimates.

umbrella and to subject these institutions to prudential standards in line with those applied to commercial banks. Supervision is also being enhanced to cover the full range of banking risks of financial institutions on a consolidated basis.[93]

The authorities strengthened prudential standards and supervision procedures—with special emphasis on the regulations of foreign exchange activities—to bring them in line with best practice as set out in the "Core Principles for Effective Banking Supervision" recommended by the Basel Committee. On June 30, 1998, the authorities introduced new loan classification standards and provisioning rules under which loans more than three months overdue will be classified as substandard, and the general provisioning requirement was increased from 1 percent to 2 percent. The Financial Supervisory Commission also introduced regulations to require the provisioning for securities losses and to cease the inclusion in Tier 2 capital of all provisions for nonperforming loans (as of January 1999). The Financial Supervisory Commission is now preparing to issue guidelines for loan classification and provisioning that would apply to banks' end of 1999 accounts. The new guidelines are designed to take into account a borrower's future capacity to repay in classifying and provisioning loans. This prospective reform is likely to lead to a need for increased provisions.

The Financial Supervisory Commission has announced the strengthening of prudential supervision and regulation of foreign exchange operations by commercial and merchant banks.[94] Regarding foreign exchange liquidity management, compliance with the guidelines that require short-term assets (less than three months) to cover at least 70 percent of short-term liabilities, and long-term borrowing (more than three years) to cover more than 50 percent of long-term assets, has been enforced for commercial banks as of January 1999 and will be enforced for merchant banks as of December 1999. A maturity ladder approach, monitored by the Financial Supervisory Commission on a monthly basis, has been implemented for commercial banks since January 1, 1999 and since July 1, 1999 for merchant banks.[95] Overseas branches and subsidiaries are included in the calculations. In addition, banks have to maintain overall foreign currency exposure limits per counterparty, including foreign currency loans, guarantees, security investments, and offshore finance. In line with international best practice, the limit on spot foreign exchange transactions of banks has been removed, leaving a global limit on spot and forward positions.[96]

---

[93]In particular, all trust accounts with guarantees are being regarded as on-balance sheet items for supervisory and accounting purposes. For capital adequacy ratio calculations, assets in such accounts are weighted at 50 percent as of January 1999 and will be weighted at 100 percent as of January 2000. The operations of foreign affiliates are also now fully consolidated.

[94]The government has amended the Foreign Exchange Act to move responsibility for the setting of foreign exchange open position limits and the supervision of foreign exchange risk to the Financial Supervisory Commission from the Bank of Korea, with information provided regularly through the Bank of Korea.

[95]This will require banks to report maturity mismatches for different time brackets (sight to seven days, seven-day to one month, one to three months, three to six months, six months to one year, and over one year), and to maintain positive mismatches for the first period. From sight to one month, any negative mismatch should not exceed 10 percent of total foreign currency assets, and from sight to three months, it should not exceed 20 percent of such assets.

[96]This measure was designed to induce an increase in turnover in the foreign exchange market, and enhance the pricing of the forward market so as to reflect interest rate differential. It has already encouraged greater swap market activity, leading to a closer link between won and dollar money markets.

The large exposure of banks to the big conglomerates has been a major source of difficulty. Exposure limits to single borrowers and groups were too generous, and the authorities passed legislation in January 1999 to tighten them. These limits have been redefined to include all off-balance sheet exposures. Both single borrower and group limits for commercial and merchant banks will be progressively reduced to 25 percent of total capital by 2004, and aggregate exposures in excess of 10 percent of total capital will be gradually reduced to 500 percent of total capital. Connected lending by merchant banks will be limited to 25 percent of equity capital by January 2001. Excesses in aggregate exposures and connected lending will be published regularly.

Increasing foreign ownership and management of banks is recognized as a means to help recapitalize banks, increase competition, and improve the management of banks. Since December 1997, full foreign ownership of merchant banks has been allowed. Nonresident purchases of equity in banks and other financial institutions (excluding merchant banks) are subject to the laws governing equity ownership of Korean companies by foreigners. Currently, the individual foreign ownership limit is set at 50 percent, although the Financial Supervisory Commission may grant exemptions. (These limits are more generous than those for residents, which are 4 percent for nationwide banks and 15 percent for regional banks.) In addition, the government has submitted legislation to abolish regulations prohibiting foreigners from becoming bank managers.

Banks have also been encouraged to adopt operational improvements. Banks' rehabilitation plans have included specific benchmarks to improve their profitability and the quality of their portfolios. Banks have lowered labor costs and reduced their staffing, and have closed down uneconomical branches domestically and overseas.[97]

---

[97]The number of bank employees decreased by 34 percent and the number of branches decreased by 17 percent as of the end of 1998, compared to the end of 1997.

Appendix III   Malaysia

Despite Malaysia's long history of outward-oriented macroeconomic and financial policies, the country did not escape contagion from the Thai crisis.[98] In addressing the situation, Malaysia has adopted some measures significantly different from those in the other countries, most notably the reintroduction of capital controls in September 1998. While Malaysia has not adopted an IMF-supported program, it has nevertheless received technical assistance from bilateral and multilateral sources, including the IMF.

Background

Macroeconomic Setting

At the outset of the crisis, Malaysia's macroeconomic performance was good. Growth was about 8 percent a year, driven in part by very high savings rates. Prudent financial policies had kept inflation low at about 3 percent, and there was a history of fiscal surpluses. The current account deficit had peaked in 1995 at about 8½ percent of GDP, but had fallen to slightly above 5 percent in 1996. External debt appeared manageable. The debt to export ratio was about 38 percent (roughly one-third of the Thai ratio). Short-term debt comprised about 60 percent of international reserves, again lower than in the other crisis countries.

Beginning with the emergence of the financial crisis in Thailand in mid-1997, Malaysia experienced increasing turbulence in financial markets (including a sharp increase in offshore ringgit interest rates). Market concerns about the economic vulnerabilities in Malaysia were reflected in a sharp fall of the ringgit and the stock market in the order of 40 percent to 50 percent by the end of 1997. Concerns included the current account deficit, rapid growth in domestic demand led mainly by large infrastructure

projects, strong credit growth, and the future course of asset prices and their potential impact on the banking system.

The authorities responded to market pressures initially through foreign exchange market intervention accompanied by an increase in interest rates, and by subsequently allowing the ringgit to depreciate. There were substantial outflows of capital, through commercial banks and sales of stocks by foreigners. By the first half of 1998, real output (year by year) had declined by 5 percent, led by sharp declines in manufacturing and construction output. Sharp decreases in imports (by more than 25 percent) exceeded the slowdown in exports (by about 10 percent), leading to current account surpluses. Gross international reserves fell to 3.5 months of imports at the end of 1997 from 4.6 months in 1996. Severe corporate and financial sector distress also led to a surge in the number of listed companies seeking court protection from creditors. Nonperforming loans soared to more than 25 percent by late 1998.

Characteristics of the Financial Sector

At the beginning of 1998, the Malaysian financial system, which is dominated by the banking system, comprised 22 domestic and 13 foreign-owned commercial banks (with about 69 percent of the system's assets), 39 finance companies (about 22 percent), 12 merchant banks (6 percent), seven discount houses (3 percent), and money and exchange brokers. Nonbank financial institutions included the National Savings Bank, pension and provident funds, insurance companies, and specialized credit agencies (Table 18). The range of activities that finance companies and merchant banks could undertake had been gradually extended with similar, but not identical, regulatory requirements—though there remains a sharp demarcation in the roles and activities of these institutions vis-à-vis commercial banks. A two-tier structure, predicated on market share and condition, was introduced at the end of 1994 for commercial banks and extended in 1996 to merchant banks and finance

---

[98]This chapter draws on an initial draft by David Marston and contributions from Patrick Downes, Michael Moore, and Inci Ötker-Robe.

Table 18. Malaysia: The Structure of the Malaysian Financial System
(December 31, 1997)

Type of Institution	Assets		Deposits		Loans		Non-performing Loans[1]
	Billions of ringgit	Percent of total	Billions of ringgit	Percent of total	Billions of ringgit	Percent of total	Percent of loans
Financial institutions	699.0	100.0	433.4	100.0	402.0	100.0	n.a.
Commercial banks (35)	481.4	68.9	300.5	69.3	276.4	68.8	4.5
Tier 1 (10)	314.2	44.9	199.0	45.9	168.5	41.9	n.a.
Tier 2 (25)	167.2	23.9	101.5	23.4	107.8	26.8	n.a.
Finance companies (39)	152.4	21.8	106.5	24.7	102.6	25.5	7.8
Tier 1 (3)	47.2	6.8	36.9	8.5	28.7	7.1	n.a.
Tier 2 (36)	105.2	15.1	70.4	16.2	73.9	18.4	n.a.
Merchant banks (12)	44.3	6.3	26.4	6.1	23.1	5.8	3.4
Tier 1 (4)	29.3	4.2	16.7	3.9	14.3	3.6	n.a.
Tier 2 (8)	15.0	2.1	9.7	2.2	8.8	2.2	n.a.
Discount houses (7)	20.9	3.0	...	...	...	...	n.a.

Source: Bank Negara Malaysia.
[1]Under the classification system in place during 1997.

companies.[99] There were restrictions on foreign ownership (30 percent) and on the activities of foreign banks. In addition to the domestic financial system, there was an offshore market in Labuan, governed under its own separate legal framework by the Labuan Offshore Financial Services Authority.

Precrisis Weaknesses in the Financial Sector

In the wake of market turbulence and contagion effects in the second half of 1997, concerns among market participants about the true condition and resilience of the financial system increasingly became a central issue, highlighted by the known frailties among finance companies.

Structural Vulnerabilities

Standard official indicators of the Malaysian financial system soundness improved significantly in

the 1990s. The ratio of nonperforming loans to total loans in banks and finance companies fell from 20 percent in 1990 to about 3.8 percent for banks, and 4.7 percent for finance companies in 1996; risk-weighted capital adequacy requirements rose to levels in excess of minimum Basel standards; and general provisions of commercial banks increased from 0.75 percent in 1990 to 2 percent of outstanding loans in 1996.[100] However, the persistent pace of credit expansion at an annual rate of nearly 30 percent (particularly by smaller Tier 2 financial institutions) to the private sector,[101] in particular to the property sector and for the purchase of stocks and shares, exposed the financial system to potential risks from price declines in property and other assets that occurred in 1997. As a result, nonperforming loans rose in 1997, and official estimates showed further deterioration in the months leading up to the announcement of the reform program. In response to these concerns, Bank Negara Malaysia had earlier

---

[99]The two-tier regulatory system was perceived to have failed to achieve the desired strengthening of the capital base of domestic banks and was abolished in April 1999. Until then, banks with at least 1 billion ringgit in equity, and which complied with Bank Negara Malaysia's CAMEL requirements, were eligible to be Tier 1 banks. These banks were given certain privileges (e.g., allowed to operate foreign currency accounts on behalf of exporters, participate in equity derivatives, undertake securities borrowing or lending, and enjoy less stringent restrictions on branch expansion).

[100]Interpretation of the indicators of improved soundness should be treated with caution because, in an overheated economy with an asset price bubble and very rapid credit growth and extensive collateralization of lending, the nonperforming loan ratio may decline even though underlying asset quality deteriorates. The deterioration only becomes obvious after the asset bubble has burst. Moreover, capital adequacy requirements are not adjusted for provisioning deficiencies.

[101]Rapid credit growth among smaller institutions in part reflected their efforts to build their asset basis to achieve Tier 1 status.

imposed limits on property lending (20 percent of total loans) and securities lending for the purchase of shares, effective from April 1, 1997. In October 1997, the authorities issued a directive that no new loans should be approved for the property sector, except for low income housing. The authorities also asked banks to submit credit plans for 1998 to moderate loan growth of the banking system to 20 percent by March 1998 and to 15 percent by the end of 1998. Nevertheless, overall credit growth remained strong, falling only slightly, to 26.5 percent by the end of 1997.

In addition to the exceptionally high level of indebtedness, the combination of the economic slowdown, decline in asset values (particularly property and stock market securities), rising interest rates, and the depreciation in the ringgit severely affected credit performance and bank profitability. Tight liquidity conditions and segmentation of the interbank money market also contributed to narrowing interest spreads, especially for finance companies, and a growing level of nonperforming loans in many financial institutions.

Weaknesses in Prudential Regulation and Supervision

After the banking problems of 1985–87, the authorities took actions to improve the legal and regulatory framework for banking supervision.[102] In 1989, a new banking law was adopted. In 1994, a new law on the Bank Negara Malaysia was enacted, and a large number of prudential regulations and circulars were issued covering enhanced prudential supervision, regulation standards, and the provision of regular statistical reports and inspections.[103] The new banking law and the Banking and Financial Institutions Act (BAFIA) provided broad regulatory enforcement and intervention powers to the supervisory authorities. Bank Negara Malaysia updated regulations, and overall a flexible framework was developed that permitted the authorities, by and large, to address prudential concerns.

One area of uncertainty in the implementation of the prudential framework related to the fact that the BAFIA provided broad exemption powers to the ministry of finance—albeit formally at the recommendation of Bank Negara Malaysia—with regard to individual prudential regulations, such as lending

to connected parties,[104] ownership of shareholdings in banks, and large exposure limits.[105] There are, however, no reports of systematic or widespread use of this power.

Impact of the Regional Crisis and Initial Responses

As regional uncertainties unfolded, concerns about the true condition of the financial system increased. These concerns stemmed from the exceptionally fast rate of growth of credit in the banking system, the private sector's high leverage (163 percent), the concentration of bank loans in real estate development and in financing share purchases, and the decline in asset qualities given the slowdown in economic activity. These worries were manifested in deposit flights to quality assets and institutions. Already vulnerable to liquidity shocks, given low excess reserves and high loan/deposit ratios, conditions in the money market were aggravated by changed perceptions of counterparty credit risks that resulted in severe money market segmentation and pressure on the payment system. Bank Negara Malaysia responded initially by acting to recycle liquidity through Bank Negara Malaysia deposit placements, supported by the announcement on January 20, 1998 of a general guarantee of deposits. There was no formal deposit insurance scheme in Malaysia.[106]

The authorities, with a view to strengthening the financial sector, announced several prudential measures, effective January 1, 1998, including a requirement for banks to classify loans as nonperforming when they were three months overdue; an acceleration of the classification of "doubtful loans" from 12 months overdue to six months, and "bad loans" from 24 months to 12 months; and a rise in the required general loan-loss reserves from 1 percent to at least 1½ percent. The requirements for booking interest-in-suspense were also tightened, so that banks were now required to reverse unpaid interest out of income and record it in the interest-in-suspense account. Banks were also required to report on a quar-

---

[102]During this episode, nonperforming loans grew to 30 percent, and institutions were restructured with government and central bank support.

[103]Prior to 1998, banks in Malaysia did not routinely report data on a consolidated basis. When activities of subsidiaries were taken into account, a number of banks announced a sharp deterioration in profitability and solvency.

[104]Lending to directors, officers, and employees was prohibited, as well as to firms in which these persons have an interest greater than 5 percent—as a partner, manager, agent, or guarantor. Also, firms in which managers, directors, or employees held shares were excluded from receiving credit from the institution.

[105]BAFIA prohibited institutions from holding shares in any corporation. Exceptions were made for shares held as security or as a result of foreclosure or as repayment or credit.

[106]At its peak in January 1998, Bank Negara Malaysia placements amounted to 34.7 billion ringgit or 13 percent of GDP. This figure declined by 15.8 billion ringgit in mid-February/March concurrent with a reduction of reserve requirements from 13.5 percent to 10 percent.

terly basis the ratio of nonperforming loans broken down into substandard, doubtful, and loss; loans by sectors; general and specific provisions for bad and doubtful loans; as well as their risk-weighted capital ratios.[107]

As of February 1998, only 10 commercial banks and four finance companies had Tier 1 status. Profits of the system varied greatly; four banks and eight finance companies made losses or zero profits while eight banks and 23 finance companies had rates of return on assets below 1 percent. In part, due to the monetary management instrument framework used by Bank Negara Malaysia (differential reserve requirements across institutions, limited reserve averaging, and differential liquid asset requirement with no averaging) but more so related to the fact that since 1994, private sector loan/deposit ratios had exceeded 90 percent, the banking system operated with very low excess reserves, suggesting very limited ability to react to adverse liquidity shocks. (Loan/deposit ratios were 96 percent for banks and 101 percent for finance companies.)

On March 25, 1998, the authorities announced a package of measures aimed at strengthening the financial sector. The measures focused on a broad-based strengthening of the regulatory and supervisory framework requirements for increased disclosure; strengthening the finance company sector through consolidation into a smaller number of core companies; and preemptive recapitalization of banks. The measures also included initiatives to improve the framework for bank liquidity management and monetary operations, and are detailed in Box 17.

Design of the Restructuring Program

Strengthening the Prudential Framework

The authorities vigorously implemented the announced program. By April 1998 targeted improvements to the loan classification and provisioning standards and the reduction in single borrower limits from 30 to 25 percent of capital had been completed and incorporated in the ongoing supervisory and regulatory framework. Moreover, in addition to its initial broad diagnostic review of the banking system in March 1998 that used stress tests (projections of capital adequacy adjusted for varying scenarios of

nonperforming loans, specific provisions, collateral values, and other measures of other balance sheet risks), Bank Negara Malaysia grouped the banks into three categories: sound banks, those on a secondary watch list, and those on a primary watch list. A program of intensified surveillance was instituted that involved reaching understandings with each vulnerable bank on a rehabilitation program. To augment its surveillance system, Bank Negara Malaysia initiated a program to develop an early warning system with the assistance of the World Bank. It also took the initiative to provide daily information to the market on its assessment of liquidity based on a daily forecast of factors affecting reserve money.[108] All disclosure requirements were observed by the end of May 1998, and a prudentially based framework for assessing bank liquidity risks was introduced effective August 2, 1998.[109]

Finance Company Merger Program

In addition to the announcement that finance companies would be subject to higher risk-weighted capital adequacy requirements, the Malaysian authorities announced a program of consolidation of the industry. The program envisaged the consolidation of 39 companies into eight, to be achieved through three modules. The first, covering 14 institutions, would involve the consolidation of finance companies into their parent banks; the second, relating to three firms, would involve consolidation through a swap of shares; and the third was a straight merger of 15 companies into six anchor institutions. Companies consolidated in this last module would carry a one-year government guarantee on the net asset value arrived at during the due diligence process. During 1998, however, as the economy and loan quality deteriorated sharply, and amid concerns about the possible open-ended nature of the government guarantee, the finance company merger pro-

---

[107]Through March 1998, no provisioning was required for substandard loans, 50 percent for doubtful, and 100 percent for bad/loss. The amount on which provisions were to be made was not based on collateral; by regulation, real estate collateral must be marked-to-market semiannually while security collateral is revalued daily.

[108]Based on this estimate, Bank Negara Malaysia also indicated its intention to either supply or withdraw liquidity and invited price or volume bids depending on the intended signal.

[109]It was envisaged that the framework would run parallel to the existing liquid asset requirement for a period of six months during which banks would be required to comply with the existing 17 percent ratio. Officials indicated that this would be applied flexibly, as there might be cases where banks—which were assessed to have adequately adapted to the new framework—internal information systems, recomposition of liquid holdings according to types of asset holdings, and forecasting capabilities—would be allowed to operate on the new system alone. Bank Negara Malaysia reserved the right to extend compliance with the liquid asset requirement beyond the six-month parallel run in those cases where it was assessed that a bank was not adequately prepared for the new framework. In early May 1999, 17 institutions migrated to the new framework.

Box 17. Malaysia: Measures Announced on March 25, 1998

Loan classification and provisioning standards. Classification standards (including three months for nonperforming loans) to be brought to best practice; 20 percent provisioning requirement against uncollateralized portions of substandard loans; off-balance sheet items incorporated in the loan classification and provisioning system.

Capital adequacy framework. Increase risk-weighted capital adequacy requirements of finance companies from 8 percent to 10 percent, with interim requirement of 9 percent; minimum capital for finance companies increased from 5 million ringgit to 300 million ringgit; compliance with capital adequacy requirement required every financial quarter.

Other prudential guidelines. Single borrower limit reduced from 30 percent to 25 percent of capital funds; prudentially based liquidity framework introduced; technical study on international practices regarding depositor protection schemes to be undertaken.

Disclosure. Aggregate statistics on nonperforming loans, provisions, and capital positions for all financial institutions to be published monthly by the Bank Negara Malaysia; all institutions to report and publish key indicators of financial soundness on a quarterly basis.

Intensified monitoring. More intensive and rigorous supervision of banks through monthly stress tests by Bank Negara Malaysia and a requirement for similar exercises by individual institutions on the basis of parameters set by Bank Negara Malaysia.

Merger program. Bank Negara Malaysia-facilitated merger program of finance companies on market-based criteria. Mergers allowed only if merged entity would be fully capitalized. Approval contingent on up-front due diligence. Government to extend a one-year guarantee on net asset value determined from due diligence, and to share in upside gains as well as downside risks. Any institution electing to stay out of the merger process was required to demonstrate its ability to comply with new capital requirements, failing which, appropriate action as provided by BAFIA would apply.

Monetary measures. Commercial bank liquidity management to be improved through widening the band for reserve averaging and providing market participants with daily information on Bank Negara Malaysia operations and liquidity forecasts; normal liquidity support operations to be separated from emergency liquidity support, and lending operations collateralized; the role of base lending rate and maximum interest spread restrictions, and liquid asset ratio, to be reviewed.

---

gram was drastically scaled back. The sole remaining requirement was that finance companies affiliated with banks be merged. Moreover, the initial schedule for compliance with the requirement for increased capital for the merged entities was postponed, and the government guarantee of net asset values, aimed at facilitating purchase, was withdrawn. Smaller finance companies not eligible for support through Danamodal Nasional Berhad (the restructuring agency) would not receive government support for recapitalization. Notwithstanding the slower than anticipated progress in consolidating this industry segment, Malaysia reports that the number of finance companies declined by eight in 1998 and is expected to decline by another 14 in 1999.

Commercial Banks: Asset Management and Recapitalization

Complementing earlier initiatives to restore sound intermediation, Malaysia established in August 1998 an institutional framework to strengthen efforts to rehabilitate the commercial banking system by using public funds to acquire nonperforming loans and recapitalizing commercial banks. It also instituted measures that were focused on facilitating the restructuring of corporate debt.

Institutional Framework

Danaharta Nasional Berhad, the public asset management company, was established in June 1998 as a public company under the Companies Act. The Danaharta Act of 1998 gave Danaharta the ability to acquire nonperforming loans through statutory vesting and to appoint special administrators who can take control and manage the assets of a borrower unable to pay its debts. Danamodal was established in August 1998 as a limited liability company wholly owned by Bank Negara Malaysia, with objectives to inject new capital in undercapitalized banks and facilitate rationalization of the system. The general policy positions of both Danamodal and Danaharta incorporate principles of economizing the use of public funds and finding least-cost solutions to government. Although Danamodal issues progress reports on its operations, it has not released a public statement as to its operational principles, criteria for selecting operations, formulae for burden sharing, or exit strategy. Danaharta's principles of operation, including valuation methodology, asset acquisition guidelines, and expected nonperforming loan sales strategy are already public knowledge. The Corporate Debt Restructuring Committee has also been established to act as an informal debtor/creditor broker to achieve debt restructuring as an alternative to companies filing for bank bankruptcy under the Companies Act. To facilitate coordination at both the policy and operational levels, an overarching Steering Committee on Restructuring is chaired by the Governor of Bank Negara Malaysia and composed of the managers of Danaharta, Danamodal, and the Corporate Debt Restructuring Committee.

Operational Process

In practice, the operations of Danaharta and Danamodal are guided by Bank Negara Malaysia's classification of banks. Bank Negara Malaysia initially classifies institutions into a primary and secondary watch list. The process is fine-tuned by Danamodal with the assistance of two investment banks acting as its advisors.[110] Danamodal has identified 14 institutions that are either currently undercapitalized or likely to be so in the future.[111] Danaharta used the same database to identify 18 institutions (including the Danamodal 14) that are most likely to sell nonperforming loans. Danamodal's intentions are carefully coordinated with nonperforming loan sales to Danaharta through ensuring that Danamodal's due diligence, and Danaharta's nonperforming loan acquisition and write-downs of capital of affected institutions occur concurrently.

Danaharta has divided its nonperforming loan acquisition process into three stages, starting with secured loans, properties, and quoted shares. A second stage will cover unsecured loans, to be followed by acquisitions of foreign currency loans. Through March 1999, Danaharta had acquired 23 billion ringgit in nonperforming loans from 37 financial institutions. The average discount at which Danaharta has purchased nonperforming loans has been about 60 percent of the principal value. As of the end of June 1999, none of the acquired assets has been sold. On July 1, Danaharta began the process of auctioning $143 million (face value) of foreign loan assets.

Danamodal has injected 6.2 billion ringgit as fresh capital into 11 financial institutions that represent approximately one-fifth of the financial system's needs. The Danamodal investment initially was as Tier 2 subordinated debt that will be converted into equity, debt, or a hybrid capital instrument.

The Corporate Debt Restructuring Committee had been set up to prevent companies from abusing the protection against creditors afforded by Section 176 of the Companies Act. The process of resolution can be initiated by either party, but once an appeal has been filed, there is a six-month moratorium on action during which credit committees will work with the affected parties to achieve a workout strategy. As of the end of June 1999, 52 applications, representing about 22 billion ringgit in affected debt, have been received by the Corporate Debt Restructuring Committee. Creditor committees had been formed to conduct due diligence studies and to formulate restructuring proposals, and these are in various stages of completion. Four cases have been rejected and turned over to Danaharta for resolution.

Public Cost of Financial Sector Restructuring

As of the end of March 1999, Danaharta and Danamodal have spent about 15 billion ringgit (5 percent of GDP) to purchase nonperforming loans and recapitalize banks (Table 19).

Managing Credit Recovery and Rehabilitation

The reforms described above were complicated by concurrent attempts by the authorities to stimulate credit growth in the face of the economic downturn. By mid-1998, the authorities were faced with a sharp decline in credit. Credit flows were negative to the extent of 1.5 billion ringgit, and undrawn commitments declined from 144 billion ringgit to 125 billion ringgit between December 1997 and July 1998. While the Malaysian authorities wished to use interest rates to stimulate credits, they were constrained by onshore/offshore interest rate differentials. While relatively stable—and in fact declining in mid-1998—these differentials limited the scope for reducing onshore interest rates without possibly triggering ringgit flight offshore. The authorities, therefore, introduced additional measures in September 1998 aimed at eliminating the offshore ringgit market, fixing the exchange rate, and improving the conditions for increased bank lending. These measures included:

- *Exchange control measures.* A broad range of measures to restrict international capital flows, which effectively eliminated the offshore ringgit market and prohibited nonresidents from repatriating portfolio capital held in Malaysia for a period of 12 months, were adopted.[112]

---

[110]Danaharta employs the services of Arthur Andersen, while the financial advisors to Danamodal are Solomon Smith Barney and Goldman Sachs.

[111]Two institutions have since been taken out of the Danamodal process.

[112]In view of continued weakness of investor confidence and concerns about the possibility of a massive capital outflow upon the expiration of the 12-month period in September 1999, the authorities in February 1999 replaced the 12-month rule with a declining scale of exit levies. Under this arrangement, for funds that entered Malaysia before February 15, 1999, repatriation of the principal of portfolio investments is subjected to a levy, with the levy decreasing with the duration of investment in Malaysia (starting from 30 percent, reduced in steps to 0 percent if repatriated after 12 months from the date of entry or September 1, 1998, whichever is later).

Table 19. Malaysia: Public Cost for Financial Sector Restructuring
(As of the end of March 1999)

	Percent of GDP	Billions of U.S. Dollars
Recapitalization including deposit guarantee	2	1.6
Purchases of non-performing loans	3	2.4
Total	5	4.0

Source: National authorities; and IMF staff estimates.

- *Exchange rate policy*. Subsequent to the introduction of capital controls, the authorities fixed the exchange rate of the ringgit at 3.8 ringgit to the U.S. dollar.
- *Reserve requirements*. Statutory reserve requirements were reduced to 4 percent of eligible liabilities—from 10 percent in February 1998 to 8 percent in August—applied to the maintenance period beginning September 15, 1998. The allowed averaging of 20 percent was kept unchanged.
- *Loan limits*. Existing limits on lending to the property sector, and for the purchase of shares, were relaxed. Loans for residential mortgages up to a value of 250,000 ringgit were made exempt from the 20 percent ceiling on loans to the property sector—the previous exemption was 150,000 ringgit. The ceiling on loans for share purchase was increased for commercial banks from 15 percent of portfolio to 20 percent. Also, financing margins for the purchase of motor vehicles were increased from 70 percent to 85 percent.
- *Credit floor target*. A floor target for credit growth during 1998 was established at 8 percent. However, the authorities indicated that weak banks on the Bank Negara Malaysia watch list would not be expected to comply, and banks that could indicate prudential constraints—for example, rising nonperforming loans or the prospect of violating prudential standards—would be exempted from the target.
- *Base lending rate*. The formula for computing the base lending rate was modified to reflect greater sensitivity to Bank Negara Malaysia policy rates, and to lower the premium that banks charge.
- *Loan classification*. Bank Negara Malaysia announced changes in the classification system so that the default period for classifying loans as nonperforming was increased from three to six months, and 20 percent specific provisions on substandard loans were no longer required.[113]

Effective March 24, 1999, Bank Negara Malaysia amended its loan classification and provisioning guidelines again so that substandard loans—those overdue between three and six months—would require provisioning of 20 percent. Doubtful loans—overdue between six and nine months—would require provisioning of 50 percent; and loss loans—those overdue for more than nine months—would require provisioning of 100 percent.[114] Provisions must cover losses in the value of securities. Nonperforming loans can be reclassified as performing when repayments are made continuously for six months, rather than 12 months as required before.

---

[113]The modifications introduced in September 1998 should be seen against the more stringent loan classification system instituted in December 1997. This system had introduced an automatic 20 percent provisioning against substandard loans defined as nonperforming for a period of three months. On the basis of that scheme, Bank Negara Malaysia classified institutions, and Danamodal and Danaharta determined estimates of recapitalization needs, and likely nonperforming loan sales. On that basis, nonperforming loans in July had increased to 14.2 percent. Banks, if they wish, can retain the more conservative three months' nonperforming loan classification. Of Malaysia's 78 financial institutions, 21 (accounting for 46 percent of total loans in the system) have retained this tight classification rule.

[114]For trade finance loans, the default periods for the classifications are shortened as follows; substandard—default between one and two months; doubtful—default between two and three months; and bad—default greater than three months.

Appendix IV   The Philippines

The Philippines has been less affected than neighboring countries by the Asian crisis and did not undergo a similar degree of capital outflows, banking sector distress, and other forms of financial upheaval.[115] Nevertheless, the combination of initial weaknesses in the banking sector, the fallout from the crisis in neighboring countries, and the possibility of more intensive contagion led the Philippines to undertake preemptive measures to address potential financial sector weaknesses. The program, developed with the support of the IMF and the World Bank, complements and deepens the efforts to improve the efficiency of financial intermediation deployed during the previous years.[116]

Background

Macroeconomic Setting

The performance of the Philippine economy prior to the current crisis had been improving. After several years of accelerating growth rates, the expansion of real GNP reached 6.8 percent in 1996. Inflation remained well below 10 percent a year. The balance of payments remained strong, and foreign reserves of the Philippines' central bank, the Bangko Sentral ng Pilipinas increased from less than $5 billion at the end of 1993 to about $8 billion (1.7 months of imports) at the end of 1997; strong capital inflows—which reached $8 billion in 1996—offset the rapid widening of the current account deficit to almost 5 percent of GDP in 1996.

In early 1997, the Philippines were faced with a large decline in the stock market and pressure on the exchange rate. From mid-1997, although to a lesser degree than in other Asian countries, the regional crisis led to a further substantial disruption in economic activity. Following the devaluation of the Thai baht in early July, the Philippines experienced a large decline in capital inflows, a further fall in the stock market, and pressures on the peso. The Bangko Sentral ng Pilipinas initially intervened in support of the peso; these efforts, however, proved unsustainable when about $2 billion in Bangko Sentral ng Pilipinas reserves were lost in a few days. The peso was allowed to float and fell from about 26 pesos per U.S. dollar at the end of June 1997 to a low of about 44 pesos in September 1998, before stabilizing at about 36 pesos per U.S. dollar. Interest rates—measured by the return on the 91-day treasury bill—increased gradually from 10.5 percent in June 1997 to about 19 percent by January 1998 as the authorities attempted to keep the depreciation of the peso under control; they subsequently fell back to about 13.5 percent by early 1999. The authorities' strategy thus initially focused on tight monetary and fiscal policies. But, as stabilization took hold, the stance shifted gradually toward supporting recovery.

Real GNP growth reached 5.8 percent in 1997—reflecting very strong growth in the first part of the year—but fell to only 0.1 percent in 1998, while at the same time inflation increased to over 10 percent, and accelerated further in early 1999.[117] Despite the significant contraction in capital inflows—the capital account surplus fell to $900 million in 1997 and $400 million in 1998—foreign reserves recovered during 1998 owing to the rapid adjustment of the current account of the balance of payments, which recorded a surplus of over 1 percent of GDP in 1998.

Characteristics of the Financial Sector

Private banks in the Philippines comprise universal or "expanded" banks (by far the largest component of the banking system), nonexpanded commercial banks, thrift banks, and rural banks

---

[115]This appendix draws on an initial draft by Enrique de la Piedra and contributions from Elizabeth Milne and Greta Mitchell-Casselle.

[116]Banking sector reform is a major component of the IMF's Stand-By Arrangement approved in March 1998, and the World Bank's Banking Sector Reform Loan, approved in November 1998.

---

[117]In addition to contagion from the other Asian countries, the Philippines was also adversely affected by the weather pattern associated with El Niño.

Table 20. Philippines: Selected Banking Sector Indicators as of December 31, 1998
(In billions of pesos, unless otherwise indicated)

	Commercial Banks				Thrift Banks	Rural Banks[1]	Banking System
	Universal	Nonexpanded[2]	Foreign	Total			
Physical Composition							
Number of banks	21	20	12	53	117	826	996
Total number of branches	3,519	650	11	4,180	1,357	1,114	6,651
Balance Sheet							
Total Assets	2,029	217	310	2,556	210	58	2,824
of which: Loan portfolio (net)	1,209	131	141	1,481	124	40	1,646
Deposit liabilities	1,318	140	128	1,586	132	38	1,755
of which: Foreign currency	480	50	71	601	8	0	609
Capital	259	44	8	311	28	9	348
Annual Income and Expenses							
Total operating income	184	21	25	230	17	3	249
of which: interest income	166	18	20	204	15	2	221
Net income before tax	22	0	4	27	0	0	27
Trust Assets	364	22	27	414	5	—	419

Source: Bangko Sentral ng Pilipinas.
[1]Data for rural banks in the Balance Sheet and Annual Income and Expenses entries are for June 30, 1998.

(Table 20).[118] Only one universal bank, the Philippine National Bank, is partly owned by the government.[119] Thrift banks cater mainly to the consumer retail market and small- and medium-sized enterprises. There are two fully government-owned specialized banks, the Land Bank of the Philippines and the Development Bank of the Philippines, which also undertakes some commercial banking functions. The small government-owned Islamic bank is currently under a rehabilitation plan. Total assets of the banking system amounted to over 2.8 trillion pesos in 1998, roughly equivalent to annual GNP; banks represented 90 percent of the banking system, up from 85 percent in 1991.

There are significant restrictions on the size and operation of foreign banks.[120] The number of foreign banks that operate wholly owned branches in the Philippines is currently capped at 14. Other foreign banks may apply for a universal or a nonexpanded bank license and can operate by acquiring up to 60 percent of the voting stock of an existing domestic bank or of a new institution incorporated locally. On average, foreign equity is about one-fifth of total equity for universal banks, 13 percent for nonexpanded commercial banks, and negligible in the case of thrift and rural banks.[121]

Precrisis Weaknesses in the Financial Sector

Prior to the Asian crisis, the Philippines had undergone a period of financial liberalization, coupled with rapid financial deepening.[122] The changes appear to have come too fast for supervision to remain fully effective. Hence, although the financial condition of the Philippine banking system in terms of capital adequacy was better than several of the neighboring countries, the corporate sector was more resilient, and the real estate boom less pronounced, there were notable weaknesses in the financial sector around the time of the crisis.[123] The

[118]Universal and nonexpanded commercial banks are jointly referred to as the commercial banks.

[119]In June 1996, the government had reduced its ownership in Philippine National Bank from 100 percent to 45.6 percent. The stock in private hands is widely dispersed.

[120]Foreign banks are not authorized to open more than six branches or to borrow from head offices more than $4 for every $1 of domestically held capital.

[121]Legislation pending before Congress as of mid-1999 would allow for full foreign ownership of distressed banks.

[122]Earlier banking sector measures included significant government assistance to resolve a banking crisis in the early and mid-1980s and a recapitalization of the central bank in 1993.

[123]In contrast to other Asian countries, property demand was flat during 1989–94 and in early 1997; the office vacancy rate was only 2 percent. In early 1997, the Bangko Sentral ng Pilipinas took steps to limit bank lending for real estate purposes.

principal weaknesses and supervisory challenges are discussed next.

Structural Vulnerabilities

Several characteristics of the Philippine banking sector that existed before the crisis appear to have made it vulnerable to shocks. They include:

- *A very rapid growth in banks' lending following gradual liberalization of banking and substantial financial deepening.*[124] The speed of this growth in lending brought about significant problems, including a decline in the average loan quality, an increase in unhedged foreign exchange operations, and for some banks, growing involvement in real estate lending. These problems have been particularly acute for smaller commercial banks, thrift banks, and rural banks.

- *A significant growth in financial intermediation in foreign currency.* Mirroring overall trends in banking sector activity, financial intermediation in foreign currency also grew significantly until mid-1997, owing in part to the prevailing significant institutional advantages for bank operations conducted in foreign currency.[125] Total foreign currency deposits in the banking system expanded at an annual rate of 38 percent from 1994 to 1996, and reached a maximum of $16.3 billion in June 1997; as a result, foreign currency deposits increased to more than half of total bank liabilities, up from only 3 percent in 1990.

- *A weakening in capital levels.* The deterioration in banks' portfolios led to a significant weakening in capital levels. Average capital levels remained still comfortable at the onset of the crisis, but capital adequacy ratios had been on a downward trend since 1993. Capital adequacy declined from 19.2 percent in 1993 to 16 percent in 1997. Moreover, average capital levels disguised problems of individual institutions—one large and several among the smaller ones—that suffered from low capital levels relative to the risk implied by their asset portfolios. Finally, a special regime granted to a few universal banks allowed them to operate with a minimum capital adequacy requirement of 8 percent instead of the 10 percent generally required.

Weaknesses in Prudential Regulation and Supervision

Despite significant progress since the early 1990s, at the onset of the crisis the banking sector still suffered from problems both in the supervisory framework and the implementation of supervision. The main areas of concern were shortcomings relative to international norms of prudential standards, the effectiveness of bank supervision, and the enforcement of the bank regulatory and supervisory framework. Finally, mechanisms for bank exit were inadequate.

Prudential standards

Problems in bank supervision included the following:

- *Loan classification and provisioning.* Until mid-1997, loan-loss provisions were not required for bank assets backed by collateral, even if such assets were classified as substandard, or for any bank assets classified as "especially mentioned."[126] There was also limited capacity of the Bangko Sentral ng Pilipinas to assess bank risks.

- *Marking to market.* Philippine accounting conventions regarding banks' portfolio investments follow closely the U.S. pattern. Banks were not required to mark to market their equity portfolios, but in contrast to U.S. norms, this included their trading accounts—thus they could defer recognition of losses. The large changes in the value of banks' securities portfolios following the onset of the crisis resulted in significant

---

[124]Total deposits and loans of the banking system increased by 27 percent and 35 percent a year, respectively, during 1993–96, and expanded a further 11 percent and 16 percent, respectively, during the first six months of 1997. Financial intermediation deepened significantly in the Philippines, as the ratio of money and quasi-money to GDP increased from 34 percent in 1991 to 61 percent in 1997, while the ratio of banking system claims on the private sector to GDP grew from 18 percent to 56 percent during the same period. Nevertheless, the degree of financial deepening in the Philippines remained among the lowest of other Asian countries affected by the regional crisis.

[125]Following a long period in which interest from foreign currency operations was fully tax-exempt, it is now subject only to a 7.5 percent withholding tax compared to 20 percent in the case of peso deposits. At the same time, profits from the banks' foreign currency deposit unit operations are taxed at a 10 percent preferential rate on gross income, compared to the standard tax rate of 35 percent on net profit from other operations. Moreover, domestic banking activity, including resident foreign currency deposit units, is subject to the gross receipts and documentary stamp taxes, while transactions in foreign currency with nonresidents and with other foreign currency deposit units are exempt. Finally, while peso deposits are subject to reserve requirements, mostly unremunerated, foreign currency deposits are not subject to reserve requirements.

[126]The "especially mentioned" classification was routinely used for loans where supervisors found minor documentary weaknesses, including for third party guarantors.

changes in their market value, but the adjustment to book values arising from marking to market was not properly accounted for. The true soundness of certain banks was thus not readily apparent.

- *Transparency.* Although banks listed in the stock exchange were required to disclose their balance sheets publicly on a quarterly basis, no information was provided on the level of nonperforming loans, classified assets, and loan-loss provisions, for instance. Unlisted banks were under no obligation to disclose their financial accounts to the public. External audits of banks were not integrated into the supervisory process, as external auditors were not under an obligation to report materially adverse factors and events to banking supervisors.
- *Consolidated supervision.* The Bangko Sentral ng Pilipinas did not address bank solvency on a consolidated basis, nor did it consolidate the banks' trust activities with on-balance sheet activities to determine capital adequacy. It also did not attempt to consolidate foreign currency exposures between banks and their affiliated foreign currency deposit units in determining compliance with prevailing regulatory limits.

Effectiveness of supervision

Although some improvements took place during the years prior to the beginning of the Asian crisis, supervisory practices in general remained weak.

- *On-site examinations.* The on-site examination process was not oriented toward an analytic approach that would allow an assessment of risk at the bank level and of the systems used by banks to manage risk.[127] Rather, it was heavily weighted toward the examination of asset quality and compliance with laws, rules, and regulations. Moreover, bank solvency was assessed on an unconsolidated basis. Finally, the scheduling of on-site bank examinations was too constrained. On-site examinations were undertaken on an annual basis, and additional examinations required Monetary Board approval. Bank secrecy legislation prevented supervisors from accessing disaggregated loan information, preventing assessments of risk concentration.
- *Off-site monitoring.* The approaches used for offsite monitoring were not well-suited to evaluate the financial condition of the institutions. The CAMEL system excluded sensitivity analysis for market risk. The individual component

ratings were applied mechanistically with no role for the supervisor's judgment; in addition, to determining the overall CAMEL rating of a bank, the supervisors normally averaged the individual component ratings; as a result, it was possible for an insolvent bank to be evaluated as "good."

Enforcement capacity

Even though the supervisory authorities generally received good compliance from banks on routine requests, their ability to require banks to adopt actions to correct problems was limited. Furthermore, penalties for noncompliance with norms and regulations were low, and there was inadequate protection for supervisors against lawsuits related to actions taken in the course of their official duties. There were also no mandatory administrative actions to be triggered when a bank's financial condition deteriorated beyond certain preestablished limits.

Framework for bank exit

The framework for bank closures was time-consuming. If the Monetary Board deemed that a troubled bank could not be rehabilitated, it would be closed and placed under Philippine Deposit Insurance Corporation (PDIC) receivership. However, there were no specific time limits for the Monetary Board to take such a decision. The PDIC had to determine within a maximum of 90 days whether to rehabilitate or close the bank; it was limited in its role as a receiver since it could not dispose of assets of a bank in receivership until the bank was closed. Even worse, the Secrecy of Bank Deposits law prevented the PDIC from gaining access to information regarding the liabilities covered by deposit insurance before it was named as receiver of the bank. All local currency bank deposits are insured up to 100,000 pesos. The actual liquidation of a bank may take several years to complete under the current system, reflecting inadequacies in the judicial system. Moreover, even when fully under way, in some cases the courts have ordered the authorities to reverse their decision and reopen a bank. Since supervisors, as well as the management and board of the Bangko Sentral ng Pilipinas, do not have explicit immunity from prosecution (although such immunity has been proposed in legislation pending before Congress), an overruling by the judiciary has had a chilling effect on the Bangko Sentral ng Pilipinas's willingness to act.

The process of closing down a bank has been complicated further by the fact that the Bangko Sentral ng Pilipinas may incur financial losses. Such losses may arise from uncollateralized overdraft

---

[127]In early 1998, a pilot test of risk-based supervision was initiated in one bank.

lending to a troubled bank; the inability by the Bangko Sentral ng Pilipinas to realize the collateral backing emergency loans to banks (in part owing to valuation problems); and the fact that, in the event it runs out of resources, the PDIC can borrow from the Bangko Sentral ng Pilipinas.

Avoiding a Crisis and Bolstering the Financial Sector

The Philippine authorities adopted a financial sector reform program in early 1998 aimed at strengthening the banks' capacity to withstand shocks, enhancing the prudential and supervisory framework, and encouraging market-based consolidation in the banking sector. Minimum capital and loan-loss provisioning requirements were tightened, regulatory standards in a number of areas were brought closer in line with international best practice standards, the focus of bank supervision was reoriented toward the analysis of risk, and bank exit policies were strengthened. The main provisions of the financial sector reform program include the following.[128]

Bank Capital Requirements

Minimum capital requirements for banks would be raised through the end of 2000, with intermediate minimum levels for the end of 1998 and the end of 1999.[129] At the same time, the lower capital adequacy requirement of 8 percent (instead of the usual 10 percent) that was allowed for certain universal banks was phased out in January 1999. The larger banks have not encountered problems in meeting the new minimum capital requirements. Several entities among the other groups of financial institutions have encountered more problems meeting the new requirements. The authorities have addressed the more severe cases by stimulating mergers, signing memoranda of understanding with the Bangko Sentral ng

Pilipinas, and setting a clear timetable for compliance or applying the policies contained in the matrices of sanctions and prompt corrective action approved recently by the Monetary Board.

Loan-Loss Provisions

Banks are now required to make a general loan-loss provision of 2 percent and specific loan-loss provisions of 5 percent for loans especially mentioned and 25 percent for secured substandard loans. The new specific provisions had to be met by April 1999 and the general provision by October 1999. To avoid an undue restriction of credit growth, the Bangko Sentral ng Pilipinas in early April 1999 temporarily freed any net increase of bank lending above the March 1999 level from the general provisioning requirement. Most institutions are complying with these new regulations. For those that are not, especially thrift and rural banks, the sanctions outlined in the newly instituted policy of prompt and graduated corrective actions, such as restrictions on branching and payment of dividends, are applied.

Marking to Market

The Bangko Sentral ng Pilipinas has required banks to start marking to market their trading securities portfolio. Accounting standards have been agreed upon with the Bankers Association of the Philippines, and the relevant price benchmarks have been discussed with market operators.

Transparency and Disclosure

To enhance transparency and market discipline, the Bangko Sentral ng Pilipinas instructed all banks listed in the Philippine Stock Exchange to disclose publicly, as of December 1998, detailed information on a quarterly basis, including the level of nonperforming loans and the ratio of nonperforming loans to the total loan portfolio, the amount of classified assets and other risk assets, and the extent of specific and general loan-loss reserves.

Consolidated Supervision

The authorities have started to supervise financial conglomerates in a consolidated fashion. Since legislative changes are needed to fully impose consolidated capital requirements and extend consolidated supervision of financial institutions to include their interests in nonfinancial ventures, the authorities have proposed an amendment of the General Banking Act in this regard. The amendment is currently under consideration by Congress. The Bangko Sentral ng Pilipinas has already begun to consolidate

---

[128]The Philippine National Bank, the only large bank in financial difficulties, is not fully subject to the regulations set out below, but the authorities have reconfirmed their intention to privatize the Philippine National Bank by mid-2000. In the meantime, the realization of losses has brought down the capital adequacy requirement to about half of the required 10 percent. An external audit is in progress that will be the basis for privatization and increase in capital adequacy requirement.

[129]Minimum capital is to increase to 5,400 billion pesos (from 3,000 billion pesos) for expanded commercial banks and to 2,800 billion pesos (from 1,625 billion pesos) for commercial banks. Rural and thrift banks will continue to have different requirements depending on the region they will operate in. The maximum capital requirement for thrift banks will be 400 million pesos (from 200 million pesos) and for rural banks 32 million pesos (from 20 million pesos).

limits on foreign currency exposures between banks and their affiliated foreign currency deposit units.

Bank Licensing

Stricter licensing guidelines for establishing banks have been in place since July 1998, focusing on the three additional requirements: the submission of the statement of income and expenses for the last three years for each of the subscribers; evidence of asset ownership; and in the case of a foreign bank, certification by the home supervisory authority that it agrees with the proposed investment.

Supervisory Methods

The Bangko Sentral ng Pilipinas has changed the focus of its supervision activities from a purely compliance-based and checklist-driven assessment of banks' condition to a forward-looking and risk-based framework. Together with the change in emphasis towards a risk-based approach, significant improvements have taken place in the area of rating methodologies. The CAMEL rating system has been revised to ensure that the composite rating will never be better than the bank's individual factor rating for capital adequacy. As of July 1998, "sensitivity to market risk" ("S") was added to arrive at a CAMELS rating system, and the composite rating system will be based on the weighted sum of the component ratings, with each component assigned a different weight depending on the size, complexity of activities, and risk profile of the institution being rated.

The Role of External Auditors

External auditors of banks have been required, since the end of September 1998, to report to the Bangko Sentral ng Pilipinas all matters that could adversely affect the financial condition of their clients, any serious irregularity that may jeopardize the interests of depositors and creditors, and any losses incurred that substantially reduce the bank's capital. Noncompliance by auditors with this requirement will lead to loss of accreditation.

Bank Resolution

The authorities also addressed problems in the recognition and resolution of weak banks:
- *Intensified bank monitoring*. The Bangko Sentral ng Pilipinas has adopted a program of intensified monitoring of selected banks and is conducting special examinations of banks without specific previous authorization on the basis of a regularly updated list of banks in potential distress, which it started to compile based on for-

ward- and backward-looking indicators in early 1998.
- *Bank receivership*. The authorities have agreed to adopt two measures to improve the ability of PDIC to act as the receiver of banks, including selling assets of distressed banks to pay for the administration costs related to receivership, and faster approval by the Monetary Board of a proposed liquidation.
- *Prompt corrective action for bank capital shortfalls*. The Bangko Sentral ng Pilipinas has adopted explicit procedures to be used when banks fail to reach certain thresholds of capital adequacy. In particular, the authorities have issued a matrix of sanctions and of graduated corrective actions to be taken according to the degree of capital shortfall and noncompliance with other prudential norms.
- *Measures to reduce Bangko Sentral ng Pilipinas financial losses*. The Philippine authorities have taken several steps to reduce the financial risk for the Bangko Sentral ng Pilipinas associated with assistance to banks in distress. A sampling includes stopping the distribution of dividends, imposing certain obligations on the banks' owners and officers, and eliminating uncollateralized overdrafts.

Bank Restructuring

Measures in the area of bank restructuring are currently limited to the privatization of the remaining government stake in the Philippine National Bank and the announcement of merger incentives:
- An important element of the authorities' strategy to enhance the overall soundness of the banking system is to strengthen the financial performance of Philippine National Bank, the second largest bank in the country in terms of assets. Philippine National Bank's financial performance has deteriorated significantly due to the effects of the current regional crisis. In early 1999, the bank retroactively recognized the impairment of its assets and wrote down its capital accordingly. Philippine National Bank's risk-weighted capital fell below regulatory norms, although it continued to meet the minimum capital requirement. The authorities intend to privatize their remaining holdings of the bank stock by mid-2000.
- The Monetary Board has granted additional incentives for banks considering the option of merging if otherwise unable to comply with the new minimum capital and provisioning requirements. The merged bank would in general be allowed time to comply with specific rules and regulations.

Linkages with Corporate Sector Reforms

Philippine companies have been affected by the regional crisis to a lesser degree than those in neighboring countries, in part because of their lower exposure to foreign debt and better corporate performance. However, there is a concentrated ownership structure in the corporate sector as well as the cross shareholdings between banks and corporations. The authorities' structural reform agenda includes some measures to strengthen the corporate sector, including a strengthening of the institutional capacity of the Securities and Exchange Commission to deal with distressed corporations while protecting the contractual rights of creditors. The new emphasis on risk-based bank supervision methods as well as the more rigorous disclosure requirements for banks will also provide an early warning system of corporate distress.

Impact of the Regional Crisis on Bank Performance

In spite of early measures to avoid a wider banking crisis, the banking sector underwent a period of increased stress. The developments include the following:

- *Activity in the banking sector decelerated.* In the first half of 1998, total deposits expanded merely by 5 percent, and the stock of outstanding loans contracted by over 2 percent. The financial crisis seemed to have prompted a more conservative attitude on the part of the banks while noticeably slowing the demand for credit. At the same time, banks started to scale down their expansion programs to ensure compliance with new minimum capital and loan-loss provisioning requirements that became effective in the fourth quarter of 1998.
- *Foreign currency deposits contracted, falling by 17 percent between June 1997 and June 1998.* Most of the Philippine banking sector's foreign currency liability exposure is to domestic residents, which may make it less vulnerable to capital flight than in other Asian countries. Nonresidents' deposits grew by 70 percent a year during 1994–97 and continued growing in the first half of 1998, but still accounted for less than 25 percent of total foreign currency deposits by June 1998.
- *The decline in the banking sector's capital adequacy requirements prior to the crisis has been reversed*; it reached 17.6 percent at the end of 1998.[130] On average, all classes of banks enjoyed healthy capital adequacy ratios; among large banks, all except one have a capital adequacy ratio well in excess of 10 percent. The improvement in the level of capital adequacy ratios reflected a slowdown in banks' asset growth, a shift in asset composition from loans to investment in government paper, and other zero risk-weighted assets, as well as the new minimum capital requirements.
- *Nevertheless, asset quality deteriorated.* The rapid increase in the ratio of nonperforming loans to total loans since mid-1997 is an important indicator of the growing problems in the banking sector. The officially reported overall nonperforming loan ratio reached 14 percent by mid-1999, compared to 4 percent in June 1997. The nonperforming loan ratio is much higher among thrift banks and rural banks than it is among commercial banks.
- *Bank earnings fell, reflecting a general slowdown in the business environment and the need to constitute the new loan-loss provisioning requirements.* The envisaged tax deductibility of loan-loss provisions was not implemented as scheduled, hence the after-tax profit of banks was much weaker than expected, making it more difficult for some smaller banks to comply with minimum capital requirements. For the banking system as a whole, the average return on equity declined to 1 percent by the end of 1998, from 1.7 percent in 1997, and an average of over 2.3 percent from 1990 to 1996.
- *Bank failures.* Since the start of the current difficulties, one small commercial bank, seven thrift banks, and 18 rural banks have failed. Their combined assets amounted to less than 1 percent of total assets.

Unlike the crisis countries, however, the structure of the financial system has seen little change: one small commercial bank was closed and several others are in talks to merge.[131] Reflecting the lesser problems in the financial system, no public funds have been needed for financial sector restructuring, except for liquidity support provided to the one small commercial bank that was subsequently closed.

---

[130]This may not fully reflect the impact of the new minimum capital and loan-loss provisioning requirements, which only became mandatory as of the last quarter of 1998.

[131]This excludes closures of thrift and rural banks, which are routine.

Appendix V   Thailand

The floating of the Thai baht on July 2, 1997 triggered a deep macroeconomic and financial sector crisis.[132] Thailand was not only the first among the crisis countries, but the first to enter into a stabilization program supported by the IMF.

Background

Macroeconomic Setting

Under the framework of a pegged exchange rate regime, Thailand had enjoyed a decade of robust growth performance, but by late 1996 pressures on the baht emerged. Pressure increased through the first half of 1997 amidst an unsustainable current account deficit, a significant appreciation of the real effective exchange rate, rising short-term foreign debt, a deteriorating fiscal balance, and increasingly visible financial sector weaknesses.

Following mounting exchange rate pressures and ineffective interventions to alleviate these pressures, the baht was floated on July 2, 1997.[133] In light of weak supportive policies, the baht depreciated by 20 percent against the U.S. dollar in July. To arrest the pressure, Thailand, on August 20, 1997, entered into a three-year Stand-By Arrangement with the IMF, augmented with funds from the World Bank, the Asian Development Bank, Japan, and other countries. Key policy measures of the program included steps to restructure the financial sector, such as fiscal adjustment and the continuation of a floating exchange rate system.

As the crisis spread to other Asian countries and the sentiment of investors toward the region remained shaky, rollover ratios of short-term debt declined and the baht continued to depreciate. Economic activity also declined, as investment, consumption, and export demand fell sharply. The increasing lack of confidence in the government's ability to manage the situation culminated in a change of government in November 1997. After a significant strengthening of the economic program there was, starting in early 1998, a gradual return of confidence, which was reflected in a firming exchange rate, although real output continued to decline.

To support the exchange rate, monetary policy was initially tight, resulting in relatively high money market rates. In March 1998, this was combined with a more accommodative fiscal stance to allow automatic stabilizers to work. By mid-1998, with a deeper recession than expected and a marked strengthening of the baht, monetary policy was eased and interest rates were gradually lowered. By early 1999, the exchange rate had stabilized and money market interest rates stood below precrisis levels. Growth for 1999 is now projected to be positive, albeit small. Notwithstanding considerable progress in financial sector restructuring, and an improved market sentiment, significant downside risks to economic recovery remain.

Characteristics of the Financial Sector

As of December 1996, the financial system in Thailand consisted of 15 domestic commercial banks, 14 branches of foreign banks, 19 foreign banks established under Bangkok International Banking Facilities, 91 finance and securities companies, 7 specialized state-owned banks, some 4,000 savings and agricultural cooperatives, 15 insurance companies, approximately 880 private provident funds, and 8 mutual fund management companies. Total assets of the system amounted to 8.9 trillion baht (190 percent of GDP), of which the commercial banks alone accounted for 64 percent (121 percent of GDP), finance companies for 20 percent (39 percent of GDP), and specialized state banks for 10 percent (8 percent of GDP). One large commercial bank and two finance companies were majority state-owned.

In an effort to make Bangkok an international finance center that could compete with Hong Kong and Singapore, the Bangkok International Banking Facilities was established in 1993 to formalize offshore banking business in Thailand. Bangkok International

---

[132]This chapter draws on an initial draft by Mats Josefsson and contributions from Carl-Johan Lindgren.

[133]Thailand had committed almost all its foreign reserves in its efforts to support the fixed-exchange rate regime.

Banking Facilities' operations mainly involved borrowing in foreign currencies from abroad and on-lending the funds locally and conducting international trade financing. As an incentive for development, the Bangkok International Banking Facilities benefited from a number of tax exemptions. As of December 1996, 45 financial institutions held licenses to operate offshore banking businesses, of which 15 were Thai commercial banks, 11 foreign bank branches already operating in Thailand, and 19 other foreign banks.

Precrisis Weaknesses in the Financial System

Structural Vulnerabilities

In response to banking sector weaknesses in the 1980s, the Thai authorities had initiated reform measures, including the creation of the Financial Institutions Development Fund, a separate legal entity within the Bank of Thailand with a mandate to restructure, develop, and provide financial support (liquidity and solvency) to financial institutions. Notwithstanding these and other reform efforts, the authorities failed to properly manage the risks in the rapidly growing banking system. Structural weaknesses that, in conjunction with the macroeconomic developments outlined above, led to the emergence of a full-blown banking crisis included:

- *The quality of loan portfolios in banks and finance companies was weak.* In banks, nonperforming loans (more than six months' overdue) were 7.2 percent of total loans at the end of 1995, and increased to 11.6 percent in May 1997. In finance companies, nonperforming loans also increased sharply over the first few months of 1997 (from 6 percent at the end of 1996 to 12 percent in May 1997). Given the weak accounting standards, market analysts believed the figures were too low, and estimated nonperforming loans to be at least 15 percent of total loans for banks, and at least twice as high in finance companies. Most finance companies' assets were related to real estate.
- *Banks and finance companies had not put aside sufficient reserves for their rapidly deteriorating loan portfolios.* There was, for example, no provisioning requirement for substandard loans: loan classification and loss provisioning was only tightened in March 1997.[134]

[134]In March 1997, the Bank of Thailand introduced provisioning requirements against substandard loans in banks and finance companies at 15 percent and 20 percent, respectively, to be implemented over a two-year period. However, under pressure from weak institutions the authorities soon extended the implementation period to five years.

Weaknesses in Prudential Regulation and Supervision

The structural weaknesses resulted, in part, from weaknesses both in the content and the implementation of prudential regulations. The main weaknesses were:

- *The rules for loan classification, provisioning, and accounting were inadequate and were applied inconsistently.* Thus, the reported capital adequacy ratios were grossly misleading since loans were not appropriately classified and provisioned for. For example, financial institutions had built up large loan portfolios of increasingly questionable quality, secured by generally overvalued asset collateral. These loans were often simply restructured ("evergreened") when payment problems arose and not reclassified.
- *Interest on nonperforming loans continued to accrue and, hence, significantly overstated financial sector earnings.* This had made it possible to pay dividends, bonuses, and taxes on nonexistent profits, effectively decapitalizing these institutions.
- *There were no prudential limits on loan concentration.* In the absence of such restrictions, banks built up excessive exposure to particular sectors such as the property market. There was also excessive lending based on collateral rather than proper credit assessment; thus, when the asset price bubble burst, banks faced rapid declines in the value of their collateral.
- *The prudential framework was generally weak and fragmented.* The ministry of finance was charged with the overall authority for supervision of banks and finance companies, but had delegated the day-to-day responsibility for supervision to the Bank of Thailand. The ministry of finance had authority to grant, suspend, and revoke banking licenses and to intervene in banks and finance companies through a control committee for each institution. Liquidation of financial institutions was under ministry of finance authority and was subject to the bankruptcy act for nonfinancial corporations.

Impact of the Crisis and Initial Resolution Measures

The Crisis in Finance Companies

Finance companies had disproportionately the largest exposure to the property sector and were the first institutions affected by the economic downturn. Much of the later spillover to other institutions, in particular to the banking sector, was triggered by the failure of the initial measures to stabilize this sector.

Financial sector restructuring was initiated on March 3, 1997, when the Bank of Thailand and the ministry of finance announced that 10 as yet unnamed finance companies had asset quality problems and insufficient liquidity, and would need to increase capital to cover weak real estate loans and finance growth. According to the announcement, there was to be a tight deadline for the increase in capital—the shortest period of time allowed in the law—and, if the finance companies were unable to raise capital, they would have to sell their shares to the Financial Institutions Development Fund. The Financial Institutions Development Fund would therefore effectively take over the finance company. The public was also assured that, apart from the 10 institutions mentioned, all other financial institutions could increase capital through their own efforts.

In the period from March to late June, the Bank of Thailand—in absolute secrecy—provided liquidity support at below market interest rates to 66 finance companies. There was also liquidity support to two banks.[135] A small part of the liquidity was provided from the Financial Institutions Development Fund's own accumulated reserves, some through Financial Institutions Development Fund borrowing in the overnight repo market, and the remainder was financed through Financial Institutions Development Fund bonds, which were purchased by the Bank of Thailand.

To stop the liquidity drain, on June 29, 1997, the Bank of Thailand suspended for 30 days the operations of 16 finance companies, including 7 of the 10 "initially targeted" institutions, based on their capital inadequacy and the need for liquidity. These 16 companies were required to submit rehabilitation plans to the Bank of Thailand by July 11. Companies that failed to submit plans, or whose plans were rejected by the Bank of Thailand/ministry of finance, would have their licenses revoked and be absorbed by Krung Thai Thanakit, a majority government-owned finance company. In addition, four other identified "core" finance companies were invited to play a role in absorbing some of the suspended companies. The government also announced that it:

- would not suspend any more finance companies beyond the 16 already suspended; and
- would guarantee all domestic and foreign depositors and creditors, of all finance companies other than those suspended.

However, these measures failed to calm the markets, mainly because there was increasing uncertainty over the exact extent of the guarantees due to inconsistencies in official statements. With inconsistencies among the different announcements unre-

solved, official assurances raised rather than reduced the market's apprehension.

Design of Initial Resolution Efforts

After the peg of the baht was abandoned on July 2, 1997, the rapidly depreciating exchange rate and falling property values led to major deterioration of banks' loan portfolios. This raised concerns about the solvency of the entire financial system. Estimates undertaken by an IMF advisory mission in mid-July 1997, based on rough assumptions of the level of problem loans and recovery rates, suggested that by mid-1997, some 500 billion baht ($17 billion or 9 percent of projected 1997 GDP) would be required to restore the legally required minimum capital adequacy of banks and finance companies. The "hole" was estimated to be about 270 billion baht ($9 billion) in banks and 230 billion baht ($8 billion) in finance companies. These aggregate figures indicated that many, if not most, of Thailand's 91 finance companies were insolvent, while banks as a group were solvent, but undercapitalized. In the absence of detailed supervisory information on individual institutions, there was an expectation that the five largest banks (representing about two-thirds of the banking system) were among the strongest in the system, so that several of the small- and medium-seized banks most likely were insolvent.

At this stage, the authorities developed a strategy to restructure the financial system in cooperation with the IMF. The strategy was based on three steps:

- exit of all nonviable financial institutions;
- issuance of a temporary blanket guarantee protecting all depositors and creditors in the remaining financial institutions, so as to calm the market and give the authorities sufficient time for restructuring measures; and
- restructuring and rehabilitating of the Thai financial system to raise to international standards.

The strategy depended on the implementation of a range of supporting measures, in particular:

- macroeconomic policies that restored fiscal and monetary control;
- establishment of the FRA to replace the Bank of Thailand and the ministry of finance temporarily as decisionmaker on all matters related to financial sector restructuring; and
- announcement of a consistent and comprehensive medium-term restructuring strategy, to be explained to the public through a professionally managed information campaign.

Implementation

On August 5, 1997, the ministry of finance and the Bank of Thailand issued a joint statement an-

---

[135]For some finance companies, the amounts involved were in excess of four times capital.

nouncing measures to be taken to strengthen confidence in the financial system. The implementation of the program to a large extent followed the steps just outlined. The policy framework was built on the separation of finance companies facing actual or imminent insolvency from those that were judged to be viable, based on the following three criteria: (1) magnitude of liquidity support (borrowing from Financial Institutions Development Fund); (2) deterioration of capital; and (3) the size of nonperforming loans.

Finance companies deemed to be facing actual or imminent insolvency were suspended and given 60 days to complete due diligence and present a rehabilitation plan to the Committee on Supervision of Merger or Transfer.[136] In all, 58 finance companies out of 91 had their operation suspended, including the 16 finance companies suspended earlier. At this stage, the authorities decided not to take any action against commercial banks, even though there were signs that at least two small banks faced serious weaknesses.

A government guarantee for depositors and creditors in all remaining finance companies and banks was announced, and the conditions were spelled out in a joint press release by the ministry of finance and the Bank of Thailand.[137] However, there were major uncertainties surrounding the guarantee, including whether it would be legal for the Bank of Thailand to provide the liquidity to honor the guarantee. Shareholders and holders of subordinated debt were not covered by the guarantee.

There were delays in initiating some of the announced restructuring measures. The magnitude of the problems, along with interagency issues of coordination and political problems, all took time to resolve, delaying the implementation of necessary policies. The committee managing the process was reorganized, and only by late September were instructions issued to the suspended companies on what information they had to submit, and which criteria had to be met before they would be allowed to resume operations.

The government through its actions made clear that it stood fully behind the Bank of Thailand. To support the restructuring/rehabilitation process, emergency decrees were passed on October 24, 1997 to: (1) establish the FRA to deal with the suspended finance companies; (2) amend the Commercial Banking Act and the Finance Company Act so as to empower the Bank of Thailand to request capital reductions, capital increases, or changes in management in troubled commercial banks and finance companies; (3) establish an asset management company to deal with assets of the 58 finance companies that had their operations suspended, or impaired assets in any financial institution in which the Financial Institutions Development Fund had acquired shares (intervened) and assumed management control; and (4) amend the Bank of Thailand Act to empower the Financial Institutions Development Fund to lend to these institutions with or without collateral, raise the fee charged to financial institutions whose depositors and creditors were protected, and make explicit the government's financial support of the Bank of Thailand (thus making the guarantee more credible).

The finance companies were given until the end of October 1997 to submit their rehabilitation plans to the FRA, which in turn had one month to assess the rehabilitation plans submitted and to make a recommendation to the ministry of finance on how many finance companies should be allowed to resume their operations. With the assistance of private consultants, the FRA refined its analysis to allow thorough technical consideration of the rehabilitation plans based on uniform criteria.

On December 8, 1997 the FRA and the ministry of finance announced the permanent closure of 56 finance companies. Only two companies were allowed to reopen, subject to the stipulated new capital being paid in. The fact that various politically attractive but financially dubious merger proposals had been rejected was a sign of the integrity of the analysis.[138] Immediately after the decision to close the 56 companies, the focus of the FRA shifted to managing their assets, in order to prevent a further deterioration in asset quality prior to disposition.

---

[136]The committee had initially been set up to handle the suspension of the 16 finance companies.

[137]The treatment of depositors and creditors in the 16 initially suspended and 42 later suspended finance companies was guided by the following principles: (1) depositors in the 16 finance companies had a choice between receiving payment under terms and conditions specified by the company in question, or to take promissory notes issued by Krung Thai Thanakit, with conditions and interest varying according to the size of deposits; (2) creditors in the 16 finance companies were not protected—they could share in the proceeds of the liquidation process, in line with the priority of their claim; (3) depositors in the 42 finance companies were given essentially the same option as depositors in the other 16 finance companies—with the exception that the promissory notes were to be issued by Krung Thai Bank and were negotiable; (4) creditors in the suspended 42 finance companies were allowed to swap their claims for notes issued by the Krung Thai Bank, under the same condition as depositors, although the interest rate was set at 2 percent.

[138]The closure of the 56 finance companies required the coordinated action of some 5,000 officials and security personnel.

Banking Sector Issues

Magnitude of the problem

Initial crisis resolution had focused solely on finance companies, but it soon became evident that banks also faced problems and that the public had started to lose confidence in the banks. Banks' asset quality was deteriorating rapidly, and many banks experienced deposit withdrawals and reduced rollover rates for external credit lines; these were facilitated through liquidity support from the Financial Institutions Development Fund/Bank of Thailand. Seven out of the 15 commercial banks were facing such severe liquidity problems that they needed liquidity support from the Financial Institutions Development Fund more or less on a daily basis. The deposit withdrawals represented a flight from private banks perceived to be weak into larger stronger domestic banks, branches of foreign banks, and state-owned specialized banks.

Based on Bank of Thailand data as of the end of June 1997, assessments of the financial condition of Thai banks were made. These assessments indicated that all banks had a capital shortfall (that is, a capital adequacy ratio below 8.5 percent); the shortfall amounted to roughly 400 billion baht if international best practices were to be applied, and approximately 250 billion baht on the less stringent Bank of Thailand criteria.

Resolution principles

On October 14, the authorities announced their strategy for dealing with the banking sector, based on the following principles:

- All banks were required to adjust (first write down and then increase) capital in order to absorb the losses that had already occurred. They had to meet the new and more stringent rules on loan classification and provisioning that would shortly be issued by the Bank of Thailand;
- None of the banks was allowed to pay dividends for the remaining part of 1997 or during 1998;
- The Bank of Thailand was to initiate discussions with each individual bank on how the bank would be recapitalized. Following such discussion, banks were required to present recapitalization plans to the Bank of Thailand;
- The requested capital would have to be injected at the latest during the first quarter of 1998;
- If a bank could not raise the capital requested within the time given, the Bank of Thailand would have the right to demand a memorandum of understanding with the bank that would give existing owners additional time to provide the capital, as long as they could furnish the Bank of Thailand with viable, legally binding, plans for recapitalization;

- Banks were encouraged to try to find foreign partners since it was unlikely they could raise all the capital needed in Thailand;
- For banks that could not raise the capital, losses would be written off against capital, ensuring that existing shareholders lose their stake, with the exception of a token position that had to be kept for legal reasons. The Financial Institutions Development Fund would then take control of the banks, recapitalize them and later privatize them (by selling them to domestic or foreign investors) or merge them with another bank; and
- The strategy clearly stated that no bank would be closed and that depositors and creditors would be fully protected by the government guarantee.

Banking sector intervention

The Bank of Thailand was initially reluctant to intervene in banks since it feared that interventions could cause a run on the whole banking system and severely deepen the crisis. With the October 1997 amendments to the Commercial Banking Act, the Bank of Thailand was given specific powers to write down capital and change management in troubled commercial banks. Based on these new powers on December 31, 1997, the Bank of Thailand intervened in a medium-sized bank, Bangkok Metropolitan Bank: management was changed, and the Bangkok Metropolitan Bank was told that if capital had not been raised within roughly three weeks, the Bank of Thailand would order the bank to reduce its capital and have the Financial Institutions Development Fund recapitalize it. In the following month, the Bank of Thailand intervened in two more small- or medium-sized banks—First Bangkok City Bank and Siam City Bank. These three banks represented 10 percent of banking system deposits. In mid-May, the Bank of Thailand intervened in seven finance companies; the government thus had become the owner of six banks and nine finance companies, which accounted for roughly one-third of total deposits.[139]

The authorities hired a financial advisor to assist them with developing a strategy to deal with the three banks mentioned above and with Bangkok Bank of Commerce. This financial advisor worked out an initial proposal for the banks to be absorbed

---

[139]In addition to the banks mentioned above, government-owned banks include Bangkok Bank of Commerce (a private bank that had earlier failed and been taken over by the Financial Institutions Development Fund) and Radanasin Bank, a bank and an associated finance company that was set up by the government in early 1998 to buy good assets from closed finance companies.

by either domestic or foreign banks. Meanwhile, in the course of 1998, these banks' assets continuously deteriorated to the point where nonperforming loans were approaching 70–85 percent in each bank. Although clearly increasingly insolvent, no decision was made on how to proceed, since more problems were emerging and there was an urgent need for the authorities to work out a comprehensive plan on how to address other outstanding weaknesses in the financial sector.

Toward a Comprehensive and Viable Financial Sector

The above measures primarily addressed the immediate liquidity and solvency problems. There was also a need for a strategy to strengthen the remaining viable financial institutions. Consequently an effort was made to focus on the longer run and more strategic needs for supporting a sustainable financial sector. Measures included revamping the prudential framework, and taking steps to restructure the sector.

Improved Prudential Framework

Following failed attempts to tighten prudential rules in early 1997, the severity of the crisis helped focus attention on a fundamental revamping of the prudential framework. The strategy was to maintain the capital adequacy requirement of 8.5 percent for banks and 8.0 percent for finance companies, but allow gradualism in building up loan-loss provisions according to a fully transparent timetable. There was to be an immediate tightening of loan classification and interest suspension rules, while provisioning requirements were to be increased every six months to bring them fully into line with international best practices by the end of 2000. This phasing was thought necessary to give the banking industry the required time to adjust and raise the new capital.

New loan classification, loss provisioning, and interest suspension rules were issued on March 31, 1998. Loans had to be classified into five categories, and strict rules on interest accrual were established. The new loan-loss provisioning requirements were gradually tightened by 20 percent every six months starting July 1, 1998, thus making it possible for the requirements to be fully implemented by the end of 2000. A new regulation was also issued on the valuation of collateral for loans above a certain size; it must now be independently appraised. Finally, to set clear incentives for banks and finance companies to actively initiate restructuring of nonperforming loans, rules for how restructured loans should be classified and provisioned for were defined in regulations for debt restructuring.[140]

A Comprehensive Plan for Financial Sector Restructuring

By mid-1998, the depth of the economic and financial sector crises raised doubts whether the measures described above, combined with the strengthening of prudential rules, would be sufficient to create the necessary private sector recapitalization and efficient restructuring of the sector. In particular, the deteriorating domestic and regional economic environment, and the associated decline in asset quality, had introduced uncertainties about the effectiveness of the market-based and private-sector-led restructuring of Thailand's financial system. While several private banks, including the two largest, had been able to secure injections of private capital in early 1998, and a controlling share in a small bank had been acquired by a foreign strategic investor, their success had not been widely shared, and it was doubtful whether the banking system would be in a condition to support the government's efforts to secure economic recovery.[141]

Hence, on August 14, 1998 the government announced a comprehensive financial sector restructuring package to address the remaining weaknesses in the financial sector. The augmented restructuring strategy focused on the following elements:

- creation of a high-level financial restructuring advisory committee (FRAC) to advise the minister of finance and the governor of the Bank of Thailand;
- the commitment of public funds to assist in the recapitalization of viable banks and finance companies;
- incentives for accelerating corporate debt restructuring at an equal rate with recapitalization;
- the efficient management of nonperforming assets;
- the exit, merger, or sale of nonviable commercial banks and finance companies;
- equitable loss-sharing arrangements and containment of public sector costs;
- the strengthening of prudential supervision and an accelerated adoption of international best practices;
- operational restructuring of state banks and their preparation for eventual privatization; and

---

[140]These regulations were based on rules used by the U.S. Office of the Comptroller of the Currency.

[141]Most new subscribers were foreign institutional investors, and foreign ownership of the two largest private banks approached 50 percent; foreign investors also acquired controlling shares in some finance companies.

- Bank of Thailand intervention in remaining nonviable institutions.

Commitment of Funds Through Capital Support Facilities

The objective of the package was to restore and maintain the solvency and credibility of the Thai financial system. The government recognized that the terms and conditions of any public support facility should be transparent and subject to the strongest possible safeguards, while facilitating the restructuring and consolidation of financial institutions and protecting the economy from further weakening. Two schemes were designed to assist with the recapitalization of the viable financial institutions. The first aimed at catalyzing new private Tier 1 capital. The second provided financial resources and incentives to accelerate corporate debt restructuring and encourage new lending through the provision of Tier 2 capital (Box 18).

To facilitate and oversee banks' efforts to raise capital, at the beginning of every six-month period, the Bank of Thailand makes an assessment of each bank's provisioning needs, profitability, and growth in assets. It then calculates whether the bank has sufficient capital to meet the required capital adequacy requirement. If a bank falls short of capital, it would be required to present plans on how, what amount, and by when capital would be raised, and those commitments would be formally agreed upon in a memorandum of understanding. Banks that cannot raise capital through their own efforts would be recommended to apply for public support under the Tier 1 scheme. The Bank of Thailand has reserved the right to intervene in any financial institution that fails to meet commitments under their memoranda of understanding.

Facilitating the Establishment of Private Asset Management Companies

Additional arrangements were needed to provide maximum flexibility for financial institutions to deal with their bad assets, while allowing them to restructure their balance sheets. Thus the government devised a plan under which institutions were encouraged to set up, capitalize and fund private asset management companies. Such companies were defined as financial institutions, which allows them to borrow, relend funds to existing customers, and provide full flexibility in setting interest rates. However, asset management companies are not permitted to take deposits. The rules also provide for a transfer of assets from the founding institution to its asset management companies without legal impediments or taxes and fees. According to the rules,

asset management companies must be fully consolidated into the founding institutions' balance sheets, provided the institution owns more than 50 percent of the shares. Two large private banks have announced that they will set up their own private asset management companies, and others are considering doing so.

On August 14, 1998, the Bank of Thailand intervened in all remaining banks and finance companies considered nonviable. This included two more banks, one small- and one medium-sized, and five finance companies. Subsequently, the authorities decided to merge three of the intervened banks into the existing state-owned banks (Krung Thai Bank and Radanasin Banks), and create a new bank (Bank Thai), from the merger of Krung Thai Thanakit, one intervened bank, and the 12 intervened finance companies.

Five banks are now in the process of being privatized and are expected to be privatized by the end of 1999. In July 1999, one additional small bank was intervened. The government is supporting the privatization process through capital injections and by offering stop-loss guarantees and/or profit and loss sharing arrangements to potential new investors. Four of the intervened banks have been closed: one formally through liquidation, and the other three indirectly through mergers with state-owned banks.

Asset Disposal

The FRA has now almost completed the disposal of assets from the 56 closed finance companies. In its first auction, it managed to sell 36 billion baht of assets (hire purchase loans, mortgages, and commercial loans) and in a second auction it sold 28 billion baht of noncore assets (foreclosed assets, repossessed vehicles, equity, and debt instruments). The recovery rate in these two auctions was 47–48 percent. In a third auction in December 1998, FRA offered 370 billion baht ($10 billion) of lower quality business loans, mainly consisting of corporate loans with or without questionable collateral. This auction was less than fully subscribed and obtained far lower prices because of the low quality of the loans. In total, 32 billion baht of assets were sold, with a recovery rate of 37 percent, and an additional 110 billion baht of assets were later allocated to bidders after profit-sharing arrangements had been negotiated guaranteeing a minimum recovery rate of about 20 percent of book value. For the first time, the government asset management company established in late 1997 was allowed to participate in the auction as a bidder of last resort, and it ended up becoming the owner of assets with a book value of 185 billion baht for which it paid about 17 percent. In sum, out of the 860 billion baht in finance com-

---

Box 18. Thailand: Capital Support Facilities

These capital support facilities apply to banks and finance companies incorporated in Thailand and deemed viable by the Bank of Thailand.

Tier 1 capital. Under this facility, the government matches capital injected by private investors (including existing shareholders). Any institution that enters the scheme is required to make full provisions upfront, in line with Bank of Thailand's end-2000 loan classification and loan-loss provisioning (LCP) rules. Existing shareholders must thus bear all the up-front losses, and the government in making its contribution will rely on due diligence performed by private investors. The Financial Sector Advisory Committee (FRAC) arbitrates on any disputes regarding the magnitude of the write-down of losses. To qualify for support, the institution must present an operational restructuring plan including measures to strengthen internal control and risk management, increase revenues, cut costs, and strengthen internal procedures for dealing with non-performing loans. These plans must be acceptable to the FRAC and the Bank of Thailand. The government will provide the capital injection in the form of equity paid up with 10-year, tradable government bonds carrying a market-related interest rate. The new government/private capital injections would have preferred status over existing shareholders. The government and the new investors have the right to change the board of directors and management of the institution. The government also reserves the right to appoint board member(s) according to the size of its equity holding, and has the right of nominating at least one board member even if this is not warranted by the size of its equity share.

Tier 2 capital. This scheme is set up to encourage corporate restructuring. At the end of each quarter, the institutions can apply to the FRAC for government injection of Tier 2 capital by reporting any debt-restructuring agreement, the original loan contract, and evidence that the borrower had been able to service the loan. The amount of Tier 2 capital provided is set at a minimum equal to the total write-down exceeding previous provisioning or 20 percent of the net increase in lending to the private sector. Each institution is eligible to receive a maximum amount of Tier 2 capital injection equal to 2 percent of risk-weighted assets. Within this limit, the amount of Tier 2 capital injection for new lending to the private sector cannot exceed 1 percent of risk-weighted assets. Also, no single debt restructuring agreement is eligible for more than 10 percent of the amount available to the institution. Institutions that bring forward the end-2000 LCP rules will be allowed to defer the cost of debt restructuring over a period of five years (20 percent per year) while those which choose not to bring forward the end-2000 rules will have to take the costs according to the existing regulation (full loss taken by end-2000). The capital injection will be provided by the government buying debentures issued by the bank with a maturity of 10 years and paid for with nontradable government bonds with matching maturity and carrying market-related interest rates. The rate on debentures is expected to be 1 percentage point higher than that carried by the government bond in order to cover administrative costs for the government.

---

pany assets managed by the FRA, 206 billion baht have been sold to the private sector and 185 billion baht to the asset management company. Total recovery to FRA is about 96 billion baht or 25 percent of face value; final recovery value will only be known after the outcome of profit sharing arrangements and asset management company liquidations are completed.

Bank Privatization and Resolution

The private sector-led recapitalization of Thai banks has worked well, and all seven of the remaining private banks, have raised sufficient capital for the next 12 months. However, all banks need to raise additional capital before they can have sufficient capital to meet the end-2000 loan classification and provisioning rules.

Of the six state-owned banks, four are in the process of being privatized with the assistance of foreign investment banks. It is expected that the privatization process will be completed this year. The government has made significant efforts to ensure that the process is transparent, and that there are proper profit/loss sharing arrangements in place to ensure a deal can be justified politically. The timetable and strategy for the privatization of the other two state-owned banks is being reconsidered to ensure that the eventual sale of shares in these banks can substantially contribute to reducing the government's final restructuring costs.

The financial sector in Thailand has been consolidated although only one commercial bank has been closed (Figure 11). The number of domestic commercial banks has declined by two as a result of mergers. The most significant change is with the finance companies—56 were closed and a further 13 (together with five banks) were merged. Some foreign capital has been invested in commercial banks and finance companies, most notably two private domestic banks that now have foreign ownership greater than 50 percent.

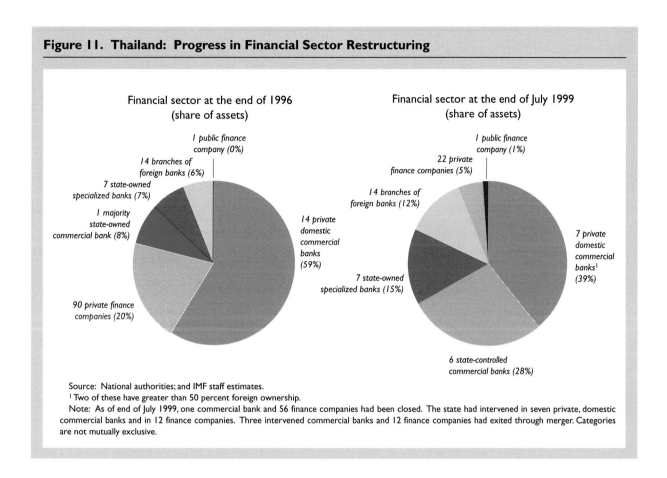

Figure 11. Thailand: Progress in Financial Sector Restructuring

Financial sector at the end of 1996
(share of assets)

1 public finance company (0%)

14 branches of foreign banks (6%)

7 state-owned specialized banks (7%)

1 majority state-owned commercial bank (8%)

90 private finance companies (20%)

14 private domestic commercial banks (59%)

Financial sector at the end of July 1999
(share of assets)

1 public finance company (1%)

22 private finance companies (5%)

14 branches of foreign banks (12%)

7 state-owned specialized banks (15%)

7 private domestic commercial banks[1] (39%)

6 state-controlled commercial banks (28%)

Source: National authorities; and IMF staff estimates.
[1] Two of these have greater than 50 percent foreign ownership.
Note: As of end of July 1999, one commercial bank and 56 finance companies had been closed. The state had intervened in seven private, domestic commercial banks and in 12 finance companies. Three intervened commercial banks and 12 finance companies had exited through merger. Categories are not mutually exclusive.

Table 21. Thailand: Public Cost for Financial Sector Restructuring
(As of the end of 1998)

	Percent of GDP	Billions of U.S. Dollars
Liquidity support assumed by the budget	15	20
Recapitalization	8	11
Purchases of nonperforming loans	0	0
Interest cost (on budget)	2	3
Total	25	34

Source: National authorities; and IMF staff estimates.

Public Cost of Financial Sector Restructuring

As of the end of 1998, the public sector contribution for financial sector restructuring was close to 25 percent of GDP (Table 21). The largest portion of this, 20 percent of GDP, was used for liquidity support; another 8 percent was used for recapitalization.

Bibliography

Alexander, William, Jeffrey Davis, Liam Patrick Ebrill, and Carl-Johan Lindgren, 1997, *Systemic Bank Restructuring and Macroeconomic Policy* (Washington: International Monetary Fund).

Baliño, Tomás, and Angel Ubide, 1999, "The Korean Financial Crisis of 1997: A Strategy of Financial Sector Reform," IMF Working Paper 99/28 (Washington: International Monetary Fund).

Basel Committee on Banking Supervision, 1999, *Supervisory Lessons to be Drawn from the Asian Crisis* (Basel: Bank for International Settlements).

Daniel, James, Jeffrey Davis, and Andrew Wolfe, 1997, *Fiscal Accounting of Bank Restructuring*, IMF Paper on Policy Analysis and Assessment 97/5 (Washington: International Monetary Fund).

Dattels, Peter, 1997, "Microstructure of Government Securities Markets," in *Coordinating Public Debt and Monetary Management,* ed. by V. Sundararajan, P. Dattels, and H. Blommestein, (Washington: International Monetary Fund).

Demirgüç-Kunt, A., and Enrica Detragiache, 1998, "The Determinants of Banking Crises in Developing and Developed Countries," *Staff Papers*, International Monetary Fund, Vol. 45, No. 1, pp. 81–109.

Ding, Wei, Ilker Domaç, and Giovanni Ferri, 1998, "Is There a Credit Crunch in East Asia?" World Bank Policy Research Working Paper No. 1959 (Washington: World Bank).

Dollar, David, and Mary Hallward-Driemeier, 1998, "Crisis, Adjustment, and Reform in Thai Industry" (unpublished; Washington: World Bank).

Downes, Patrick T., David Marston, and Inci Otker, 1999, *Mapping Financial Sector Vulnerability in a Non-Crisis Country*, IMF Policy Discussion Paper 99/4 (Washington: International Monetary Fund).

Eichengreen, Barry, Donald Mathieson 1998, *Hedge Funds and Financial Market Dynamics*, IMF Occasional Paper No. 166 (Washington: International Monetary Fund).

Enoch, Charles, and John Green, eds., 1997, *Banking Soundness and Monetary Policy* (Washington: International Monetary Fund).

Enoch, Charles, Gillian Garcia, and V. Sundararajan, 1999, "Recapitalizing Banks with Public Funds: Selected Issues," IMF Working Paper 99/139 (Washington: International Monetary Fund).

Escolano, Julio, 1997, "Tax Treatment of Loan Losses of Banks," in *Banking Soundness and Monetary Policy,* ed. by Charles Enoch and John H. Green (Washington: International Monetary Fund).

Feldstein, Martin, 1998, "Refocusing the IMF," *Foreign Affairs*, Vol. 77, No. 2, (New York), pp. 20–33.

Folkerts-Landau, David, and Carl-Johan Lindgren, 1998, *Toward a Framework for Financial Stability,* World Economic and Financial Surveys (Washington: International Monetary Fund).

Frécaut, Olivier, and Eric Sidgwick, 1998, "Systemic Banking Distress: The Need for an Enhanced Monetary Survey," IMF Paper on Policy Analysis and Assessment 98/9 (Washington: International Monetary Fund).

Furman, Jason, and Joseph Stiglitz, 1998, "Economic Crises: Evidence and Insights from East Asia", *Brookings Papers on Economic Activity: 2*, Brookings Institution.

García-Herrero, Alicia, 1997, "Monetary Impact of a Banking Crisis and the Conduct of Monetary Policy," IMF Working Paper 97/124 (Washington: International Monetary Fund).

Garcia, Gillian, 1999, "Deposit Insurance: A Survey of Actual and Best Practices in 1998," IMF Working Paper 99/54 (Washington: International Monetary Fund).

Ghosh, Swati R., and Atish R. Ghosh, 1999, "East Asia in the Aftermath: Was There a Crunch?" IMF Working Paper 99/38 (Washington: International Monetary Fund).

Goldstein, Morris, 1998, *The Asian Financial Crisis: Causes, Cures and Systemic Implications* (Washington: Institute for International Economics).

Guitián, Manuel, 1997, "Bank Soundness: The Other Dimension of Monetary Policy," in *Banking Soundness and Monetary Policy*, ed. by Enoch and Green (Washington: International Monetary Fund).

Hardy, Daniel, and Ceyla Pazarbaşıoğlu, 1998, "Leading Indicators of Banking Crises: Was Asia Different?" IMF Working Paper 98/91 (Washington: International Monetary Fund).

Ingves, Stefan, and Göran Lind, 1997, "Loan-Loss Recoveries and Debt Resolution Agencies: The Swedish Experience," in *Bank Soundness and Monetary Policy*, ed. by Enoch and Green (Washington: International Monetary Fund).

International Monetary Fund, 1997, *World Economic Outlook, December 1997: Crisis in Asia*, World Economic and Financial Surveys (Washington).

———, 1998, *World Economic Outlook, October 1998: Financial Turbulence and the World Economy*, World Economic and Financial Surveys (Washington).

Kaminsky, Graciela L., Saul Lizondo, and Carmen M. Reinhart, 1997, "Leading Indicators of Currency Crises," IMF Working Paper 97/79 (Washington: International Monetary Fund).

Lane, Timothy, A. Ghosh, J. Hamann, S. Phillips, M. Schulze-Ghattas, and T. Tsikata, 1999, *IMF-Supported Programs in Indonesia, Korea, and Thailand: A Preliminary Assessment*, IMF Occasional Paper, No. 178 (Washington: International Monetary Fund).

Leipziger, Danny M., 1997, *Lessons from East Asia* (Ann Arbor: University of Michigan Press).

Lindgren, Carl-Johan, Gillian Garcia, and Matthew Saal, 1996, *Bank Soundness and Macroeconomic Policy* (Washington: International Monetary Fund).

Lirio, Ricardo P., 1998, "The Central Bank and Non-Bank Financial Intermediaries" in *Philippine Financial Almanac 1997/98* (Manila).

Merrill Lynch, 1999, *Asia-Pacific Banks: Progress and Issues in Bank Restructuring,* Global Fundamental Equity Research Department, February.

Nascimento, Jean-Claude, 1991, "The Crisis in the Financial Sector and the Authorities' Reaction: The Philippines," in *Banking Crises: Cases and Issues,* ed. by V. Sundararajan and Tomás J. T. Baliño (Washington: International Monetary Fund).

Nellor, David C. L., 1998, "Tax Policy and the Asian Crisis," (Washington: International Monetary Fund).

Quintyn, Marc, 1997, "Government Securities Versus Central Bank Securities in Developing Open Market Operations," in *Coordinating Public Debt and Monetary Management,* ed. by V. Sundararajan, P. Dattels, and H. Blommestein (Washington: International Monetary Fund).

Radelet, Steven C., and Jeffrey Sachs, 1998, *The Onset of the East Asian Financial Crisis* (Cambridge, Massachusetts: National Bureau of Economic Research).

Samsung Economic Research Institute (SERI), *Korean Economic Trends*, (Korea, various issues).

Sheng, Andrew, 1996, *Bank Restructuring: Lessons from the 1980s* (Washington: World Bank).

Sundararajan, V., and Tomás J.T. Baliño, 1991, *Banking Crises: Cases and Issues* (Washington: International Monetary Fund).

———, 1990, *Issues in Recent Banking Crises in Developing Countries* (Washington: International Monetary Fund).

Sundararajan, V., Dong He, and May Khamis, 1999, "Crises, Policy Responses and Steps to Increase Transparency—The Case of Asia," Thomson Bank Watch Conference on Banking Systems in Chaos (Washington: International Monetary Fund).

World Bank, 1998, *East Asia: The Road to Recovery* (Washington).